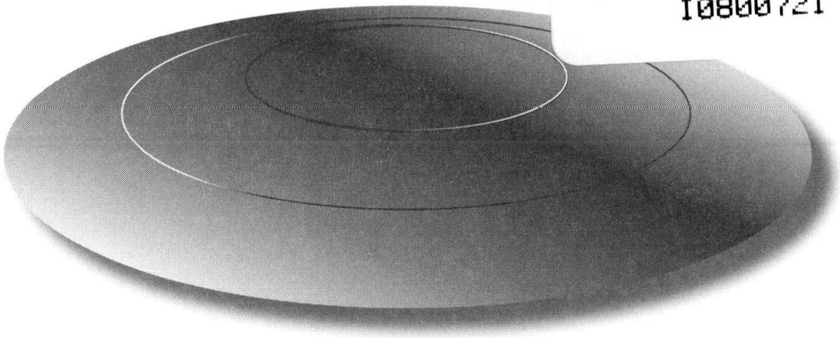

Midwest UFOs and Beyond

Tom Baker

Schiffer Publishing Ltd
4880 Lower Valley Road • Atglen, PA 19310

Dedication

This book is dedicated to the idle dreamers, the sky watchers, the true believers, the seekers of distant shores, and all those who ever looked into the star-strewn sky above, and wondered.

Schiffer Books are available at special discounts for bulk purchases for sales promotions or premiums. Special editions, including personalized covers, corporate imprints, and excerpts can be created in large quantities for special needs. For more information contact the publisher:

Published by Schiffer Publishing, Ltd.
4880 Lower Valley Road
Atglen, PA 19310
Phone: (610) 593-1777; Fax: (610) 593-2002
E-mail: Info@schifferbooks.com.

For the largest selection of fine reference books on this and related subjects, please visit our website at **www.schifferbooks.com.**

We are always looking for people to write books on new and related subjects. If you have an idea for a book, please contact us at ***proposals@schifferbooks.com***.

This book may be purchased from the publisher.
Please try your bookstore first.
You may write for a free catalog.

In Europe, Schiffer books are distributed by
Bushwood Books
6 Marksbury Ave.
Kew Gardens
Surrey TW9 4JF England
Phone: 44 (0) 20 8392 8585; Fax: 44 (0) 20 8392 9876
E-mail: info@bushwoodbooks.co.uk
Website: www.bushwoodbooks.co.uk

Other Schiffer Books By The Author:

Midwest Maniacs
ISBN: 978-0-7643-3942-4 $16.99

Indiana Ghost Folklore
ISBN: 978-0-7643-3334-7 $14.99

Scary Urban Legends
ISBN: 978-0-7643-3587-7 $14.99

Haunted Indianapolis
ISBN: 978-0-7643-2747-6 $14.95

Library of Congress Control Number: 2013938832

Designed by Mark David Bowyer
Type set in Lemonade ICG / NewBskvll BT

ISBN: 978-0-7643-4390-2
Printed in the United States of America

Contents

Acknowledgments

Acknowledgments must be given to my excellent family, my mother Brenda Durham, my father David Baker, my good friend John Titchenal, Dinah Roseberry and the folks at Schiffer Books, Margie Kay at Missouri MUFON, William Neff, and old friends who I don't see much of these days: Jason Leonard, Matt Losure, Chris Bennett, Adam Glass, Mr. Derek Edwards of the White Rabbit bookstore in Muncie, Chris and Aly Vyain, Abe Sandoval, Josh Lund, Joe King, Crystal Kidd, and last, but certainly not least, my aunt Terri Lynn Juarez, who was with me the night I learned the truth.

Special acknowledgment should be made to Marla Brooks, the Rev. Tim Shaw, the people at Spirit Finder's Radio Network, Dave Wilson, and those wonderful writers who have kept me interested in this subject for several decades: John Keel, Frank Edwards, Dr. Jacques Vallee, Whitley Strieber, Jim Marrs, Budd Hopkins, Charles Fort, Daniel Cohen, Erich von Däniken, and old gents with names like Heinlein, Hubbard, Lovecraft, Wells, Asimov, Herbert, and Bradbury. I wish us all peace, wherever we may, respectively, be.

"I believe in them now;
I didn't…until I saw it."

~Anonymous

Foreword

The Footsteps of the Mystery

John Pickman

We lie cheek and jowl with the Unknown. It's a part of our everyday existence, a theme more powerful and universal than any we create for ourselves. It's so omnipresent, in fact, that we have a hard time seeing it. You know how farmers who work with chickens will eventually stop noticing the smell of the chicken coop? Same with us, only more so. Not only do we not notice the miasma of the Unknown about us, we've forgotten there ever was anything there in the first place. From grade school onward we are fed a line of comforting patter—by science, by religion, by the endlessly prattling voice of the television. Everything is explainable; everything is understood. Anything we don't understand we have experts working on, so don't worry about it. We'll probably explain it tomorrow.

No.

A rational, explainable Universe? Give me a break. We don't know where we come from, or what lies beyond the zygote. We don't know where we go to, or what lies beyond the pine box. We don't know why we fall asleep at night, or how we wake up again in the morning. We don't know what our dreams are, or why they happen. And, of course, we don't have a clue about the biggest question of all: Why everything?

Ancient peoples had shamans and portents to interpret the inexplicable. The Greeks had their gods, meddling in the world of mortals. Even in the middle ages, we had demons and witchcraft to point to when things went all strange. But now, in this modern world, we have done away with all of those things. We no longer have a framework with which to deal with the mysterious; and instead of rectifying this problem, we've spent the last three centuries pretending it doesn't exist, like a child hiding under the blankets in the belief that anything we can't see isn't there.

And yet.

Imagine it. You're walking along a country road, late at night. You see a strange light in the sky that seems to be behaving oddly, moving in ways no airplane would ever move. It comes closer. Strange thoughts begin bubbling up in your mind, surreal and nonsensical thoughts that don't seem to come from you at all. Everything seems full of a significance that you can almost understand, everything about to open up like some marvelous lotus—

You find yourself a mile down the road. You look at your watch and realize that three hours have passed. Three hours that you cannot remember. You stagger home, fall into bed, and by the next morning, it seems distant and unreal, almost like something that happened to someone else, or something you may have seen in a movie.

We have no framework, no language for these kinds of things, and yet they happen every day. Visions and trances, synchronicity and eerie connections, unsettling bumps in the nighttime of our subconscious.

Terence McKenna breaking into DMT space and finding a world of living machines. Philip K. Dick lying stunned on his bed, struck by a beam of pure information from an orbiting source. Robert Anton Wilson staring in wonder at his own television. "And how are you tonight, Mr. Wilson?" You can't be Sirius.

Jim Keith, the conspiracy writer, coins his eponymous Law: "All conspiracy authors must die under unusual circumstances." In 1999, at the Burning Man festival, he falls down and breaks his leg, has to go in for surgery. He confesses to his friends that he is afraid to be put under for this fairly ordinary surgery, that he will somehow die. He claims he did a Tarot reading, and the cards came out all wrong. During the operation, a blood clot is released in his leg and he dies there on the operating table, another victim of the very law he gave a name to.

Something weird is going on here.

People have been seeing strange things in the sky, communicating with strange entities, and having inexplicable experiences for as long as human history can record. The Celtic countries speak of changelings, little people who steal babies and replace them with withered imitations. Three hundred years later, a rash of people claim aliens stole the fetuses from their wombs. The UFO community is obsessed with alien/human hybrids. People are abducted by beings that convey information that seems so important, so vital...if only they could remember what it was...

The Other has always been with us. The unnamed something waiting behind the door. It has always been a source of fear, because—as H. P. Lovecraft so aptly pointed out—the most powerful kind of fear is fear of the Unknown. The unspeakable thing that lies beyond the veil. "Ghosties and ghoulies and long-leggedy beasties and things that go bump in the night."

Things that go bump in the night.

We could turn away from all this easily enough, and most people do. Apart from campfire stories and Halloween night, no one wants to hear spooky tales, and no one ever wants to hear spooky tales that don't make sense. Alan Moore, the author, once ran into a character he had created—DC Comics occultist John Constantine—in a sandwich bar in Westminster. "Constantine" looked at Moore, and smiled, and walked away. What is anyone to make of that? What about the woman who reported a UFO and claimed she knew it was a UFO because it had "UFO" written on the underside of it?

We can turn away, but that doesn't make the Other go away. In the quiet hours of the night, we wake in the dark and remember who we are. We remember how scary it was outside the firelight, how dark. We remember how the bigger we built the bonfire, the more darkness we uncovered. And something seemed to be out there. Something not us.

And yet.

So many of our problems, as a race, evolve from our fear of the new, the unknown, the alien. Psychologist Carl Jung claimed that the UFO represented a symbol of wholeness, a mandalic representation of our own alienation from ourselves. Our darkness. Our mystery.

Whatever it is, it's been with us since the very beginning, and if we're ever to grow up as a race, we must confront it. Not to understand it, but to claim the mystery as our own. Our mystery. Our darkness.

Become the Other.

I know it's dark out there. Don't be afraid. Take my hand; we'll go together.

"We have been to the moon,
we have charted the depths of the ocean
and the heart of the atom,
but we have a fear of looking inward
to ourselves because we sense
that is where all the contradictions flow together."

~Terence Mckenna

Introduction
An Enigma

"By a route obscure and lonely,
Haunted by ill angels only,
Wherein an Eidolon, named NIGHT,
On a black throne reigns upright,
I have reached these lands but newly
From an ultimate dim Thule–
From a wild weird clime that lieth, sublime,
Out of SPACE–out of TIME."

~Edgar Allen Poe

The Midwest, with its endless miles of lonely fields and its wide-open expanses of bright blue sky, is the perfect setting for UFO stories, and indeed, many, many such accounts have come from this area in the past 100 years. One such account, chronicled in the report *Regional Encounters*, has a UFO landing outside of my own hometown of Gas City, Indiana in 1897. The object, which landed about a mile and a half (two kilometers) outside the farm of a man named Roush, carried a number of occupants, who were said to emerge from the craft, work around it as if trying to repair it, and then reenter, only to mysteriously fly away. Whether or not there is any truth in this story depends strictly on what you believe. At the time, the country was being inundated with stories of "mystery airships" carrying mad inventors and crews said to look "just like ordinary folks."

Of course, the present author has been blessed (or, alternately cursed) with having seen UFOs for himself, having witnessed one close-up many years ago, and having a pretty good knowledge of the subject from intense interest that has alternately waxed and waned over the years. The book you are about to read, in fact, is the second version of the book I've set out to write, as the first version did not seem to do justice to the subject, or cover it in a way that was acceptable to my own standards. Thus, we have here a second book that is more personal, less of a "book report" type book, and one which, I hope, will spare the reader the intense boredom of reading a book that seems as if it should have been written in 1977. The book that follows then, is one that involves my own experiences, as well as the documented experiences of others. I hope that it might make a believer out of some of you, or, at the very least, teach you to look at a subject that most find laughable in a new, more conscientious way.

It might even teach you to stop and consider the wonder of the vast vault of the heavens, and look skyward each night, with new, and child-like eyes.

Submit it for your approval: A man on a trip cross country, with his wife and child in tow, stops for a few hours of rest at a roadside motel, eager for a little relaxation, a little shuteye, a chance to get off the road. He curls up in bed next to his wife, but for some strange reason finds that he cannot sleep. He goes down to the lobby, walks out to the parking lot, lights a cigarette, and plays over in his head exactly how much more driving he has ahead of him.

Off in the distance, he notices something strange. It looks like a shooting star. A weird, bouncing ball of light. He thinks maybe it is an airplane; hell, maybe it's a satellite. He stares at it with bleary eyes for a few moments, shrugs his shoulders, and goes back in the lobby. He makes for the elevator, goes up to the room to wake his wife up. He wants to get back on the road before sunup; something is making him edgy.

His wife crawls out of bed a perfect bear, stretches, yawns, and finally forces herself to get patched up and dressed. They make a quick breakfast in the all-night diner downstairs, and hustle their little man into the backseat as Dad warms up the car and the sun starts to peep, gradually, out from the edge of the old field across the road.

They pull out of the parking lot, and, by now, the man isn't thinking about the strange light that he saw anymore. In fact, he is just thinking about reaching his destination in a good amount of time, of his gas mileage, of the condition of the car, of how much this little excursion has cost them, and a million other things. But anomalous lights in the sky aren't one of them.

He wishes for a coffee, tries to make some small talk, finds it is better just to let the radio fill up the silence. In the backseat, Junior has fallen asleep, and it looks like wifey is about to fall back to sleep as well. He smiles; he loves his family a lot. Life is good.

He looks out the driver's side window and across the field. He suddenly notices that strange light again. Now, it seems to have grown bigger. He wonders what on Earth it could possibly be. He thinks he can almost see a shape behind the light, but he isn't sure. He laughs nervously to himself, thinking wild thoughts about "little green men." He has always felt such claims were nothing but the products of overheated imaginations and deranged minds.

But that light seems to be tailing them, pacing them; even stalking them. He speeds up a little, unconsciously trying to outrun it, but the damn thing seems to get closer, and there is no getting away from it. He feels the first few stirrings of panic grip his chest. He suddenly realizes that something unusual is going on, something quite extraordinary in fact. He wakes his wife.

"Honey," he says, trying to control the tremor in his voice, "what is that?"

She groggily looks out the windshield at the light, which has now grown enormous. She is silent for a few moments, then says, "I haven't the faintest idea. But it looks like it's about to land on top of us!"

The light has now resolved itself into a disc-shaped craft, alternating red and green flashes, with a dome on top and what appears to be portholes along the sides. Dad brings the car to a screeching halt at the side of the road, and Junior now rouses himself. Seeing the object in the sky, he is silent, seemingly awed with wonder.

Dad moves to get out of the car, but his wife grabs his shoulder.

"No, Bill, are you crazy! You don't know what in hell that thing is!"

"I just want to get a better look at it, is all!"

He gets out, suddenly remembering the old field glasses he keeps in the glove compartment. He gets these and gets out of the car. The thing is hovering so close he hardly needs them.

He can see vague shapes at the portholes, moving. It looks like there are occupants on board, operating the thing, whatever the hell it happens to be. Bill can't believe his eyes. His hands shake, and he suddenly remembers that he has a camera stowed away in the trunk. Will he have time to get it before the thing disappears? He figures he at least better try, as no one, but no one, will believe this without some sort of photographic proof.

He drops the field glasses in the driver's seat, gets his keys, and goes back to the trunk. The UFO (for that is undoubtedly what it is) is still hovering silently above the road, almost as if it is putting itself on display. Bill goes around to the trunk while his wife is begging him, pleading with him, to get back in the car and drive away. Now Junior is crying, as scared as his mother, but Bill is determined to get at least one good photograph of the thing. He goes back to the trunk.

Suddenly, something strange happens.

The world suddenly seems to grow dark.

Bill remembers putting the key in the trunk. Then, things just sort of go dim. The next thing he remembers he is behind the wheel, driving, in the opposite direction from where he needed to go. The wife is silent, the kid has apparently fallen back to sleep. They discuss, quietly, what they have just witnessed, but it all seems fuzzy now, somehow—dreamlike. Eventually, they just stop talking about it.

They finally stop for lunch, and they both decide to put the strange sighting out of their minds. Just don't talk about it, they think. No one will ever believe it anyway.

Bill and his family enter the busy restaurant, and Bill suddenly catches a glimpse at the clock on the wall. Puzzled, he looks down at his watch. It seems to have stopped.

His watch stopped at eleven-fifteen. It is now nearly two o'clock. Even given the distance from the motel to this roadside eatery, they should have arrived here much earlier than that, nearly an hour earlier. Somehow, Bill realizes, they have lost just over an hour of time while on the road. This begins to disturb him.

Later, Bill and his wife are plagued by troubling dreams. These dreams invariably involve UFOs (which are referred to by Bill and his friends as "flying saucers"), and seem to involve being taken on board the thing for some sort of "medical exam." The UFO occupants themselves are an ugly, big-headed lot with scary, large eyes. They look a little like mongoloids. Bill and his wife compare their dreams, and come to the conclusion that something must have happened, something they can't quite remember.

But what can they do? Who will ever believe them? And, most importantly, how will they ever come to grips with this frightening, bizarre new reality that seems to have manifested, quite unexpectedly, in their lives?

The above story, of course, is a sort of composite, but it illustrates well the reality behind so many UFO encounters—encounters that have been happening, with greater and greater frequency for the last sixty years. Ever since Kenneth Arnold spotted nine disc-shaped objects flying aerial acrobatics over Mt. Rainier, Washington in 1947, the subject of alien visitation has been one that has fascinated, delighted, and terrified millions of people. Yet, is there any truth to any of this?

There are, of course, many different types of paranormal phenomena that are fascinating and fun to speculate about. People believe in ghosts, Ouija boards, séances, strange creatures, mental telepathy, even magic and time travel. Yet, no phenomenon known to us has quite the same fascination and appeal as UFOs. Perhaps that is because hundreds of thousands of witnesses, for decades upon decades, have reported seeing them in the skies, on the ground, and have even reported meeting their occupants and being taken aboard the craft. Some of these stories seem silly; some are frightening. All of these stories are fascinating.

People seem to be under the impression that UFOs are a relatively new phenomenon, that, somehow, beginning in the 40s, the "aliens" (if that is what they truly are) decided to come to Earth to warn us about our atomic experiments and our propensity to make war. These people seem to think that UFOs just appeared in our skies as a response to the bombing of Hiroshima and Nagasaki.

Nothing could be further from the truth. UFOs have always been with us, as the following section of this book will amply demonstrate.

Chapter 1
Ancient History

The roots of the UFO problem go back into the mists of antiquity. Most people are already aware of this, to some degree, thanks to television specials on the History Channel and other networks. It is supposed by many that "ancient astronauts" first came to Earth some 450,000 years ago, that they helped create the first great civilizations in lower Mesopotamia, and that they helped erect the many breathtaking monuments that cover the face of the Earth, mysterious monuments such as the Great Pyramid of Giza.

It is undeniable that a civilization, a lost civilization, existed on Earth many thousands of years ago. It is here that we return to our stories of the lost civilization of Atlantis, that paradisiacal place where man cavorted with the "gods" in perfect harmony, before the advent of a great cataclysm destroyed his hopes and dreams.

There are many mediums (people who claim to be able to speak with the dead) who claim to be in communication with lost souls from Atlantis. Apparently, the Atlanteans lived in a high state of spiritual and technological development for their time, had a utopian government, and lived in perfect harmony with each other and with nature. Occultists such as Helena Blavatsky hinted at such a "golden period" in books such as *Isis Unveiled,* and the Nazis took inspiration from this for their insane theories about perfecting the world for the "Aryan Race." Whatever the case, there are troubling archaeological finds, such as machined cubes of metal of impossibly ancient origin, screws and coins found in layers of rock many thousands of years older than where, by logic, they should have been found, and, of course, the massive megaliths like the three stones at Baalbeck (each weighing an estimated 800 tons) that are placed high on a wall. Since no modern crane could possibly lift such stones, how did the ancients manage to do it?

According to "ancient astronaut" theorists such as Erich von Däniken, they didn't. These anachronistic technological marvels are the result of galactic intervention on the part of space visitors from long ago.

Of course, Atlantis, if it existed at all, is rumored to have sunk beneath the waves, and certain finds like the Bimini Wall seem to suggest that something indeed sank beneath the waves during some cataclysmic shift in prehistory. It is also rumored that the Atlanteans destroyed themselves through their advanced (alien?) technology. Perhaps they had a nuclear war, or a war using weapons so terrible that they would boggle the mind of modern man, whose own destructive capability is considerable. Whatever the case, one theory, put forward by Brad Steiger in his excellent book *The Fellowship*, has the Atlanteans learning of an imminent disaster about to befall their great civilization. In desperation, they build an "ark," a spaceship, capable of combing the stars in search of a hospitable new home world to colonize. A remnant quickly escape in the space ark, leaving behind the rest to die in the cataclysm. But there are survivors among the Atlanteans, and this is where the scenario becomes most interesting.

After perhaps hundreds or thousands of years, the escapees aboard the space ark, having perhaps now settled on a distant planet hospitable to life, begin to yearn for the rolling green hills of Mother Earth. They organize a return visit to the stricken home world, only to find, to their horror, that the survivors of the cataclysm have regressed to the point of primitives living in caves. They slowly begin to help the primitives rebuild.

But that is just one theory.

All human civilization seems to trace back, 7,000 years, to ancient Sumer (the Biblical land of Shinar), which is located in present-day Iraq. The ancient Sumerians experienced an incredible transformation in the way they lived, from primitive nomads and hunter-gatherers to the founders of an advanced civilization that made great strides in architecture, astronomy, mathematics, and other sciences.

The Sumerians, whose "gods" were depicted riding winged discs, surrounded by stars and other astral bodies, charted the heavens with astounding measurements that do not fail to impress modern researchers. For instance, their measurements of the rotation of the moon are said to deviate only 0.4 percent from our modern measurements. They likewise had a heliocentric model of the universe—meaning they realized that the earth and the other planetary bodies revolved around the sun.

The Greeks, whose highest number was 10,000, were long before outdone by the Sumerians, who recorded a 15-digit number—195,955,200,000,000—on a stone tablet found in the Kuyunjik hills.

How did the ancient Sumerians rise up from simple nomads to the builders of great temples and ziggurats, from wandering primitives to scientists determined to plot the course of the heavens? Well, according to the Babylonian priest Berossus, they did so with the help a strange being called Oannes, a being that lived on land by day, but took to the water at night.

Described as utterly repulsive, Oannes was said to have had the feet of both a man and a fish, to have a fish head and a human head, and to "take no nourishment by day." The Sumerians, who Berossus describes as living "like the beasts of the field," spent the day being instructed by Oannes, who taught them the finer points of civilized living. Of course, it has been suggested by some that Oannes must have been an extraterrestrial visitor.

Brad Steiger, from his book *The Fellowship*, states:

> Let us assume that you are an extraterrestrial sent to Earth to instruct the primitive inhabitants on the rudiments of civilization. Let us also presume that Homo sapiens was seeded there many generations ago; it is now time to pass along knowledge from the mother planet. You will need a safe, secure headquarters for your crewman and the spaceship, which is capable of underwater propulsion. Wouldn't you consider submerging your craft in a quiet lagoon and emerging on land each morning in an underwater diving suit? If we allow our imagination to expand we can see ancient scribes attempting to describe what is today a conventional diving suit, "both a fish head and a human head."[1]

The late biblical scholar, Zecharia Sitchin, had his own theories concerning the rise of Sumerian culture, which he chronicled in a number of popular books beginning with the *12th Planet*. His theory? In his opinion, the Sumerians were aided by the intervention of ancient space visitors from a planet called Nibiru, a planet with an elliptical orbit that came close to earth once every 3,600 years. He refers to Nibiru as the "12th Planet" because of the cosmology of the Sumerians, which counted eight planets, plus the Moon, the sun, and Pluto. Sitchin interpreted the ancient cuneiform writing of the Sumerians to decode what he felt were the beginnings of the Earth itself, a time when one of Nibiru's moons, Tiamat, collided with a planet between Mars and Jupiter, creating the asteroid belt. A further collision created the Earth.

The advanced extraterrestrials of Nibiru, called Annunaki, came to Earth some 450,000 years ago, primarily to mine gold and other minerals in Africa. They founded a colony of workers, but, because of labor struggles, decided to experiment with the genetic engineering of Homo erectus, a primitive ape. The Annunaki known as Enki and Ninkharsag thus created, in what sounds in modern terms suspiciously like a test tube, a new being: Homo sapiens sapiens. They called this first being a "Lulu."

The addition of this genetically-engineered slave labor force did nothing to quell the burgeoning rebellion among the Annunaki worker class, and struggles between various factions led, eventually, to what Sitchin believed was a nuclear war. He believed this war was responsible for the "evil wind" reference that is referred to in the "Lament of Ur." Ur was destroyed, according to Sitchin, in 2024 B.C.

The Annunaki not only created man, but also created his government. According to Sitchin, they established the "divine right of kings" among men, setting up intermediaries as royalty between themselves and their human slaves. Conspiracy theorists today posit that this "underground stream" of knowledge exists as the "secret society network," and that there may even be a hidden, extraterrestrial or "ultra terrestrial" hand in human politics and affairs. More on this later.

Ancient Indian literature also gives us "gods" flying about on miraculous UFOs, called "vimanas." These texts, primarily in the *Ramayana* and the *Rig Veda*, offer descriptions of events that sound suspiciously like nuclear war:

> Elephants burst into flames...the rivers boiled. Animals crumpled to the ground and died. The armies of the enemy were mowed down when the raging of the elements reached them. Forests collapsed in splintered rows. Horses and chariots were burned up....The corpses of the fallen were mutilated by the terrible heat, so that they looked other than human...never before had we heard of such a ghastly weapon.[2]

Indra, called the "fort destroyer" because of the magnificent power of his space-age weaponry, was the god who flew the Vimana. These craft are described in awesome technical detail in ancient passages such as the following:

> The secret of constructing aeroplanes, which will not break, which cannot be cut, will not catch fire, and cannot be destroyed. The secret of making planes motionless. The secret of making planes invisible. The secret of hearing conversations and other sounds in enemy planes. The secret of receiving photographs of the interior of enemy planes. The secret of ascertaining the direction of enemy planes' approach. The secret of making persons in enemy planes lose consciousness. The secret of destroying enemy planes...Metals suitable for aeroplanes, light and heat-absorbing, are of 16 kinds...Great sages have declared that these metals alone are the best for aeroplane construction.[3]

Did ancient man have the capability of flight? Puzzling ancient structures, such as the famous ground markings at Nazca in Peru (which can only be seen from the air), seem to give some credence to this idea. If some ancient, pre-flood civilization *did* have the power of flight, from where did they acquire the technological know how? These are puzzling questions.

UFOs in the Bible

No one should be surprised to find that UFOs make appearances in the Bible; after all, we've all seen those television programs on the History Channel, right? However, in case someone out there reading this is not on the same wavelength as the rest of us, we can briefly recount a few of these Biblical UFOs as an example.

The prophet Ezekiel is renowned for his own spectacular vision of the "wheel within a wheel," which was ringed about with "eyes" and which was under the control of the "four living creatures." Let's look at the Biblical text from Ezekiel Chapter 1:

> Now it came to pass in the thirtieth year, in the fourth month, as I was among the captives by the river of Chebar, that the heavens were opened, and I saw visions of God...
>
> Out of the midst thereof came the likeness of four living creatures... they had the likeness of a man...
>
> Now as I beheld the living creatures, behold one wheel upon the earth by the living creatures...
>
> The appearance of the wheels and their work was like unto the color of a beryl: and their appearance and their work was as it were a wheel...
>
> And when they went, they went upon their four sides: and they turned not when they went.
>
> As for their rings, they were so high that they were dreadful; and their rings were full of eyes round them four.
>
> And when the living creatures went, the wheels went by them: and when the living creatures were lifted up from the earth, the wheels were lifted up.[4]

Of course, Ufologists have speculated much about what Ezekiel meant, even suggesting that the "four faces" of the "living creatures" might be the insignia of a star-voyaging race who accosted Ezekiel while dressed in modern space suits. One NASA scientist, Josef Blumrich, went so far as to build a replica of what he thought Ezekiel's UFO might possibly look like; he came up with something that looked like a lunar Lander with four helicopter blades.

Much has been made of the term "pillar of cloud by day, pillar of fire by night." This was the description of how Yahweh led the Children of Israel through the wilderness and out of bondage in Egypt. During this grueling forty-year period, Yahweh caused a certain substance, called "manna," to drop from the sky and feed the Israelites. Moses originally saw and spoke with God in a "burning bush," that burned and was not consumed; he later went up on a mountain to commune with God, a mountain that was ringed with light all about it.

God commanded the children of Israel to build the Ark of the Covenant. Author Barry Greenwood, in his book *The Bible and Flying Saucers*, speculates that Yahweh (who he contends was a space visitor in a UFO) used this device, which conducted a powerful electric charge, to communicate with the ancient Israelites; that it was in essence his two-way radio.

Going back even further in the Bible, Greenwood posits that the destruction of Sodom and Gomorrah was accomplished by UFOs, who vaporized both cities with atomic weapons of some sort.

There are dark hints, too, in the book of Genesis, of mankind and his early mating with "fallen angels" or "Nephilim": beings cast out by God for their sexual lust for human females. These beings are said to have begat children with human women, and these children were legendary monsters who indulged in all manner of cruel practice and cannibalism before being killed off by the great deluge.[5] As many already know, author Zechariah Sitchin has identified these "Nephilim" with the Annunaki extraterrestrial colonists of the ancient Sumerian legends.

Angels are treated strangely in the Bible, having both a physical and spiritual essence. The angels apparently looked "just like humans," as do many accounts of space brothers as given to us by the contactees. Like the space brothers, the angels in the Bible are said to be able to turn on and off their divine essence, appearing in their true nature only when it serves the purpose of God.

The prophet Zechariah saw a "flying scroll" that he proclaimed to be the "curse that goeth around the world." The apocryphal Book of Enoch records an interstellar tour provided by fallen angels. Later, in the New Testament, we have the "Star of Bethlehem," which Greenwood has credited as being a UFO. Also, the Ascension of Christ upon a "pillar of cloud" is thought by some to refer to a UFO (those, at least, who think of Jesus as another "ascended master space brother" in a long line of them), a notion that strikes the more religious as utter blasphemy.[6]

The "four living creatures" make another appearance in Revelations, apparently sitting in the throne room of God. Most bizarrely, we have a final vision of a strange flying vehicle in the Bible in the form of the "New Jerusalem," an aerial city (mothership?) that descends from the clouds at the end of time.

Now, because we've had quite enough of this subject, we're going to move on.

Ancient Astronaut Theories

The lead proponent of the theory of "ancient astronauts," or that space visitors came to Earth in the distant past and aided ancient man in his development, is author Erich von Däniken, who interprets the ancient art and inscriptions of early man in light of his ancient astronaut beliefs. The result is a number of startling and intriguing works, which paint the bizarre headdresses and ceremonial costumes of distant tribes as representative "space gear," worn to give them the same semblance of power as the extraterrestrial visitors of long, long ago.

To give a few examples of von Däniken's interpretations, we have the cave etchings found in the Tassili mountains of the Algerian Sahara. These ancient etchings consist of hundreds of pictures of men wearing what appear to be round helmets with antenna on their heads. Von Däniken interprets this as being the dress of space visitors, and also interprets another etching, a round vehicle-like object with four concentric circles and a hatch on top, as being that of an ancient extraterrestrial spacecraft.

He likewise interprets the plateau of El Enladrillado in Chile as being an "extraterrestrial landing base." The plateau, which was discovered in 1968, is only accessible by horseback, but when visitors finally reach the place, they are often astounded by what they find. The plateau is covered by massive, rectangular stone blocks, twelve to sixteen feet high and twenty to thirty feet long, with smooth surfaces; 200 of which are grouped into a sort of amphitheatre. Remember: the plateau itself is only accessible by horseback. *Who could have erected these ancient stones?* Von Däniken wonders, as it is not thought, generally, that the natives could have ever accomplished it.

There are many such wonders, of course, spread out across the continents of the world. At Baalbeck, in Lebanon, according to researcher David Icke, there are three massive stones positioned high upon a wall. Each stone weighs an estimated 800 tons; no modern crane could possibly lift them. How then did the ancients manage to do it? (One might likewise ask how a man like little Edward Leedskalnin managed to build the remarkable Coral Castle in south Florida by himself, in modern times.)

To von Däniken, the ancients didn't erect such monuments; or, if they did, they had help from extraterrestrial visitors who had the technology to move the massive stones into place effortlessly. This has also been suggested as the answer to the enigmas of the building of the Great Pyramid of Giza, of Stonehenge, and other massive, ancient wonders.

Von Däniken likewise speculates about Tiahuanaco. At Tiahuanaco there is an ancient city atop a plateau, with an elevation of 13,000 feet. The ancients, despite the fact that working conditions at such an elevation must have been brutal, were able to construct buildings made of massive sandstone blocks. Some of these blocks weigh a hundred tons, and are topped with blocks of similar height and weight. Yet, they are smooth and perfectly fitted together, held with metal clamps. Who among the ancient peoples of South America had the ability to construct such marvels?

There is a massive monument at Tiahuanaco called "The Gate of the Sun," a monument hewn from a single stone block. The inscriptions upon the face of the stone tell of an alien visitor called Oryama, who came to the Earth long ago in a "golden spaceship." According to these legends, Oryama had four webbed fingers, gave birth to seventy children, and, in time came to miss her home among the stars. She soon decided to return to it.

One apocryphal story of "ancient astronauts" has recently been denounced, by UFO researcher Dr. Jacques Vallée, as a hoax. The story goes thusly: In China, in 1938, the archaeologist Chi Pu Tei discovered a series of strange graves, placed in orderly rows, in the Sino-Tibetan border district. The walls of the cave in which these graves were found were decorated with curious pictures, depicting helmeted men dancing amid the Sun, Moon, and stars, each of these linked by a series of dots. Inside the graves, he found a series of granite plates with a hole in the center and a spiraling groove coming out to the edge. Von Däniken has compared them to phonograph records.

What was most remarkable about the graves were the skeletons themselves, for, while the bodies of the skeletons were slight, their heads were oversized, leading Chi Pu Tei to theorize that they were a species of extinct mountain ape. But, if they were simply a species of ape, how could they have managed to dig out a graveyard in orderly rows? Finally, part of the inscription on the stone slabs was deciphered, and revealing a very peculiar history.

It told of a spaceship that crashed on earth 12,000 years ago, bearing friendly visitors from another planet (the "Dropas") who tried to make peace with the native inhabitants. However, the natives killed some of the extraterrestrials, so the others hid in caves.[7]

Did the archaeologist accidentally stumble upon the burial ground of an ancient alien race? Von Däniken certainly seems to think so, and this is only one example he gives, over his series of bestselling books, as proof that extraterrestrials visited us in the distant past, helped us create civilization, erect massive monuments, and begin our long, arduous journey back to the stars.

Here is von Däniken expounding upon his own ideas of man's origins based on an idea of a spaceship discovering the planet:

> The crew of the spaceship soon found out that Earth had all the prerequisites for intelligent life to develop. Obviously the "man" of those times was not homo sapiens but something different. The spacemen artificially fertilized some female members of this species, put them into a deep sleep, so ancient legends say, then departed. Thousands of years later the space travelers returned and found scattered specimens of the genus homo sapiens. They repeated their breeding experiment several times until finally they produced a creature intelligent enough to have the rules of society imparted to it.[8]

Von Däniken's books are wildly popular, and have sold millions of copies.

UFOs and the Native Americans

UFOs are important in the folklore of many Native American cultures. The Hopi, for instance, speak of a race of sky visitors called Kachinas and make reference to these beings riding on "flying shields," or paatuwvota, objects which sound remarkably similar to our modern stories of flying saucers.

Native American belief pictures the world as "Turtle Island," a place surrounded by dimensional portals, a void referred to as "the ocean of pitch," and various races of extraterrestrial beings. Several tribes, including the Dakota, the Hopi, and the Iriquois, locate their place of origin as the Pleiadies star system, and even pray to the Pleiadies for happiness. The Hopi refer to the Pleiadies as Chuhukon, the Navajos as Delyahey—a place which they claim from a "Black God" originates—and the Cree claim they descended from the Pleiadies in spirit form before obtaining flesh and blood bodies.

(Those familiar with UFO folklore know the Pleiadies to be the professed home of many extraterrestrial contacts.)

Native legend speaks of the "ages of destruction" that mankind must pass through, and the shaman is tasked with the responsibility of descending to the achiva, or underground world, there to commune with the "Ant People," a race that sound suspiciously like Grey aliens.

The home of the Kachinas was said to be a mountaintop where there are "great cloud formations." The Hopi believed that they would be gathered there, on the Day of Purification, and that the Kachinas would return for them from their home among the stars.[9]

Author Gary A. David relates the Hopi legend of "flying shields," called paatuwvota. These "flying shields" existed in the "Third World," a time when the Hopi believe their people lived in a utopian paradise of great wonders and technology. This paradise, unfortunately, was devastated by a great flood. The "flying shields" were devices that were associated with Sotuknang, the Hopi sky god, who figures in a legend about Palatkwapi, the "red city to the south," which, David states, was possibly located near modern-day Sedona, Arizona.

The legend states that a man named Tiwahongva and his sister Tawiyayisnima both fled the destruction of their city. They made camp in the wilderness when, one evening, just getting ready to eat, they heard a great roaring overhead. They looked up, and what should they see to their amazement, but the "flying shield." This landed and a fantastic being emerged "glittering like ice" with a face that "shone like a star." He told them not to fear, that he was Sotuknang, and that he was greatly touched by their plight. He told them that he would take them to safety, and invited them for a ride aboard his "flying shield."

They then traveled through the heavens, astounded that they could see for many miles in every direction. Sotuknang told them that they must listen to his teachings, which would "arrive in dreams." He then brought them to the camp where their parents were, and rose into the sky, departing.

The similarity to UFO contact stories and the above folktale should be apparent to anyone.

Quoting author Frank Waters' book *Mexico Mystique*, David writes:

> On Second Mesa near Mishongnovi an ancient petroglyph depicts a dome-shaped object resting on an arrow which represents travel through space, and the head of a Hopi maiden who represents pristine purity. As the Hopis believe that other planets are inhabited, this petroglyph represents a paatuwvota or a "flying shield" similar to a "flying saucer" that came here in the Beginning. So now at the End the sacred ones will arrive from another planet, said to be Venus, by flying saucers. Many Hopi traditionalists recently have reported seeing flying saucers, all piloted by beings they call kachinas.[10]

Interestingly, much like today's UFO abductors, the Kachina were, at times, enamored of human women and used them sexually. This theme of humans mating with nonhuman entities is recurrent through *all* world folklore it seems, from the "Nephilim" of Genesis to the fairy folklore (see next section) of ancient Europe. The wilder claims of alien abduction and molestation feature alien/human rape, sometimes by Greys and sometimes by the sort of Satanic, "reptilian" entities that feature prominently in the conspiracy theories of David Icke and several others.

However, to return to the subject at hand, author Robert Morning Sky, in his book *The Terra Papers*, relates a bizarre story of his Hopi grandfather and four other men, who, while camping in the desert, saw a UFO crash land. They sought out the object, and found a survivor, a being in a silvery suit that communicated with them through the use of a strange crystal. This being, who they named the "Star Elder," told them a tale of a galactic war raging in space. Apparently, the "Star Elder" had been one of the warriors, although David notes that this material is "unconfirmed."

He further notes that "hundreds" of UFO sightings occurred southwest of the Hopi villages in 1970, and that, more recently (March 13,1997), a gigantic delta-winged craft was sighted in Phoenix by many, many witnesses (the "Phoenix Lights"). That object was said to be a mile across.[11]

Other native legends hint at UFO intervention. The Eskimos apparently believed that their ancestors were flown to the polar regions by a race of beings that were god-like, possessing metallic wings. There is also a Mayan tale of a "great eagle." The eagle landed with a mighty roar, and the beak of the eagle, which was made of iron, opened, revealing four people who were not human. The four apparently did not breathe the "same air."

The Popol Vuh, the Bible of the Quiches tribe of Guatemala, lays out an old Mayan story concerning a race of sky visitors who used the compass and knew "the secrets of the universe." This race of sky visitors knew that the world was round (something it took Galileo and Keppler some time to hammer out), and, when the people attempted to steal their secrets, the sky visitors "fogged their minds," or rendered them unable to complete the task.

Returning to the United States, the Yakima Indians have a legend of a curious healer with red eyes, who came to help the tribe before finally growing too old. The man realized that he was going to die, so, had the tribe carry his body to a secret location. It was here that a curious craft landed, and took the body away to the stars. Interestingly, the Yakima Indian reservation (which is in Washington) has, in the past, been the site of many UFO encounters and is even considered by some Ufologists to be a "window area"; in other words, a place where UFOs frequent. The reservation recorded, between 1964 and 1984, 186 UFO sightings, most of which were made by the "lookouts," or those tasked with watching for forest fires.

These UFO sightings consisted of red, orange, or sometimes white lights that would be seen skittering and hovering over the area, and sometimes performing odd aerial maneuvers. The presence of these puzzling lights convinced Dr. J.

Allen Hynek to back a study of the Washington Reservation headed by volunteer UFO researcher David Akers.

The study was carried out with an assortment of high-tech equipment, including cameras for both motion and still-shots, a magnetometer, a camera fitted with a grating to analyze light wavelengths, and equipment for measuring nuclear and infrared radiation as well as ultrasound frequencies. Akers spent two weeks there in 1972, but managed to only obtain a few disappointing, indistinct photographs.

UFOs and Fairy Folklore

Not to be left out, ancient Europe certainly had its hands full with flying phantoms. The folklore of fairies, leprechauns, elves, sylphs, and other mythological creatures bears a striking resemblance to modern UFO folklore, particularly if you believe in the idea of UFO abductions. Fairies were inordinately interested in human affairs, particularly birth and reproduction, and a human unlucky enough to stumble upon these terrible creatures could well find him or herself abducted and taken to the "fairy mound." There he or she would be put through the ringer before being let loose to tell their friends and neighbors of strange events in a land where time passed differently.

The fairy entities were said to wear uniforms, wage war, create art and music, have their own cities and kingdoms, their own special ranks, and to take "human wives" upon occasion. These beings were variously described as tall and beautiful, or small and repugnant. They were mischievous, and often came knocking at the door with odd requests. This is an occurrence that is echoed, somewhat, in some modern UFO accounts, like that of Joe Simonton. His flying saucer visitors requested and received a jug of water. They repaid him with a handful of "space cakes." Similarly, there is an airship account wherein a witness was requested by the captain of a landed airship to retrieve for him a "bluestone chisel." Yet another UFO account has beings that were inordinately interested in fertilizer. They requested a bag of the stuff, and one was left for them at the sight where the witness had seen the UFO land. The next day it was gone. But it was considered unwise to have anything to do with those who came knocking, as encounters with the fairies sometimes ended quite badly. Like UFO occupants, the fairies (or "Gentry," or "Good People" as they were called, because supposedly they did not like to hear their proper name used) would sneak into the home in the middle of the night, often to steal a human infant and replace it with one of their own.

The fairy lore was widely believed in Ireland, Scotland, Wales, and Brittany; however, one account comes to us from a man in the early part of the last century. Harry Anderson was walking in his hometown of Barron, Wisconsin, when he saw a strange vision: twenty little men, all walking in single file, wearing suspenders, leather knee pants, and having bald heads. They were bare chested and were making a sound that he interpreted as "mumbling." Apparently, the sight so frightened him he hurried past as quickly as he could, but the vision of the little men stayed with him. And he was not the only one.

Edward Williams had a fairy experience at the age of seven, in 1757, while he was playing in a field in Wales. He was with a few other children when they spied a group of "tiny couples" (sixteen little people in all), all dressed in red and carrying white kerchiefs. The strange little people were a hundred yards distant, he estimates, but the children could hear them speak to one another in an unknown tongue. Suddenly, realizing they were being spied upon, one of the little men gave pursuit, chasing (but not capturing) one of the children. The child who was chased got a good look at the face of his pursuer, which Williams described as "ancient, swarthy, grim." Although it is not made clear how the episode ended, it apparently troubled Williams for the rest of his life.

Another fairy encounter, that of the Rev. Sabine Baring-Gould is recorded as:

> legions of dwarfs of about two feet high running along beside the horses; some sat laughing on the pole, some were scrambling up the harness to get on the backs of the horses.

Baring-Gould was apparently alone in his fairy vision that day, but reportedly his wife and son also had encounters with the Gentry.

A man in England reported fairies in 1842. While passing through a meadow, he saw a number of small figures, some as small as "dolls," dressed in garments that "sparkled as if with spangles." The beings were moving around hand in hand, in a ring, and the man suddenly became afraid. Screwing up his courage later (at the local pub perhaps), he brought a number of companions back to the spot, but the alleged fairies were gone. The man told a local historian:

> They seemed light and shadowy, not like solid bodies…no sound came from them.

On Walpurgisnacht (April 30, a day important to those who practice the occult) of 1973, another Englishwoman, Mary Treadgold, reported sighting a fairy while taking a bus through the Scottish Highlands. The figure was a "miniature man" dressed in bright clothing, with a sack by his side. He was in the act of digging (UFO occupants have been reportedly seen digging soil samples by some witnesses), his foot pushing a spade into the earth as the bus drove away. Mary Treadgold was insistent that she had not seen a "dwarf, child…or a plastic garden gnome," but a real, miniature man. When she later told locals about what she had witnessed, she was told that such sights were "common on the Mull," and that other people had seen "little men" as well.

Robert Kirk catalogued the various aspects of the Sleagh Maith and their strange behavior in his book *The Secret Commonwealth*, in 1691. This book has been pointed to by Vallee and others as a veritable compendium of information regarding man's contact with otherworldly beings over the centuries. There are sixteen individual characteristics of the "Gentry" that, Vallee points out, are also somewhat characteristic of UFO occupants. Those include:

1. They have a nature that is intermediate between man and the angels.
2. Physically, they have very light and fluid bodies, which are comparable to a condensed cloud. They are particularly visible at dusk. They can appear and vanish at will.
3. Intellectually, they are intelligent and curious.
4. They have the power to carry away anything they like.
5. They live inside the earth in caves, which they can reach through any crevice or opening where air passes.
6. When men did not inhabit most of the world, the creatures used to live there and had their own agriculture. Their civilization has left traces[12] on the high mountains; it was flourishing at a time when the whole countryside was nothing but woods and forests.
7. At the beginning of each three-month period, they change quarters because they are unable to stay in one place. Besides, they like to travel. It is then that men have terrible encounters with them, even on the great highways.
8. Their chameleon-like bodies allow them to swim through the air with all their household.
9. They are divided into tribes. Like us, they have children, nurses, marriages, burials, etc., unless they just do this to mock our own customs or to predict terrestrial events.
10. Their houses are said to be wonderfully large and beautiful, but under most circumstances, they are invisible to human eyes. Kirk compares them to enchanted islands. The houses are equipped with lamps that burn forever and fires that need no fuel.
11. They speak very little. When they do talk among themselves, their language is a kind of whistling sound.
12. Their habits and their language when they talk to humans are similar to those of local people.
13. Their philosophical system is based on the following ideas: nothing dies; all things evolve cyclically in such a way that at every cycle they are renewed and improved. Motion is the universal law.
14. They are said to have a hierarchy of leaders, but they have no visible devotion to God, no religion.
15. They have many pleasant and light books, but also serious and complex books dealing with abstract matters.
16. They can be made to appear at will before us through magic.[13]

Thus did Kirk leave a profile of the standard "extraordinary being." As far as comparing UFO occupants with mythological "little men" though, one could not go far wrong in pointing out that, at least in South America, "hairy dwarfs" are a very common form of UFO entity, and have been reported frequently in close encounter and abduction cases.

The Belo Horizonte abduction case, where a Brazilian soldier who was out fishing was accosted by two entities, was said to fit the "hairy dwarf" description. The entities took him to a machine that looked like an "upright cylinder" for a bizarre close encounter that included corpses, a room with rocky walls and strange paintings, an upside-down race car, and a vision of Christ.

Of course, we don't suggest to readers that fairies, elves, gnomes, trolls, or any of the denizens of "the Secret Commonwealth" are or were objectively "real," only that ancient people might have been interpreting visits by UFO occupants in the only way they could: that is, through the cultural conditioning of their own folk beliefs.

Wizards of the Air

Of course, in those days, people really did believe that witches rode broomsticks back and forth to the Sabbath, where, in the form of a hen or a goat, they might commune and have sexual intercourse with the Devil. Such fantastical beliefs do not for good witnesses make, yet, there are a small number of accounts from this era that do smack of the strange or genuinely paranormal.

One example includes that of Agobard, Bishop of Lyons, who in 840 A.D. issued a proclamation denouncing belief in "Magonia," a mythical kingdom in the clouds from whence, reputedly, issued "strange ships" containing mischievous pirates who spirited away corn and crops, and were thought to be responsible for whirlwinds and foul weather. All of this could be taken, out of hand, to simply point to a learned man putting off a popular primitive superstition, were it not for the intervention of Agobard in the execution of several men and women who had been jointly condemned to death due to their having been seen to emerge from a "Magonian airship." For their part, the men and women claimed to have been abducted.

Agobard saved them from being burnt at the stake. (Hence, Jacques Vallée has suggested that Agobard should be declared "the patron saint of abductees"!)

A similar story comes to us from 1270. In Bristol, England, a fantastic aerial ship was said to have sailed overhead (a foreshadow, perhaps, of the American airship sightings that were to come hundreds of years later) and dropped an anchor which caught in a steeple. The vehicle is said to have dropped a ladder which a man quickly scurried down. The man attempted to free the anchor, but the crowd, enraged by the absurdity of the spectacle, stoned him to death. They later burned his body, as they were convinced he was a demon.

Going further back, there is a quite similar Irish legend, which reads:

> It befell that an anchor was dropped from the sky, with a rope attached to it, and one of the flukes caught in the arch above the church door. The people rushed out of the church and saw in the sky a ship with men on board, floating before the anchor-cable, and they saw a man leap overboard and jump down to the anchor, as if to release it. He looked as if he were *swimming in water* (emphasis mine). The folk rushed up and tried to seize him; but the priest forbade the people to hold the man, for it might kill him, he said. The man was freed, and hurried up to the ship, where the crew cut the rope and the ship sailed away

out of sight. But the anchor is in the church, and has been ever since, as a testimony.[14]

Whatever the case, Agobard, for his part, wrote a book condemning belief in Magonia and her crew of piratical airmen in the strongest possible terms. Thus did Agobard become the first authority to engage in OFFICIAL DENIAL.

In an interesting side note, Jacques Vallée has used the designation "Magonia" (in his book *Passport to Magonia*) as a name for the other-dimensional "reality" from which UFOs and their occupants might well originate.

In Japan

UFO sightings were reported in ancient Japan; they were taken as ill-omens and seemed to precede periods of intense revolution and social unrest. One interesting factoid, brought out by Jacques Vallée in his groundbreaking book *Dimensions*, is the existence of earthen statues from the Jomon period, dating to about 3,000 B.C. These statues, which were at first made to represent humans, underwent a gradual shift, depicting strange beings with small legs, broad chests, long arms, and oversized heads covered in "complete helmets." The helmets, said by some archaeologists to simply be burial masks, depict what appear to be "sunglasses," eyes with a peculiarly insect-like slant to them, and a kind of "perforated grate" that seems to be a breathing apparatus. The resemblance to modern UFO occupant descriptions is striking.

In the book *UFO's: Past, Present and Future*, Robert Emenegger gives examples of ancient Japanese UFOs:

August 3rd, 989

> A mysterious object sighted in the heaven had three round objects that were said to later join together. It is likewise said that this occurred during one of the periods of "social unrest" when UFO sightings seemed to be most prevalent.

October 27, 1180

> A luminous object flew out of the mountains of the Kii province, going "beyond the northeast mountain of Fukuhara," before disappearing into the distance. The object, described as looking like an "earthenware vessel" left a luminous trail behind.

September 24, 1235

General Yoritsume, perturbed at the odd aerial displays seen around his encampment, which consisted of lights in the southeast that swung in loops, called together an investigation of the phenomenon. He was reassured by the learned investigators that the phenomenon was nothing to worry about, that it was only "the wind making the stars sway." [Such official denials, Vallee observes wryly, continue to this day.]

September 12, 1271

At Tatsunokuchi, Kamakura, the famous priest Nichiren found himself a very lucky man when, about to be beheaded, a giant object that looked "like the moon" rose up in the sky, convincing the authorities to spare his life.

1361

An object said to be shaped "like a flying drum, about twenty feet in diameter" rose up off the inland sea of western Japan.

January 2, 1458 forward

An object said to be like the "full moon" arose, followed by curious signs and wonders in the heavens. People were said to be amazed by the celestial manifestations. Two months later, on March 17th, five objects that looked like stars appeared, circling the moon, and changing color before vanishing. This upset the citizens of Kyoto very much, who took them to be portents of calamity. The aerial prodigy apparently even troubled the emperor.

Ten years later, on March 8th, a "dark object" making a "sound like a wheel" flew at midnight from Mt. Kasuga. On January 3, 1569, a "flaming star" appeared in the evening sky, and was heralded as a portent of calamity, perhaps signaling the fall of the Chu Dynasty. In May of 1606, during a rash of "fireballs" floating over Kyoto, an object said to be like a "flaming wheel" hovered over Nijo Castle, astounding many of the samurai; the next day, tongues wagged with dark forebodings of doom and despair.

It was at noon, September 1702, when the sun took on a weird, "bloody" color, and strange cotton-like threads began to drift down.

Finally, all hell broke loose on January 2, 1749, when three objects "like the moon" rose in the sky for a period of four days. The government, in an attempt to quell the resulting insurrection, began to execute the rioters, but the situation only grew worse as more aerial objects, three "moons" and later two "suns," were spotted.

Chapter 2:
History Into the Modern Age

I have given you a wealth of information proving the great antiquity of the UFO and "alien visitor" phenomenon, but, just to be thorough, I thought I might give here a few parting shots. The following examples are taken from *Visitors from Outer Space* by Stemman.

Columbus got into the UFO act; he saw a UFO on board the *Santa Maria* on October 11, 1492. The object, which he described as "a light glimmering at a great distance," played hide and seek with Columbus and a second man, who also witnessed the prodigy.

In 1561, people in Nürnberg Germany reported seeing red, blue, and black balls and "discs" floating in the vicinity of the sun; these aerial objects floated for an hour before seemingly falling to the ground in a blaze of fire.

Edmund Halley documented an early UFO report. In March of 1676, a mathematician in Italy documented a "vast body bigger than the moon," which made a "hissing noise," and a noise like a "cart rattling over stones." The sound notwithstanding, the thing was really moving—it was reported as being forty miles up, and traveling at an estimated 100 miles per minute.

Halley himself saw a UFO in 1716: "a light in the sky so bright" he could "read a printed text by it." This light maintained itself for two hours, until it seemingly "reactivated…as if new fuel had been cast in a fire."

On April 5, 1800 a bright object passed over Baton Rouge Louisiana. Described as "big as a house," it left heat to be felt on the ground, and took fifteen minutes to disappear into the sky, headed northeast.

In 1883, Jose Bonila, an astronomer at the Observatory of Zacatecas, was taking photographs of sunspot activity when he noticed upwards of 283 "luminous objects" traveling east to west across the face of the sun. He quickly took photographs of them, but this did little to explain, exactly, what they were. Astronomer Camille Flammarion pronounced them misperceptions of insects, birds, or dust.

Coming back to the modern world, in 1906, while floating in the Persian Gulf near Oman one summer, a British steamer reported an immense wheel of light emerging from the water. The wheel, which seemed considerably bigger than the ship, rose completely silently, shot shafts of intense light through the ship (which didn't, at any rate, seem to affect it) and revolved in the sky before departing. Such reports had been made off and on since 1769; there were eleven such reports between 1848 and 1910.

Finally, few people realize that the term "flying saucer" *did not* originate with pilot Kenneth Arnold, but had been coined much earlier, in 1878, by a Texas farmer named John Martin, who spotted a shiny, disc-shaped object fly over him while on a hunting trip. He described this object as a "flying saucer," seventy years before the term came into popular use.

Author Note: I know that, so far, I have given short shrift to ancient Egypt, and the fact that their deities rode on "winged disks." Likewise, we have said little about the construction of the pyramids and the debate as to whether or not they originated due to extraterrestrial intervention. For this I apologize. I have limited space here, and to include everything would not only be a Herculean task, it would make this book many thousands of pages long. I advise those interested in the pyramids and UFOs to check out the work of Richard C. Hoagland, an eminent researcher whose book, *The Monuments of Mars*, details his theories concerning the "Face on Mars" (the weird Sphinx-like structure photographed by NASA) and other Martian "structures." Hoagland theorizes that those structures could be evidence of an ancient space-voyaging civilization.

Mystery Airships of the Midwest

It was in 1896 that mysterious "airships" began to be seen over Sacramento, California, by scores of confused witnesses. Author Daniel Cohen, in his terrific book *The Great Airship Mystery: A UFO of the 1890s*, explores the mystery in detail. A number of crazy people and attention seekers stepped forward, most notably a lawyer (or two) who claimed to be representing the mad inventor of the airship, who would soon be revealing to the world his astounding creation. Claims were made that the airship would be used to lead an assault on Cuba, and newspapers at the time fought a circulation war based on whether or not they supported or ridiculed the idea of the airship.

What is uncontestable is the fact that, beginning in 1896, a number of people in the West and Midwest sighted three strange, glowing orbs in the sky. When examining these orbs, many people claimed to see what they took for a large, cigar-shaped body resembling a dirigible behind the lights. Witnesses varied in their reports, but some of them claimed fantastic things, such as seeing an airship that was manned by two men riding bicycle contraptions (to keep the propellers running!), and airships that seem more like flying Rube Goldberg inventions than anything capable of interplanetary travel. Although the airship phenomenon was short-lived, it has left Ufologists with a buried treasure trove of intriguing and titillating accounts to examine.

Of course, one thing can be said about the airships: as absurd as their appearance, they somehow managed to fly leisurely over major metropolitan areas, astounding and confusing witnesses, who often gathered in great numbers to watch the peculiar aerial spectacle. For example, in Chicago, the airship made its debut on April 9, 1897, where eager crowds turned out to watch the night sky in amazement. Some people even took to rooftops, and others peered through telescopes and field glasses to get a better look at it.

The *Chicago Times Herald* reported:

> One who was among the first to observe it says the object had all the appearances to him of being composed of two cigar-shaped bodies attached by girders...

A man named Lowen of Evanston observed:

> four lights a short distance apart and moving in unison. The first was a bright white light and appeared to be operated like a searchlight. Behind it was a green light and farther to the rear were green and white lights set closely together.

The *Chicago Tribune* added:

> At several points, the moving wonder was observed by persons with small telescopes or powerful field glasses, and these persons claim to have described the outlines of a structure bearing the lights...the main body of the night flier was about seventy feet in length, of slender proportions and fragile construction. To this body, it is reported, were attached the movable headlight and the other lights described. A few observers claim that they also saw, a short distance above the body, lateral structures resembling wings or sails. These appeared to be about twenty feet in width...

The airship left South Chicago around 9:30, but was spotted in a variety of other places. It was described, in the pages of the *Quincy Whig*, by an observer who noted that it was "shaped like a cigar" and that it was made of some "bright metal, perhaps aluminum," which reflected the moonlight. It was furthermore noted that, "on either side of the hull, extending outward and upward, are what appear to be wings" and that, above this, were the "misty outlines of some sort of superstructure." It goes on to describe "small lights...midway of the hull," and a "green light on the starboard or right hand side, and a red light on the port or left hand side, the same as on smoke stacks of steamboats."

On April 11th of that year, news dealer Walter McCann managed to get a photograph of the object as it flew over the Chicago suburb of Rogers Park, thereby making history with what must, surely, be the first UFO photograph ever taken. The papers at the time derided the photograph as a fake (which has become a common enough practice today) but unfortunately, according to Daniel Cohen, the photo may no longer even be in existence. We do still have an etching of it from one of the newspapers, though.[15]

The airship was sighted by thousands, poked fun of in the papers, and was generally forgotten about after a short time. There were accounts of the airship landing, as if the crew needed to stop for repairs, and some accounts, like those documented by Vallée , tell strange stories of airship crews asking for "bluestone chisels," (mentioned earlier) among other things. The airship crews were almost always described as looking like normal humans; albeit, often with abnormally long whiskers, "smoked glasses" (the old-time equivalent of sunglasses), and other bizarre accoutrements.

Scientists and astronomers pooh-poohed the airship stories; others thought Edison was behind it. He even inspired a story of an airship expedition to Mars which became a popular dime novel of the time.

Skeptics pooh-poohed it all, putting it down to mass-hysteria, whiskey, or misperceptions of the planet Venus. Not much has changed, it seems, in a hundred years.

After the American sightings, there was a spate of airship sightings in Europe.

Charles Fort, Ghost Rockets, and Green Fireballs

"If there is a universal mind, must it be sane?"

~Charles Fort

Charles Fort was a man with a great moustache. He was also, quite likely, the world's first Ufologist.

Fort labored over four volumes of unexplained phenomena, *The Book of the Damned* (1919), *New Lands* (1923), *Lo!* (1931), and *Wild Talents*(1932), chronicling such mysterious freaks of nature as fish falling from the sky and thunderstorms of frogs. He also documented the weird archaeological finds that hinted at forgotten races of giants and dwarves, found articles and factoids about falling flesh from the heavens, and rhapsodized on showers of red rain, among other things.

Fort also expounded on the phenomenon of "aerial ships" and weird sightings on the moon. He floated the idea that gravity only extended about twenty miles from the surface of the Earth, and that there were "lands in the sky" from which aerial ships and flying phantoms originated.

He called this the "Super-Sargasso Sea." He felt that this theory might more adequately explain rains of frogs, flesh, fish, and giant hailstones than the stoic science that refused comment on such a procession of "damned datum."

Fort was a mischievous writer and researcher, spending hours pouring through the files of old newspapers, looking for the strangest items he could find to chew and spit back in the face of "conventional science." Indeed, he once wrote that, "Every science is a mutilated octopus." He felt certain that all phenomenon were simply rats "in an all-inclusive cheese."

He died May 3, 1932. His name would live on in the term *fortean*, the designation given to unusual scientific phenomena. Today, the Fortean Society carries on his work, keeping his name and ideas alive.

One intriguing series of episodes chronicled by Charles Fort in his book *Lo!*, and reprinted in the book *Extra-Terrestrials Among Us* by George C. Andrews, is the puzzling series of occurrences that happened in rural England between the years 1904-1905. The countryside was apparently swept up in a religious revival, and a popular female lay minister was said to manifest "floating orbs" or lights in the air, whenever she felt the spirit move her. At the same time as this was going on, animals (primarily sheep) were being found mutilated, exsanguinated, and the culprit, much as in mutilation cases today, remained a mystery. Likewise, mysterious "abductions" began to take place, with odd strangers turning up in the streets, muttering to themselves, and being unable to give an account of where they had been and what they had been doing.

The religious revival spread panic among the populace, with teenage shop girls suddenly stopping their work and breaking out into song, or running up and down the aisles of the stores. An ugly spirit of anti-Catholic bigotry began to take shape, with near-riots breaking out against Catholic churches, and, all in all, it was as if some invisible force was manifesting itself through strange phenomena, driving the people temporarily batty. John Keel would go on to write about similar occurrences in West Virginia and other places—places he theorized that the "super spectrum" was working to communicate with, or feed off of, human energy, and was manifesting itself as "strange lights," hysteria, and mutilated animals.

Fort's pessimistic philosophy might best be summed up with the quote: "The Earth is a farm. We are someone else's property."

Moving forward from the days of Charles Fort, beginning in 1933, in Norway, Sweden, and Finland, an epidemic of "phantom planes" and "ghost rockets" began to be reported by an increasingly nervous populace. These planes, which were often seen to perform under the most hazardous of conditions, prompted some to speculate about the foolhardiness of pilots that would fly in snowstorms and thick fog.

The ghostly flights were investigated by the air forces of the three countries, who were very forthcoming about sharing information with each other. The phenomenon, which continued up to and after the war, was extensive, and fueled fears of Nazi or Soviet secret weapons. The "phantom fliers" were said to look just like normal airplanes, but to have no identifiable markings, and to sometimes shine weird lights down from the sky. It was reported they flew under the most dangerous conditions.

The "phantom fliers" were mostly a phenomenon of the years leading up to World War II, but the "ghost rockets" of Sweden made an appearance as late as 1946. So many sightings of the ghost rockets were reported (around 12,000) that the government found themselves at a loss to investigate or explain them. The rockets, some of which were described as cigar-shaped and having a red light and flames coming out of the tail, disappeared after a short time.

Here is a short description of an eyewitness to one of the ghost rockets:

> All of a sudden one of my comrades shouted and pointed to the sky. Out from a cloud came a smoking torpedo dashing over the blue sky towards another cloud. I switched to the telephoto lens and turned the camera to the object.
>
> I could see the object clearly in the camera as I filmed it. It disappeared into the cloud, came out again and eventually we lost sight of it somewhere in the north. Not a sound was heard.[16]

This man, a camera technician, then continued on his trip to Stockholm. He turned his film over to the authorities, but later found, to his great disappointment, that none of the pictures had turned out. They were all blanks.

The Battle of Los Angeles

Aliens invaded the skies over LA in 1942. Whether due to a flock of seagulls, an excess of "war nerves," or a genuine alien invasion, the resulting tale is instructive, if for no other reason than to illustrate just how much terror an unknown coming from the sky can bring.

It was February 25, 1942, and the country was still reeling from the damage done to the national psyche by Pearl Harbor. Citizens in Santa Monica and Culver City, California, looked up into the night sky to see a "surreal, giant, magic lantern" hanging above them menacingly. The night was suddenly broken by the piercing wail of the air raid sirens, as the city started gearing up for what they assumed must be some sort of Japanese invasion. The volunteer Air Raid Wardens headed into action; so did the Army's 37th Coast Artillery Brigade.

Though it was early in the morning, seemingly all of Southern California was outside looking up at the night skies. Above them, what appeared to be a "large object" floated by with no noise. The wail of the air raid sirens was soon joined by the sound of a barrage of artillery, as the 37th shot everything they had at the aerial intruder.

For over thirty minutes, hundreds upon hundreds of rounds were fired at the object, leaving shell fragments to fall over civilian areas (which reportedly killed six people). The object took direct hits, but seemed to remain undamaged, at last floating out over Long Beach before disappearing into the night. The artillery fell silent, and the military and government must have found themselves mystified.

A volunteer air raid warden later described what she had seen as, "Huge... enormous. And it was practically right over my house! I had never seen anything like it in my life." She went on to say, "It was just hovering there in the sky and hardly moving at all...It was a lovely pale orange and just about the most beautiful thing you've ever seen. I could see it perfectly because it was very close. It was big!"[17]

She also claimed she saw fighter planes scrambled to attack the object, but that they "turned away." They "fired upon it" she said, but the attack didn't seem to affect the object at all.

Some have tried to float the theory that the "Battle of Los Angeles" was caused by a flock of highly-reflective seagulls.

Incidents such as The Battle of Los Angeles, combined with the widespread panic that greeted Orson Welles' radio adaptation of H.G. Wells' *The War of the Worlds*, must have gone a long way to convincing the government that UFOs, whatever else might be believed about them, could incite the masses in a way that few other topics could.

Foo Fighters

Allied pilots during the Second World War found themselves troubled by a curious phenomena. Little balls of light, or "foo" (from the French word *feu* for "fire") were pacing their vehicles, following close at their wingtips, and making them nervous. There was no telling, from their perspective, what the things were; conventional logic held that they were German secret weapons. Often, the little lights would change color as they flew, and perform other impressive aerial feats. They seemed essentially harmless, however, so the pilots just ignored them. After the war, it was found that the explanation of their being German secret weapons was completely erroneous, as the German pilots saw them, too!

Various conventional explanations have been touted for what the enigmatic lights may have been, but the Ufologists have pointed to them as possible extraterrestrial craft, curiously monitoring the military activities of Allied and Axis pilots during the war.

No explanation has ever been found to adequately explain what the "Foo Fighters" were.

Nazi UFOs?

There are apocryphal stories (circulated to a great degree on the fringes and by those who give credence to conspiracy theories) that the Nazis were either constructing their own fleet of UFOs at the end of the war, or were, more fantastically, even in contact with a race of perhaps malevolent extraterrestrial entities. There are sketches of supposed Nazi UFOs circulating the internet, craft with names like the Flugelrad and the Kugelblitz. I can not vouch for the veracity of any of these claims, but I can relate to you the information I have gleaned from supposed sources who know.

Of course, Hitler and the Nazis are often said to have been mad for the occult, borrowing much of their symbology and mystical philosophy from the occult lodges from which their early leadership grew. Hitler, in particular, has been said to have been obsessed with the Spear of Longinus, the spear that pierced the side of Christ at the Crucifixion, and is even said to have been a mystical initiate in a secret brotherhood that found its inspiration in the pages of the great saga *Parsifal* by Wolfram von Eschanbach.[18] Himmler was known to be mad about psychical research, and established the S.S. school at Wewelsburg to train his elite corps in the occult secrets behind National Socialism.

These secrets included the performing of rituals, one of which, at least, according to author Dusty Sklar, included human sacrifice. Of course, I have no way of knowing how much of this Gothic horror scenario is actually true, but the claims are made, and they are made upon seemingly solid evidence.

One of the philosophical underpinnings of Nazi philosophy was *The Secret Doctrine*, by medium Helena Petrovna Blavatsky, a massive esoteric tome that postulated that man once lived in a state of perfection, but that intermingling with "inferior races" had caused him to lose his supernatural fellowship and fall into a degraded state. This theme would be carried on by French neo-Nazi Savitri Devi, a Hindu priestess who worshipped Hitler as an incarnation of the god Vishnu. Her book, *The Lightning and the Sun,* is considered a classic in fascist circles.

Whatever the case, it is an unquestionable fact that Nazism has deep roots in esoteric and occult thought. Vallée has suggested, in his book *Messengers of Deception*, that contact between man and UFO entities may be part of a long-range plan to promote a sort of neo-fascism, enacted by a shadowy or mysterious group to serve its own purposes.[19]

Vallée gives his readers the example of American Nazi sympathizer William Dudley Pelley, leader of the Silver Shirts, who was interned during the war on suspicion of being an enemy agent. Pelley later became a trance channel and the founder of "Soulcraft" Publishing. His understudy in later life was George Hunt Williamson, a spiritualist and early writer on UFOs and esoteric subjects, who was with George Adamski the day he went out to the desert to meet "Orthon," a tall, blond-haired, blue-eyed Venusian who, according to Adamski, landed in a scout ship with a universal message of peace and brotherly love. Williamson himself channeled a bewildering variety of "space brothers."[20]

So the idea of an "Interstellar Fascist Cabal" is not that far off, perhaps. Today, it is chiefly discussed in the New Age conspiracy theories of author and researcher David Icke (with a few modifications).

To return to the topic at hand, Nazi UFOs supposedly did exist. The story about them (at least, one story about them), is this:

In the early part of the Twentieth century, a number of German occult societies sprang up, their doctrines a loose mixture of politics, racial science, and mysticism, their driving aim to establish for the German people a mythological pedigree that connected them to a glorious, Viking past. Hitler was probably exposed to the ideas of these societies while living in Vienna, through the pages of *Ostara*, his favorite magazine.

At any rate, one of these societies, Thule, had an offshoot called the "Vril Society." The Vril group took its inspiration from the pages of a strange science fiction novel by Edward Bulwer-Lytton called *The Coming Race*, the plot of which concerned a subterranean race who had mastered a form of supernatural energy called "vril" with which they could perform miracles. The members of the Vril Society actually believed in this possibility, and so Vril member Dr. W.O. Schumann, in 1920, contacted the renowned medium Maria Ortish (or Orsic, as her name has also been given), and another medium called simply "Sigrun."

Ortisch, so the story goes, claimed that she had made contact with otherworldly entities or "gods," who had given her instructions on how to build an "interdimensional flying machine." This machine, of course, was disc-shaped, and was supposedly actually constructed. These beings were high extraterrestrials from the Aldebaran star system.

According to aircraft historian Henry Stevens, this vehicle was at first thought to have been designed by "gods," but later members of the Vril group felt they were really in contact with a race of extraterrestrials. Stevens says:

> The craft basically would work because of the interaction of two spinning—not just alternating—magnetic fields. They believed this interaction would cause not only the craft, but the entire region, to

function outside the physical laws that we are bound by. In other words, they felt they could surf on gravity. And indeed, the Vril Society built this machine in the mid-1920s, and it levitated.[21]

Dr. Schumann, not content to rest on his laurels, continued working on his vril-powered electromagnetic antigravity device, finally constructing a flying disc called the Vril 1, which was allegedly tested in 1934. A pilot named Veitz was supposedly the man at the helm, but the machine, though it flew, proved to be erratic; it crash landed and then self-destructed. But the Vril Society, and now the German government, found themselves interested.

The story gets even weirder with the addition of a crashed UFO that supposedly went down in the Black Forest. The German government alledgedly discovered this wreck, and the technology from back-engineering was given to the Vril Society to put with the channeled material they already had. The result? A large flying saucer called the Haunebu 1. This vehicle was purportedly flown for the first time in 1939.

There were other scientists, such as Miethe, Victor Schauberger[22] (who was apparently working on a design that could be powered on tonal frequencies, or "cosmic vibrations"), and Epps who were all working on saucer-based designs. Miethe (who would go on to build the Avrocar, a failed flying saucer hover car tested for the United States government) was supposedly successful, and bragged to Hitler in a memo that he had tested his device the V7 in Prauge, that it had flown to 24,000 meters, and claimed that it could be run on "unconventional energy," perhaps a reference to the earlier vril-powered craft of Dr. Schumann.

Alas, the end of the war saw the plans and prototypes for these miraculous vehicles destroyed; usually, this was done by their creators, as in the case of a Czech scientist named Schriever, who pushed his saucer out onto the tarmac near the test area and dynamited it. He had heard the Red Army were in the suburbs of Prague, and realized that "all was lost."[23]

Of course, all was not lost for the Allies, who took home every bit of military intelligence or captured technology they could lay their hands on as they swept through Germany at the end of the war. This alone has led some UFO researchers to speculate that, just perhaps, the flying saucer phenomenon could be accounted for by captured Nazi technology. Whatever the case, the years immediately after the war would see the beginning of an awesome wave.

Kenneth Arnold

The modern UFO era begins on June 24, 1947, with the sighting made by Kenneth Arnold, a Boise Idaho businessman who was flying a search and rescue mission over the Cascade Mountains in Washington. At approximately 3 p.m., at 9,200 feet, Arnold saw a brilliant flash through his cockpit window and thought, instantly, "Explosion!"

He waited for the sound of the impact, thinking perhaps a plane had gone down in the mountains…but heard and felt nothing. There was, according to Arnold, a lone DC-4 at his rear, to the left.

The bright flash happened again. This time, he saw something that he found intriguing. There was a formation of nine, delta-winged aircraft of unknown origin, skimming through the mountain peaks, and reflecting sunlight off their bright, shiny surfaces. The objects, which Arnold could only surmise were a formation of the new experimental jets he had heard the Air Force was testing, flew past the peak of Mt. Rainier to Mt. Adams at an astonishing speed; Arnold calculated it at somewhere in the vicinity of 1,656 miles per hour. This was three times the speed of any aircraft that Arnold had ever heard of. He likewise judged their distance to be some twenty miles away.

Amazed, he landed at Yakima and immediately informed his friends about what he had seen. Al Baxter, the manager of General Aircraft called in a circle of experienced pilots to listen to the tale, with one of them suggesting that what Arnold had seen might have been the testing of guided missiles. However, other pilots pooh-poohed this idea, pointing out that Arnold had seen planes that banked and turned, performing incredible aerial maneuvers, and that this seemed quite beyond the capability of guided missiles.

By the time Arnold got to Pendleton, Oregon, he landed to find himself surrounded by reporters asking tough questions. Arnold, a solid citizen who made his living selling fire-fighting equipment, and who had logged more than 4,000 hours of flight time (much of it due to flying search and rescue operations) seemed beyond reproach. At least, he didn't seem as if he would willfully make up a story or tall tale just to get in the newspapers.

When asked to describe the look of the objects he had seen, Arnold struggled to put the sighting into words. Finally, he hit upon a description that would stick in the public consciousness for decades to come.

"They moved like a saucer would if you skipped it across the water!"

The term "flying saucer" had been coined.

Many people debated on what Arnold had actually seen; experts argued that his estimation of the speed and distance of the odd aircraft were inaccurate, and that they were either military jets or bombers flying a routine training mission. However, the floodgates had now been opened, and within a short amount of time, a deluge of reports came in from all across the country, some from witnesses who seemed every bit as solid and reliable as Arnold. The modern UFO era had begun.

Chapter 3:
Green Fireballs Over New Mexico

An epidemic of "green fireballs," or objects that looked like meteorites but moved in an erratic, frightening fashion, occurred over New Mexico in 1948. The various reports of the fireballs were investigated by the eminent Dr. Lincoln La Paz, who himself sighted one. He later stated that the mystery fireballs didn't seem to be meteors, and confessed himself baffled as to what, exactly, their true nature was.

The "green fireball" mystery began December 5, 1948, when two pilots reported some kind of strange, green "flare" in sightings that were twenty-two minutes apart. The next day, a sighting over Sandia Base, a super-secret nuclear installation, convinced the military there might be something to worry about.

A sighting was made of a "green fireball" on December 6 by two pilots flying at 2,000 feet, who noted that the object was "definitely larger and more brilliant than a shooting star, meteor, or flare."

That object apparently burned itself out, but in its trail left a cloud of strange reddish-orange "fragments" floating to the ground.

It was the next day that Lincoln La Paz was called in. La Paz was considered an authority by the government on meteors, and was a consultant on many top secret matters. He did not know what could possibly be their origin, but, after seeing one himself, he became satisfied that they were, most definitely, *not* meteors.

La Paz eventually informed the military that the fireballs were not "naturally-occurring" phenomena, but had almost certainly been launched by "somebody."

The AESS (Atomic Energy Security Service) set up a special unit to get photographs, and scientists at Los Alamos set about studying the phenomena. In April, officials with the Pentagon set up a meeting between physicist Joseph Kaplan, Dr. La Paz, and other experts at Kirtland AFB. The "fireballs" and what to do about them were the chief topic of discussion, and the scientists agreed that a special network of observers should be set up at various locations in New Mexico. This came in the aftermath of several sightings of tiny white "flares" over restricted nuclear installations, including one in Camp Hood, central Texas. It was decided by the military that the "flares," much like the "fireballs," could not be attributed to natural causes.

This worried them a great deal. However, in the final assessment, they actually did very little about it. The resultant project, "Project Twinkle," was the military answer to the fireball/flare phenomenon, consisting of a couple of observers stationed "at an operations post at Holloman AFB." It folded in 1951.

Many of the scientists who had worked on the green fireball problems later gave their opinion that the fireballs were "artificially created." When Captain Ed Ruppelt interviewed some of them years later as head of Project Blue Book, they confessed they felt the objects were "fired from extraterrestrial spacecraft."

Chapter 4:
UFO Crashes, Contacts, and Men in Black

The folklore of UFO crashes and retrievals goes all the way back to 1884, to an apocryphal tale of four cowboys recovering a cog and some other debris from a weird cylindrical object said to have crashed out on the plains. While this story is almost certainly a hoax devised by bored newspapermen, the idea of the "crashed flying saucer and dead occupants" refuses to die, and is believed by many people. There are a number of different accounts, but two of the most well-known are the hoax perpetrated on author Frank Scully, and the famous Roswell case, which has been the center of heated debate, speculation, and fascination for many decades now.

Frank Scully

The Scully case begins in March of 1950, with the lectures delivered by one Silas Newton, who claimed to be an oil man and a millionaire, as well as a scientific expert. Newton had been going around giving lectures on scientific topics to university students, but it was at the University of Denver where he would make his biggest hit.

One of the subjects Newton lectured about that day was the subject of "flying saucers." The students, who had been instructed on about five points on which to judge the truth or falsehood of what Newton related, decided that, for the most part, they didn't believe a word he said.

That day, Newton managed to relate a particularly impressive incident, allegedly told to him by a "Dr. Gee" (the "top magnetic research specialist in the United States") about a flying saucer that had supposedly crashed in New Mexico (where else?) containing the bodies of a number of "little men." This Dr. Gee had apparently been called in later to examine a number of other crashed UFOs, and more alien corpses, which numbered, altogether, about 36.

Newton's story hit the local papers, and quickly gained traction. Newton himself supposedly wrote a few articles, but it was decided that another writer should be brought in to really tell the story in the way it deserved to be told. Enter Frank Scully, who cobbled together a bestselling book of the account called *Behind the Flying Saucers*. The book gave the readers what they wanted: tales of dead aliens.

Scully's book claimed that the aliens were "completely human," only smaller than us, averaging about three feet. They all apparently had perfect teeth, wore dark blue uniforms with shiny metal buttons, and had been found carrying something that looked like a "timepiece." "Books and pamphlets" were found amid the wreckage, but they were written in a language that was indecipherable.

The ships themselves were described as anywhere from 100 to 36 feet across, and made of a very strong, unknown metal. Dr. Gee went on to claim that he had actually, at one point, seen one of these vehicles land, but that it had sped off before the scientists could get to it.

Dr. Gee claimed that the material recovered from the saucer wrecks was sent to government laboratories for testing, but that he himself was finally closed off from access to it. He claimed that the government was holding the evidence of said saucer crashes for its own purposes, and that they were sitting on the information in hopes of averting a national panic if the truth got out. All familiar enough claims.

Newton continued to lecture, and the book did very well. Then something happened. Newton, who had claimed to have been an "oil millionaire" was revealed in the press not to have been a millionaire at all. In fact, he was trying to sell a phony device for discovering oil when he was arrested for fraud. With him was a Mr. Gebaur, or, the mysterious "Dr. Gee." Gebaur was no scientist, and the hoax fell apart for the tissue of lies that it was.

The Roswell Incident

The mother of all UFO crash stories is the Roswell case. It may, in point of fact, be the most famous UFO story of all time, so it deserves inclusion here.

The events of Roswell begin on or around July 2, 1947, when, during a violent storm, a disc-shaped object was sighted by witnesses over tiny Roswell to the northwest. Witnesses describe hearing a loud explosion, which has since been attributed to the crashed saucer. The next day, seventy-five miles to the north of town, some strange debris was found, and the legend begins.

The debris was discovered by W. "Mac" Brazel, who found a great amount of strange wreckage scattered over a wide area of his ranch. He was perplexed about what it might be, and irritated because, whatever it was, his sheep wouldn't cross it. Brazel did not, at first, bother to report his finding, but eventually collected a box of the stuff. It seemed to him to be uncommonly weird material, consisting of an aluminum-like foil that could not be dented or cut; material that once wadded into a ball would unfold with no creases; material that could not be burned; thread-like material; a number of weird I-beams containing what seemed to be hieroglyphics; and a parchment-like paper. Other alleged pieces of wreckage included a tube-like material that acted suspiciously like fiber optics—a flashlight beam could be shined down it, and, no matter which way it was twisted, the beam came out the other end.

Puzzling.

Brazel ultimately reported his finding to the local sheriff, thinking that, perhaps, it might be something that belonged to the local Air Force base. The sheriff contacted Roswell Air Force Base, and the base dispatched two officers, one of whom was Major Jesse Marcel, whose testimony would do so much to revive interest in the Roswell incident decades later. Allegedly, it was Marcel's opinion that the material was "not made on this earth." Marcel then did something unprecedented: he took a box of the wreckage back home to his son, announcing that they had found pieces of a "flying saucer" in the desert, and allowed him to view and handle the wreckage. Jesse Marcel, Jr. would go on to corroborate his father's story decades later in television appearances.

A press release, issued on orders from Roswell Air Base Commander colonel William Blanchard, announced to the world that the USAF had captured a "flying disc," and the story was picked up from coast to coast, and even ran in the *London Times*.

The government, however, had other ideas. The wreckage was loaded onto a B-29 and flown to what was then called Wright Field Air Base in Dayton, Ohio (Now Wright-Patterson AFB), but first made a stopover at the headquarters of the 8th Air Force at Forth Worth, Texas. It was here where a switcheroo was enacted, and, according to believers, a cover-up was put in place.

The crew of the B-29 were sworn to secrecy, and a second press release was issued, contradicting the first, and announcing that the wreckage was *not* that of a "flying saucer" but was, instead, the wreckage of a simple weather balloon. A press conference was called, the wreckage of a weather balloon was brought into General Roger Ramey's office, and Marcel was ordered to bend down, pick up pieces of the substituted wreckage, and pose for embarrassing photos with it. Of course, the implication was that a man who worked for the 509th Atomic Bomb Group had actually managed to mistake the wreckage of a weather balloon for a "flying saucer."

Marcel would, decades later, claim that the wreckage he handled in General Ramey's office that day was *not* the same wreckage he discovered on Brazel's ranch.

The wreckage was then flown by armed guard (!) to Wright Field AFB, and Marcel returned to Roswell.

In Roswell, Mac Brazel was being held in detention (he was released after a week) by the Air Force,[24] a move that must make even the most skeptical of individuals wonder exactly why. After all, if it was simply a case of mistaken identity of a weather balloon, what could he possibly know that would constitute a "threat to national security"? The "crash site" was cleared of all debris, and a press wire announcement from Albuquerque confirming the original crashed flying saucer story was halted, the radio station in question having been warned against broadcasting such information again. All the bases seemed to be covered as far as the government was concerned, and, for a time, the story simply died.

It seemed as if the "Roswell Incident" was a closed book.

Years later, however, people began to talk. A man named Grady Landon "Barney" Barnett told an incredible tale of being out in the desert when he noticed the sun glinting off of metal in the distance. Going to investigate, he was soon joined by some passing archaeology students, who, together, found a bizarre tableaux laid out on the desert floor.

It was the wreckage of a delta-winged style craft of unknown origin, with a gash in the side and a number of "little bodies" strewn about. The bodies were unlike anything the witnesses had ever seen: small, hairless, with strange large eyes and weird, one-piece suits without pockets or zippers. The witnesses had no idea what they had stumbled upon, but they were soon joined by a cordon of military, who sealed off the crash site and swore them all, upon pain of death, to secrecy.

Or so Barnett claimed.

However, he was not the only one.

In the mid-seventies, witnesses began to come forward, some with stories that seemed to have the ring of eerie truth about them. One such witness was Roswell mortician Glenn Dennis, who was working late on the night of or around July 4th when, he claimed, he got a call from someone at Roswell Air Force Base that they needed five "hermetically sealed little caskets." The man on the other end of the line went on to ask how best to preserve bodies, and Dennis found himself more and more baffled as the conversation progressed.

Thinking there might have been an air accident, and that he might lend assistance, he drove out to the air base, and was surprised to find that it was in a flurry of activity. He went into the main facility and walked around, noting the state of confusion and panic in the air. Suddenly, he ran into a female friend of his who was a nurse at the air base, and she got a panicked look on her face.

She told him, in no uncertain terms, to get away from the air base as quick as he could, and that she could tell him no more. The two planned to meet later. Then, as if in answer to this, Dennis found himself unceremoniously hustled out of the place and back to his car by military police.

Later, he met his nurse friend in a bar, and she described to him the nature of the emergency situation he had happened upon.

She described, while doing her duties, of happening upon the autopsy[25] of a "little creature," a being with a large head and eyes and a slit for a mouth that she was certain wasn't human. She drew a picture of the creature for Dennis, and described the terrible odor emitted by the body. Later, Dennis claimed, he had tried to find his nurse friend again, but had been unsuccessful; he was later told she had died in a military plane crash.

And that is just one of the stories making up the legend of Roswell. William Moore and Charles Berlitz would go on to write a book, alleging that the military was in possession of the wreckage of an alien spacecraft and the bodies (presumably on ice after all these years) of its crew. The terrific television program *In Search Of*, with Leonard Nimoy of *Star Trek* fame, would do an episode covering Roswell, and the story would sink into the public consciousness.

Jesse Marcel was interviewed by *In Search Of*. He claimed that the wreckage that he found was of a genuine UFO. He maintained this until his death.

Later, the Air Force would come out and publicly admit that they had staged a cover-up, but they claimed it was not of a "flying saucer," but of the wreckage of a super-secret Project Mogul weather balloon…an assertion that did nothing to convince the true believers. As recently as fifteen years ago they produced a report called "Roswell: Case Closed," which floated the claim that what witnesses have described as "alien bodies" were, in fact, high-altitude crash test dummies, dropped from airplanes in a military experiment.

(Of course, the fact that the alleged dummies looked *nothing* like "big-headed, big-eyed, little aliens" did nothing to deter the government from making this claim. Leaving one to wonder who was more intelligent, the government or their crash test dummies.)

Today, Roswell is a tourist attraction for "true believers," boasting the International UFO Museum, as well as an annual festival commemorating the 1947 "Saucer Crash." Out in the desert, at the supposed site, there is a commemorative plaque for the dead alien crew. You could, at one point, get a guided tour out there.[26]

Author Note: There are a number of deathbed confessions associated with Roswell, one of which, that of Walter Haut, happened recently. This man claimed that he had participated in a cover-up of the crash of a genuine UFO... And then he died. Although it's not clear who Walter Haut was or what he did during the Roswell incident, I can't think of a more powerful way to end this chapter than that.

Saucers Over Washington

In 1952, UFOs buzzed the United States Capitol, and were caught on radar. The story goes something like this:

On the nights of July 19 and 26, 1952, unidentified craft were picked up by the radar screens at Washington National Airport and Andrews Air Force Base. These objects were "fast walkers," some of them being tracked at speeds in excess of 7,000 miles per hour. Others just seemed to hover, their objective undetermined. What was unquestionable, however, was that the craft were violating the highly restricted airspace over the White House, the Capitol, and the Pentagon.

The UFOs were spotted both on the ground and by commercial airline pilots. Al Chop, the Pentagon's official spokesman on UFOs, stated:

> They moved slowly at first, about 100 to 200 miles per hour. And then, one target shot away at a fantastic speed...estimated speed 7,300 miles per hour. The tower operator at Bowling Air Force Base sighted one of the objects drifting low in the sky southeast of the base. Also,

> several airliner crews reported seeing the object: Capitol Airlines Flight and National Airlines Flight. Flight T807 sighted three at level flight, moving at terrific speed. Casey Pierman on that Flight T807 saw "several flying objects with bright lights." By this time, the tower had numerous unidentified blips on radar too, about seven, and their speeds were…"phenomenal." One then followed National Flight SP610 up to within four miles of touchdown. I remember one tower operator was frantic. Some of the unidentified objects then flew over the restricted air corridors here above the White House and Capitol. My office, to say the least, was swamped with inquiries from the press.[27]

On the next Saturday, the 26th of July, Chop was called by the FAA and told that the UFOs were back. He drove to the airport, where known flights were being tracked by little plastic flags. The unknowns, which comprised between six and twelve, were moving at astonishing speeds, performing aerial acrobatics, disappearing and reappearing suddenly, and flying over restricted air space.

Two F-94s were scrambled. The planes were at a disadvantage though, because, as soon as they got within range of the objects…there was nothing to see. The UFOs had disappeared, both from the skies and from the radar screen. After the planes left to return to base, the UFOs appeared again as radar blips, and the people in the control tower found themselves deeply disturbed.

Al Chop said:

> About 3 a.m., I called the Pentagon Command Post and explained the situation. They said: "Stand by—a second scramble is on the way."' This time, the "unknowns" stayed on the scope and we directed the intercepts to the exact compass readings.[28]

One of the pilots radioed in that "he couldn't see anything"; just minutes later, he radioed that "he could see them" and that they appeared to be "tremendous blue-white lights." Suddenly, the pilot sounded slightly panicked, as the UFOs were "all around me…closing in. What do I do?" He reported in that the UFOs were "moving off" and that he was returning to base. The UFOs stayed on the radar scope until five that morning.

The official Air Force explanation was to debunk the sighting as a "temperature inversion" (i.e., an atmospheric condition that can cause false returns on radar screens), but Al Chop later stated:

> About one week later, Major Lewis Norman, Jr., an Air Force radar specialist, told Major Fournet, Captain Ruppelt, and myself that the temperature inversion present in the Washington area on the night in question was not sufficient to cause the radar to pick up reflections of ground objects. Major Norman was a specialist working with the Air Force Aircraft Control and Warning Branch. He said an inversion of the order of ten degrees Fahrenheit was required before the radar would react to ground clutter.

The U.S. Weather Bureau figures for the two nights in question showed the temperature inversion present over Washington to be not more than one-tenth of one percent different on the Fahrenheit scale.[29]

Regardless, the public seemed to largely buy the Air Force's official explanation. The Air Force, on the other hand, doesn't seem to have believed itself, for their internal report casts doubt, in the first paragraph, on the idea that the sightings could be explained away by "natural causes."

Adamski and the Contactees

The most interesting phenomenon to emerge from the post-1947 flying saucer wave was launched by an eccentric hamburger cook from California named George Adamski. Adamski, who was exploring the Mojave Desert with his friends one day in November 1952, found his attention arrested by a large, cigar-shaped object that seemed to be surrounded by military jets.

This object ejected a smaller one, a "scout ship" it was later decided, and Adamski was driven to where he felt he could make contact with the pilot. His friends went along with him, and Adamski quickly unloaded his telescope and photographic equipment. He began to take pictures as the scout ship came to rest within a cove. Suddenly, a few military jets flew overhead, and the ship seemed to vanish. Adamski, deciding that the ship had probably gone back to the cigar-shaped "mothership," was about to pick up his equipment and signal to his friends (who had been instructed to watch him) when, suddenly, he noticed the figure of a man coming toward him, about half-a-mile away. Adamski recognized this, immediately, as the pilot of the scout ship, and approached him.

The being was described as human, even handsome, with a strong, athletic build and gorgeous hair that spilled down past his shoulders. He was dressed in a one-piece suit, and (perhaps unsurprisingly) did not seem to speak much English. Instead, he and Adamski used telepathy to communicate,[30] and Adamski learned that he was "specially chosen" to carry the message of the "Space Brothers" (who were Venusian) to the people of Earth. This message consisted primarily of concern over atomic testing and radiation, and the same dire warnings of calamity that UFO entities seem to repeat, over and over again, to this day. Adamski furthermore learned that the flying saucer that "Orthon" was piloting operated on the principal of "attraction and repulsion," and, as if to underscore this, Adamski stepped up to the edge of the hovering craft, put his arm out, and found it caught by an inexplicable force. He managed to free it, but found that it pained him. Orthon told him this small injury would fade in a short time, however.[31]

It was soon time for Orthon to depart, but before he went, he asked Adamski if he could have one of the photographs that he had taken, saying that it would be returned to him at a later date. Adamski agreed, and gave him one of the photographic plates, after which, climbing up onto the flange of his saucer, Orthon disappeared inside. The ship took off, and Adamski went back to his friends.

The witnesses later signed sworn affidavits attesting to what they had witnessed. Among the witnesses was spiritualist medium George Hunt Williamson, who made plaster casts of the footprints left by Orthon in the dust. The soles of Orthon's boots, they decided, had a special encoded message to the people of earth, and, indeed the images provided of these alleged Venusian bootprints reveal a plethora of strange symbols—most notably, a swastika in the heel of the right print.[32] (Williamson would try to interpret these arcane symbols in his book *Other Tongues—Other Flesh*.)

On December 13, the "scout ships" were back, and Adamski was able to take a series of photographs that established his style of flying saucer as the legitimate artifact in the minds of thousands of people. Showing a dome-shaped object atop a saucer, the underside of which was decorated with three balls, Adamski's photos were met with amazement by some and derision by most. Critics howled that they were unconvincing fakes, but that did not deter George, who quickly came out with a book called *Flying Saucers Have Landed*. The speaking engagements and radio interviews on shows such as that of Long John Nebel (the Art Bell of his day) soon followed.

Adamski's claims grew weirder. Soon, he was claiming trips to the moon, which he took after meeting with two normal-looking individuals dressed in regular clothing who happened to be lounging around his favorite hotel. These individuals took him to a scout ship, where "Orthon," "Firkon," and "Ramu" treated him to an interstellar expedition to a moon that was populated with animal life, cities, vegetation, and, was claimed by his contacts, to be a place hospitable to human life, which was the "most adaptable…in the Universe."[33]

Adamski continued to share his strange stories and odd photographs until his death on April 23, 1965. His claims about cities on the moon were soon discredited by our voyage there, four years later. One intriguing side note: Adamski described his alleged space flight thusly:

> I was amazed to see that the background of space is totally dark. Yet there were manifestations taking place all around us, as though billions upon billions of fireflies were flickering everywhere, moving in all directions, as fireflies do. However, these were of many colors, a gigantic celestial fireworks display that was beautiful to the point of being awesome.[34]

Astronaut John Glenn, during the first manned orbital space flight, described his experience in this way:

> When I glanced back through the window my initial reaction was that the spacecraft had tumbled and that I could see nothing but stars

> through the window. I realized, however, that I was still in the normal attitude. The spacecraft was surrounded by luminous particles. These particles were a light yellowish green color. It was as if the spacecraft were moving through a field of fireflies.[35]

Notice a similarity in descriptions? How, if Adamski were a complete fake (and his absurd stories are almost impossible to swallow today), did he manage to invent this one small, crucial detail?

Paranormal investigator John Keel has theorized that contactees, despite most people characterizing them as frauds and charlatans (which no doubt many are), are actually, for the most part, being completely honest in their descriptions of what they experience, but that it is the UFO occupants themselves who are engaging in deception. Thus, Adamski may not have been the greatest con man of all time, but one of the greatest *conned* men of all time!

Adamski was not the only man at the time claiming contact with flying saucer occupants. One man, engineer Daniel Fry, actually predated Adamski by a few years; he claimed contact with an alien named "A-lan", who came in a ship described as an "oblate spheroid." A-lan warned Daniel to keep away from the "hot hull," flew him from New Mexico to New York City and back in half an hour (which meant his craft would have been traveling at 8,000 miles an hour), and dropped him back off in the desert, where he told him there would be further contacts. Fry was then told he was "chosen" to deliver the alien philosophy of peace and brotherhood to the Earth children, and so founded an organization called Understanding, Inc. to disseminate his channeled messages. Fry failed a polygraph test on live television, and faded into obscurity.

George King, or "Master Aetherius" was a London cabdriver who practiced Yoga religiously, and was contacted by spaceman "Aetherius" in his flat when King was thirty-five. They allegedly told him he was about to become, "The voice of Interplanetary Parliament." He went on to found the Aetherius Society, which has branches in many countries.

King channeled new teachings from Master Jesus and other ascended entities that lived on Venus, Mars, and a myriad of other worlds. The Aetherius Society use a number of strange devices in their worship, including a "prayer battery," and claimed that they have helped divert the ill-effects of many natural disasters. Since confronted with evidence that many of the planets they claim to be populated by life are, in point of fact, barren hells inhospitable to life, they have adapted their philosophy to include the possibility that life exists on these worlds at a "different vibration" than the physical realm.

Contactee Frank Stranges was a strange man that combined his evangelistic Christianity with his UFO contact beliefs. His space brother was Valiant Thor, who apparently was known to creep about the Pentagon. Stranges describes Thor thusly:

> As I gripped his hand, I was somewhat surprised to feel the soft texture of his hand...like that of a baby. His eyes were brown and his hair wavy brown, also. He was in all appearances like an Earth man, but he had no fingerprints.

Thor was Venusian, and hinted to Stranges that he might in fact be the Second Coming of Christ.

Sign painter Howard Menger claimed that space aliens gave him the instructions to construct a "free energy" device (not the first time such a claim has been made). He produced a bundle of "space potatoes," recorded an album of Saturnian music, cut hair, and delivered bundles of bras to gorgeous space sex kittens who all dressed as if they were at an Aspen ski resort, etc.

He later divorced his wife and married another woman; they were both convinced they were really from another planet. Perhaps anyone that knew them thought the same thing.

One of the more interesting of the contactees of the period was aerospace expert George Van Tassel, who lived in a house dug out of the ground near Giant Rock, a huge boulder in the desert near Landon, California.

Van Tassel, who had taken possession of the rooms at Giant Rock after the builder, Frank Critzer, was killed on suspicion of being a "German agent," was no mental slouch. According to his Wikipedia entry, he at various times worked for Douglas Aircraft, Hughes Aircraft, and Lockheed. He built a café, home, airstrip, and dude ranch beside Giant Rock, and lived a comfortable existence there.

In 1951, Van Tassel was meditating beside Giant Rock when a curious thing occurred. He was transported astrally to a giant spaceship orbiting the earth, where he made contact with the all-wise, all-knowing "Council of Seven Lights." It was a year later that Van Tassel reported that the "Space Brothers" had visited him in the flesh.

They suggested that he build the "Integratron," a machine for rejuvenating human cells, so as to increase longevity. This would be in preparation for the coming of a space "Lord." Van Tassel took the plans imparted to him from the aliens, and set to work.

The result was a wooden-domed structure that still stands today, a place of pilgrimage for many New Agers that feel they receive help and healing from the powerful cosmic vibrations there (despite the fact that Van Tassel never actually completed his plans for the Integratron). Van Tassel hosted the annual "Giant Rock Spacecraft Convention," which at one point boasted 10,000 attendees. This was basically a massive festival and convention for flying saucer buffs and true believers, and every notable contactee spoke there. The last festival was held in 1978.

He wrote a number of books, including the now-rare *I Rode a Flying Saucer*, and founded an organization called "The Ministry of Universal Wisdom." He kept up a steady stream of channeled messages from his space contacts until his death in 1978.

As far as other contactees of the period, those interested can research such names as Truman Bethurum, Eduard "Billy" Meier,[36] and Orfeo Angelucci, among others, or look into some of the material channelers are currently getting from "Ashtar," a blond-haired, blue-eyed Venusian who is usually depicted the way Adamski described Orthon.

Few people give any credence, however, to the claims made by today's contactees, outside of New Age circles.[37]

Author Note: For a penetrating examination of the contactees and their channeled messages, the interested reader is invited to search out a copy of the 1988 book *The Fellowship: Spiritual Contact Between Humans and Outer Space Beings* by Brad Steiger. Steiger is a heavyweight who has authored hundreds of books and articles on UFOs and paranormal topics, and the book makes for insightful and informative reading.

Projects Sign, Grudge, and Blue Book

The Air Force, despite its official position that UFOs are not, in the sense of being extraterrestrial craft, "real," at one point conducted a twenty-two year study of the phenomenon, called, at various times, "Project Sign," "Grudge," and finally "Blue Book." Although critics contend that the object behind these various projects was to simply debunk UFO sightings, Blue Book set important standards for field investigation, as well as amassing a spectacular amount of case files.

The Air Force first got into the UFO business in the late forties, more out of concern that the Soviets might be developing secret weapons than for any other reason. They had a number of reports of strange aerial objects made by quite credible and competent personnel, and wanted to know if there was something to the growing body of weird anecdotes. They quickly surmised that the subject was bigger than the resources they were currently spending on it, and the Pentagon decided a more full-scale, penetrative study was called for.

It was then that General Nathan Twining, who was at that time Commander of Air Materiel Command, in a top secret discussion, suggested the formation of a permanent group to perform a more penetrating examination of the reports.

The result was Project Sign, which was only two weeks old when the Mantell tragedy occurred. Investigators for Project Sign were desperate to avert what they perceived was a growing national uneasiness (rumors that Mantell had been killed by a "flying saucer death ray" were circulating), so they quickly produced some statistics to show that the UFO Mantell was chasing when he died was actually Venus. Needless to say, this explanation did little to satisfy the rumormongers.

Captured Nazi scientists were interrogated, to see if, perhaps, anything the Germans had been working on when the war ended could possibly be responsible for the spate of UFO reports. In each case, the scientist answered in the negative, swearing that nothing their colleagues could create (perhaps for the Soviets) could possibly perform the kind of aerial acrobatics attributed to the UFOs.

In 1948, the Chiles-Whitted case became national news, and Sign had a new headache to deal with: a close-up observation of an unidentified object by two reliable witnesses. After investigating the case, members of Project Sign decided that, indeed, the UFO problem was extraterrestrial in origin, and wrote their opinion in a top-secret report.

The report was summarily rejected by General Hoyt Vandenburg, Air Force Chief of Staff, as well as others within the ranks of Project sign, and it was felt that a reorganization of the project was called for. It was rechristened Project Grudge, and given a new mission: solve as many UFO cases as possible, show that the objects were no threat to national security, and then get out of the business of investigating UFOs altogether. Thus, Project Grudge offered the most likely explanation for reports, but still found that about twenty-three percent remained "unexplainable."

The government stated publicly that they felt a great number of these unexplainable sightings could be attributed to "a mild case of…war nerves," and recommended closing down the project. However, the reports began to come in at a growing pace, and the media was paying attention.

It was in 1952, a year when UFOs buzzed the Capitol (and were picked up on radar), that Cold War fears lead to the CIA getting involved in the UFO business.

The Robertson Panel

The idea that communist agents could use UFOs as propaganda or terrorist tactic fueled concerns at the highest levels of government. Hence, the Air Force, jointly with the CIA, convened a panel of scientific inquiry to assess the situation. This panel was called the Robertson Panel, and its findings were, essentially, that the Air Force should drop the subject of UFOs.

The panel noted that most sightings could be explained away as misperceptions of natural aerial phenomena or conventional aircraft, and recommended that the public be "educated" as to that fact, come hell or high water. An attitude of "explain it away, whatever it is" prevailed, and Project Grudge was reorganized, yet again, as Project Blue Book.

Project Blue Book received sharp criticism from the public for many years, partly because of the fact that all reports gathered, due to the nature of military intelligence, were thus "classified," and unavailable to the general public. The more paranoid thought, too, was that Blue Book was an excellent way for the government to amass information on private citizens.

Dr. J. Allen Hynek, who was the scientific advisor for Blue Book, met howls of criticism when he suggested that a wave of UFO sightings in Michigan might be attributable to "swamp gas," and Gerald Ford, then a congressman, called for a congressional hearing. The result was the controversial University of Colorado UFO Project, better known as the "Condon Committee," chaired by Dr. E. U. Condon. The committee, which most researchers accept as a "whitewash," was controversial from the get-go: Condon gave interviews in which he stated that, as for UFOs, he thought there was "nothing in it," but that he "wasn't suppose to reach a conclusion" until the end of the project.

A leaked memo from one of the committee members was more candid, explaining that the "trick" of the project was to basically debunk every sighting. Project members grew disgusted with all of this and resigned. Nobody seems to take the final, massive Condon Report seriously.

Conspiracy theorists argue that the only reason the government ever entered the UFO "investigating" business to begin with was as a smokescreen for their actual involvement in back-engineering crashed UFO technology, or working closely with extraterrestrials in secret bases, or allowing aliens to abduct humans (as if they could stop them?), or some combination of the three. It is beyond my powers to chronicle all the conspiracy theories swimming around the internet and other places, so I won't even try.

Sky Watchers and Flying Saucer Clubs

At one time, people used to actually gather together in groups, instead of in front of the television—they would go out and do things in the real world. One such group of people were the UFO enthusiasts ("flying saucer nuts," to some) who gathered together in fields where UFOs had been seen, to aim their binoculars and their hopes at the night sky.

These "saucer clubs" flourished through the fifties and sixties, and more sophisticated operations included a printed newsletter, or a team of civilian "investigators" who would go out in the field and pioneer the burgeoning science of Ufology. Some of these civilian groups included NICAP (National Investigation Committee on Aerial Phenomena, a rather grand name for a group with no government backing.), APRO (Aerial Phenomena Research Organization, a group started in the home of Jim and Coral Lorenzen), IFSB (International Flying Saucer Bureau) and something called Ground Saucer Watch, among others. It is the IFSB, headed by Albert Bender, which has an interesting story attached to it.

Albert Bender and the Men in Black

Bender had started the group in 1952, and it had steadily grown in prominence, attracting a hardcore group of true believers and enthusiasts eager to solve the UFO riddle. Suddenly however, less than two years later, Bender announced that he was closing down, and wrote in the bureau's newsletter, *Space Review,* a statement, saying:

> The mystery of the flying saucers is no longer a mystery. The source is already known, but any information about this is being withheld by

orders from a higher source. We would like to print the full story in *Space Review*, but because of the nature of this information, we are sorry that we have been advised in the negative.[38]

Bender went on to caution his fellow saucer-enthusiasts to be "very cautious."

It was deeply puzzling, and it was not until ten years later that anyone had any explanation for Bender's strange behavior. That explanation came in the way of Bender's book *Flying Saucers and The Three Men*. The book, supposedly a true story, aroused even more suspicion, as it read like the most juvenile of science fiction yarns.

Here is a brief synopsis:

Bender begins to experience strange, paranormal phenomena soon after founding the IFSB, receiving bizarre phone calls, smelling sulfur,[39] seeing weird lights and floating eyes in his room, and twice being followed to the movie theatre by a bizarre man with "eyes like light bulbs." Among other things, Bender was a confirmed horror movie and science fiction fan, so perhaps some of this could have been the product of a slightly overactive imagination.

Next, while Bender is experimenting with sending telepathic messages to UFO occupants, he feels a strange pain in his head, and suddenly feels as if he has left his body. Floating above his bed, he hears a strange voice speaking to him, telling him he must, "no longer explore the mysteries of the Universe." When Bender protests this voice telling him what to do, he is told: "We are among you and know your every move. So please be advised we are here on your Earth."

Bender then gets a special visitation. One day blue lights swim in front of his eyes, and he is swept off his feet by a profound feeling of sickness and discomfort. He describes his skin as feeling icy, and then says the room grew darker. Materialized in the room, says Bender, are three men, dressed in black, with homburg-style hats and glowing eyes. The men levitate above the floor by a few inches.

While this nearly sounds like an image out of a Clive Barker novel, the mysterious revenants are, in fact, aliens, sent here to reveal their message to Bender, who they think is so painfully "ordinary" that, were he to tell anyone, no one would believe him. (So if there is any doubt, why tell anyone in the first place?)

The Men in Black (who were first introduced in Gray Barker's book *They Knew Too Much About Flying Saucers*), tell Bender that they are on earth for a special purpose and must not be disturbed, that they are, currently, only occupying a human form but that this is not what they truly look like, and that they sometimes find it necessary to carry off human bodies to disguise their own. They claim to have "many contacts' with Earthlings, and to have established a base here.

Bender claims that the three MIB gave him a metal disk the size of a coin, and that, should he hold it in his hand and repeat the word "Kazik," he could make contact with them when he chose. Next Bender describes going to a room that looks like a glass dome, and being introduced to a man that said they (the aliens) were on Earth to extract a chemical from the sea, and that they "had their people" in many high places "including the Pentagon." The man then shows Bender a series of images on a screen, the last of which was a hideous monster, too repulsive to even look at. Bender recoils in terror, but not before the image of the monster speaks with his new friend's voice. Bender is told that this is the actual appearance of the aliens.

It is explained to Bender that the alien race has three sexes: male, female, and a third sex that grows to over nine feet tall and has shining eyes. He is told that the females lay eggs. Then he is escorted on a tour of the aliens' secret base in the Antarctic. It is there he gets to examine a flying saucer close up.

One of the "Exalted Ones"[40] —the third sex—tells him they have been on Earth since 1945, and will carry some humans back to their home world to put in a zoo. He tells Bender that, if he doesn't cooperate, the same thing will happen to him.

Bender has further strange adventures: meeting invisible entities and monsters, getting an oil massage from three extraterrestrial sex kittens, and becoming exposed to a ray that would, supposedly, give him perfect health. Bender has such outlandish adventures, in fact, he could have competed with any contactee for whose flying saucer stories were the wildest.

The one area in which Bender had some credibility was the Men in Black. Frequently, the cause of harassment and intimidation of UFO witnesses and investigators, the Men in Black were, at one time, thought to be CIA or secret government agents. They wore dark suits and hats, had oriental features, wore dark sunglasses, and drove Cadillacs. They also had official-looking cards and credentials.

Of course, as time progressed, and reports of the Men in Black grew stranger, it became apparent to some researchers, such as John Keel, that they were something far stranger than mere "government spooks." Bender's saga seems to suggest that they are alien in origin, as is the conventional theory about them today.

Bender confessed that it had taken him so long to come clean with the story because the aliens had shined a ray on him which they could use to destroy him, simply by pressing a button. They said that once they were finished, he could talk, and that he would know it when the disk they had given him self-destructed. Finally, around 1960, Bender claimed that he smelled sulfur again in his room quite strongly, and when he checked the box in which the disk was kept, it had disintegrated. He felt free to tell what he knew, despite the fact that he knew no one would ever believe it.

After publishing his book, Bender faded into obscurity.

Chapter 5:
Cultural Invasions

Science fiction books, magazines, and films had long been preparing people, especially the young, for the eventuality of space travel and alien contact. Beginning with H.G. Wells in *War of the Worlds*, and continuing on for decades in pulp magazines like *Weird Tales* and *Amazing Stories*,[41] the idea of alien visitation was one that appealed to the imaginative side of a young audience, who grew up with a more accepting attitude toward the idea that we were not alone in the cosmos. During the heyday of the cinematic chapter plays, children could thrill to such cosmic adventures as *Flash Gordon Conquers the Universe* and *Buck Rogers* (both heroes portrayed by Buster Crabbe), and marvel as he flew rocket ships to alien worlds populated by sword-slinging bad guys and giant lizards. Later, comic books, radio, and television would all come to play an important role in this cultural transformation.

The science fiction movies of the fifties were fraught with paranoid themes, playing on Cold War fears of Soviet aggression and communist subversion. Thus, aliens are depicted as menacing baddies in films like *Earth Vs. The Flying Saucers, War of the Worlds, I Married a Monster from Outer Space,* and *Attack of the Saucer Men*. The only good alien to speak of from that period is Klaatu from *The Day the Earth Stood Still*, and he still comes off as menacing, coming to Earth with his killer robot Gort to warn us that if we don't stop messing with atomic power, our world will be reduced to "a burned-out cinder." Despite the warning against nukes, this is hardly the logic of a friendly space brother.

(In *The Thing From Another World*, James Arness plays a blood-drinking vegetable man from another planet. Insulting, if you happen to be an alien.)

Television shows from the late fifties and early sixties brought aliens and UFOs into the home each week. Shows like *Twilight Zone, Outer Limits* and later *Lost in Space, The Invaders* and the ever-popular *Star Trek* (which featured the sympathetic alien Spock, played so excellently by Leonard Nimoy), all brought glimpses of a future where man was confronted with the reality of alien contact. In 1967, Stanley Kubrik's monumental classic *2001: A Space Odyssey* gave a mind-bending tour of a world where aliens had been present since the dawn of man.

In the Seventies, science fiction and UFOs became big business, as films like *Star Wars, Close Encounters of the Third Kind,* and *Star Trek: The Motion Picture* broke box office records, and revived interest in UFOs for millions of people. *Close Encounters*, with its (for the time) dazzling special effects and soaring musical score, seemed to really strike a chord in people, and it no doubt did much to bolster the idea that Earth was being visited by technologically-advanced beings from another planet. In most people's minds, *Close Encounters*, and the benevolent almond-eyed aliens it portrayed, was probably close to reality.

However, benevolent aliens were *not*, for the most part, being reported by frightened people who thought they'd had an experience of being abducted aboard a UFO. For them, the movie *The UFO Incident*, starring James Earl Jones as Barney Hill, was a little closer to reality (at least, *their* reality). The film, which played just a couple of weeks before the famous Travis Walton UFO abduction case, is thought by some skeptics to have inspired Walton's story.

Whatever the case, the film marks the first real mainstream media treatment of the abduction phenomenon. Later, the excellent television series *In Search Of* with Leonard Nimoy, would do numerous specials on UFOs and UFO-related themes, including one episode on alien abductions.

With the possible exception of Stephen Spielberg's mega blockbuster *E.T.*, during the next couple of decades, man's cinematic interaction with extraterrestrials grew unremittingly bleak.

Director Ridley Scott's *Alien*, with its intensely disturbing and gory scenes and its disgusting and hideous extraterrestrial menace, became a huge blockbuster, while John Carpenter's remake of *The Thing From Another World* went one step beyond and gained notoriety for its utterly repulsive special effects. Both films portrayed aliens so well and so alien that, like the Lovecraftian monstrosities that inspired them, they could not possibly evoke anything but repulsion and loathing.

V, a popular mini-series that spawned a short-lived television series, portrayed disguised alien invaders that looked like reptilian[42] monsters, ate human flesh (and swallowed guinea pigs whole) and were here for the water. Later, they are defeated by a band of intrepid human resistance fighters.

In the late eighties a film of *Communion*, based on the bestselling book by Whitley Strieber, starred actor Christopher Walken as the tormented writer, confronting a bizarre episode in which he seems to be the center of some otherworldly visitation. The film was eerie, but didn't do well at the box office. Later, *Intruders*, based on a book written by abduction researcher Budd Hopkins, would pick up where *Communion* left off, showcasing such things as "hybrid children," and probably getting at the American psyche in a way that *Communion* did not. The eighties also brought us actor Robert Hayes as *Starman*, in a television series based on a movie. Hayes portrayed a gentle, kindly alien with a hybrid son, who was merely looking for his way home while trying to avoid capture by a government investigator. The series was short-lived.

A popular paranormal series from the nineties, *Sightings*, kept viewers up to date on what was going on in Ufology, and a film version of the Travis Walton case, *Fire in the Sky*, used the abduction account as an excuse to throw hideous images on the screen for fascinated audiences. At about the same time, Showtime aired a movie called *Roswell*, starring Kyle McLachlan as Jesse Marcel, and pushed the already popular idea that the government is hiding, possibly back-engineering, crashed UFO technology. And, of course, hiding alien bodies.

Meanwhile, the *X-Files* brought the paranormal, conspiracies, UFOs, and abductions into the American living room in a big way, becoming one of the most successful television programs of all time, and spawning a popular, alien-themed movie. It was followed by the less-successful Roswell-themed *Dark Skies*.

Independence Day revived the old "Us vs. the Aliens" theme of movies like *War of the Worlds*, but was little more than an action picture. Perhaps because of this, it was an immense blockbuster.

An "alien autopsy" video (which was really quite graphic and disturbing) aired on Fox, causing a minor stir, but was later widely derided as a fake. Numerous spin-offs and sequels of *Star Trek* (*The Next Generation, Deep Space 9, Voyager*) kept aliens, of a sort, in the public mind, but, with the possible exception of a low-budget quickie called *The Fourth Kind*, there have been no recent UFO or alien abduction pictures made, as far as I know.

(One possible exception might be the 2001 film of *The Mothman Prophecies*, starring Richard Gere. The movie, which completely leaves out the subject of UFOs—something anyone who has ever read *The Mothman Prophecies* knows is an integral part of the story—nevertheless has some chills and atmospheric touch that makes it worth seeing.)

However, the complete media saturation that has been going on ever since the fifties, and particularly the sci-fi boom of the late Seventies and early eighties, has ensured that, in the public consciousness, there is a certain way an alien looks and acts, and certain things that happen in an alien encounter. So, does the media feed the phenomenon, or vice versa? You have to answer for yourself.

Chapter 6:
Accounts from the Midwestern States

"Every time I would drop to sleep I would see the cursed thing, with its big lights and hideous people. I don't know whether they are devils or angels or what; but we all saw them, and my whole family saw the ship, and I don't want anymore to do with them."

~Alexander Hamilton

Author Note: The excellent article by George A. Filer, "Major UFO Wave in Midwest Including 'Fleet of Discs'," found at http://www.rense.com/general10/filers42501.htm, helped immensely with the preparation of this chapter.

I begin this chapter with a little note: The following cases are a random sampling of UFO sightings and encounters from each of the twelve Midwestern states, some cases going back over a hundred years. I chose the Midwest to illustrate the average, run-of-the-mill nature of the witnesses involved, and to show that the UFO phenomenon is not merely province of California cranks or folks who have spent too much time in the desert. However, this should not be taken to imply that UFOs are simply an American phenomenon, as UFO sightings have been reported in EVERY COUNTRY IN THE WORLD.

That said, the Midwest has long been a hotbed of UFO activity, as I'm sure some of the selected following accounts will demonstrate.

Springfield, Missouri

Adolph Wencke Episode

Sometime the strangest things happen while we are just walking along, minding our own business. This can be attested to by farm worker John Halley, who, on April 14, 1897, was making his way along Jefferson Street in Springfield, when he happened to notice a strange light in the sky. He initially thought this light to be nothing more than a balloon, but soon decided that it was something very different, as it grew closer and closer.

Adolph Wencke, a man that owned a local vineyard, also noticed the light, and came over to where Halley was standing to watch.

Both men were amazed to see the light begin to slowly descend, and resolve itself into the most unusual vehicle either of them had ever seen.

The men were quaking in terror as the thing landed with a hissing sound, only a few hundred feet from where they were standing. Finally working up the courage to approach it, they slowly walked toward the object, not quite certain what to make of it all.

They were soon greeted by the captain, a peculiar man with a long beard, who climbed out of the craft and inquired as to where he might be. The men answered that he was just outside Springfield, and the man took some satisfaction in this, noting that he had been 100 miles to the west, in Quincy, only a half an hour before.

The craft, which carried another man and the captain's wife, had, the bearded man reported, a carriage made of aluminum covered by canvas, and they used a common locomotive headlamp for the purposes of navigation. Other electrical apparatuses were vaguely alluded to, and the man (who went by, based on the letter painted on the side of the craft, the initial "M") explained that his wonderful machine would, undoubtedly, be used against Cuba, as soon as Congress permitted. The man then jumped in the carriage of the vehicle, manipulated some controls, and slowly took off, being lost to distance.

Kansas

Alexander Hamilton Episode

Such accounts were endemic in Midwestern newspapers in the period between 1896-1897. While we're on the subject of the old-time airships, we might as well go ahead and tell about the events that supposedly transpired on the farm of one Alexander Hamilton that year of 1897. Now thought of primarily as a hoax, the account has been much-discussed in UFO literature over the decades, although if this is the first book you've ever read on the subject of UFOs, you've probably never heard of it.

Alexander Hamilton was startled from sleep that April night by a "noise among the cattle." Thinking that his dog was tormenting the livestock, he bounded from bed and went out into the barnyard, where, to his astonishment he saw, "an airship was slowly descending upon my cow lot, about forty rods (600 feet) from the house."

Hamilton got a good look at the strange craft, claiming that it was cigar-shaped, pulsating red, and 300 feet long, approximately. He claimed that there was a carriage underneath, made of some sort of glass, and that the whole of the interior was brightly lit. He also claimed that, inside, he could see "six of the strangest beings I ever saw," and that they were "jabbering together but we could not understand a word that they said."

Hamilton claimed that a noise seemed to attract the attention of the strange beings, and that they "turned a light on" him and his son Wall—presumably a searchlight. As soon as the strange visitors got a look at the men assembled (which also included a farm hand), they flicked some sort of a switch that left a huge turbine wheel at the bottom of the craft spinning. The craft rose slowly and silently, and then seemed to hover, at about a distance of 300 feet, above a two-year-old heifer, who appeared to be caught in a wire fence. The men raced to the animal, to find, inexplicably, that there was a sort of noose made of strange, wire-like material looped around her neck. The men found themselves unable to remove the noose, so cut the heifer free from the fence, and watched in amazement as airship and heifer rose silently into the night sky and disappeared. (Already, this old account has all the earmarks of a classic close encounter.)

The next day, according to Hamilton, he was filled with apprehension, and rising early, went out to investigate the happenings of the night before. He had little luck, but coming home, discovered that another man, whom he identifies as Link Thomas, found the hide, legs, and head of the animal in his field, and had brought it to town to try and identify whether or not someone had stolen and butchered an animal. Hamilton claims to have identified the cow by his brand, and was told by Link that he was mystified, for he could find no tracks in the snow around the remains.

The Hamilton account will be familiar to students of cattle mutilations, an ongoing phenomenon that is endemic to Western states and seems to have, in the last few years, traveled south of the border.

Cattle that are found to have been "mutilated" are said to have had their blood drawn without spilling a drop, to have had their eyes, tongue, and sexual organs removed with precise cuts, and to have mysterious burn marks upon them that some say point to the use of a laser. These cattle are found in remote areas, often after the presence of UFOs or even black helicopters have been reported. Stranger accounts of cattle mutilators have hooded beings or tall aliens bounding over fences and trying to molest cattle, while frightening the wits out of whoever happens upon the scene. Skeptics argue that cattle mutilations are the result of predators; believers of various stripe have blamed UFO occupants and Satanists for the activity. Whatever the explanation, the cattle mutilation continues, with little in the way of a solution to the enigma.

Hamilton sums up his account thusly:

> ...Every time I would drop to sleep I would see the cursed thing, with its big lights and hideous people. I don't know whether they are devils or angels or what; but we all saw them, and my whole family saw the ship, and I don't want anymore to do with them.

Of course, so far the account is not only plausible, it is eerily compelling, in a way that the best science fiction stories often are. It was reprinted in papers all over the country, and affixed to the end of the account was an affidavit by some of the most prominent local citizens that Alexander Hamilton's story was true. In researching the account, author Daniel Cohen found that Hamilton himself was a respected man, a lawyer before becoming a prosperous farmer, and that he was generally held to be, within the community, a man whose reputation was beyond question.

Furthermore, the account has all the earmarks of a classic UFO story, complete with strange beings, brilliant red lights, a cigar-shaped object, and the abduction of an animal that later turns up bizarrely killed. What researcher couldn't be thrilled by the prospect of such a story emerging, dated not in 1997, but 1897, an era when even dirigibles had yet to take to the air?

Sadly, the tale is now thought to be a hoax, the product of an inventive round at Alexander Hamilton's club, a gathering of esteemed citizens who met weekly to concoct tall tales and pass them off to the unwary. Hamilton admitted as much when, in 1897, at the height of the hysteria involving the airship, he came in from the fields one day and informed his wife and a young visitor that he had come up with a real whopper, and that it would even be in the papers the next day. The young visitor remembered this particular conversation decades later. The story not only made the papers worldwide, it existed in Ufological circles and was reprinted in countless books as truth, time and time again.

Strike a blow for the skeptics, I suppose.

St. Louis, Missouri

Joseph Joslin Episode

The year of the "airship," 1896-97, is one rich in anecdotes and lore, and two of the strangest cases reported to us come from Missouri, the "Show Me" state. One of them is the bizarre tale of a man in St. Louis named Joseph Joslin, who was walking along Skinker Road at Forest Park when, suddenly, he espied before him an airship, as it was coming down in the distance. The young man must have been terrified, but how much more horrified must he have been when what emerged from the airship was a two-legged, but otherwise inhuman being!

Joslin claimed that the creature used some sort of hypnosis against him, thus luring him onto the craft. It was here that Joslin was held a captive for three weeks, though, sadly, because of the amnesiac effects of the hypnosis, he was unable to recall many details of his experience.

Today, of course, we would say that Joslin was just one of thousands and thousands of UFO "abductees," and he would promptly be given regressive hypnosis to try and reclaim the memories of his startling experience.

The preceding was reported in the pages of the *St. Louis Globe-Democrat*, April 23rd, 1897. It was reported as truth.

Springfield, Missouri

"Golden-haired Girl is in It"

The following was reported in the pages of the *St. Louis Post-Dispatch* for April 10th, 1897. It was also reported as truth.

This account is so like many of the accounts of contactees of the 1960s that it bears revisiting here. It was sent in as a "Letter to the Editor" of the *Post-Dispatch* from a man named W. H. Hopkins, who worked for the Hartford Steam Boiler Company. The newspaper vouched for the universal regard in which Mr. Hopkins' respectability was held. At any rate, according to Daniel Cohen, an examination of the St. Louis directory of the period yields a Hopkins who did, indeed, work for the Hartford Steam Boiler Company, and who lived at said location.

At any rate, according to Hopkins, while he was traveling in the hills east of Springfield, he came upon a strange landed vessel. It was twenty feet long, he claimed, and had three large propellers. He quickly deduced that this must be the strange airship that he had read about in the papers and disbelieved, and he felt himself apprehensive at approaching it.

As if in response to his fear, he suddenly saw two occupants appear on the outside of the vehicle. One of them, he saw, was a woman of rare and intense beauty, covered in long, golden hair…and completely naked!

"Near the vessel was the most beautiful being I ever beheld," he writes in his letter. "She was rather under medium size, but of the most exquisite forms and features such as would put to shame the forms as sculpted by the ancient Greeks. She was dressed in nature's garb and her golden hair, wavy and glossy, hung to her waist, unconfined excepting by a band of glistening jewels that bound it back from her forehead."

This vision of loveliness incarnate must have stunned the simple, church-going Hopkins, but what must he have felt when the second apparition appeared? This was a "godlike" being of "noble proportions," a heroic-looking man with a long beard, who sat beneath the ship. Both of these surreal characters, Hopkins noted, seemed to be bothered by the heat.

Hopkins approached them warily, and started to make gestures, but it was difficult to get the two UFOnauts to understand what he meant. He finally asked them where they came from, and the two, looking to a place in the sky, pointed, and in an unknown tongue, said a word that, to Hopkins' ears, sounded suspiciously like the word "Mars."

It was then that the two beings ascended back into their vehicle. It rose slowly from the ground, and then zoomed off into the sky at a great speed. Hopkins stood there, dumbfounded at what he had just seen, and later declined to be interviewed, although interviews with his wife and friends appended the article. All attested to the veracity of his claims, and to the fact that, despite the ridicule often heaped upon those who claimed to have seen the mystery airship, Hopkins himself was a teetotaler.

Missouri

The Reedsburg Encounter

A few years later, in 1900, we have an interesting anecdote told by a young boy riding home from a dance. The dance had been an outstanding success. The young man had made quite a few new friends, and turned the heads of not a few local girls, as he winged his way across the floor, the collar of his shirt turned up and his heels clicking against the boards. It seemed like the night might never end, and he was happy to get a chance to get away from his chores and celebrate life, if only for a little while. There had been much good food and good fellowship, and now the boy was plum tuckered out, and ready to retire.

He said his last goodbyes to his new friends, unhitched his horse, and started out with a final wave. He took the road through town slowly, yawning, taking his time to appreciate the deep, black cloudless sky above with its multiplicity of twinkling stars. Tonight had been quite a night, but, unknown to the boy, it was only going to get more interesting.

He soon came to the old bridge, and crossed over into a stand of trees, when, suddenly, his patient old nag seemed to start. He pulled the reigns tight and tried to figure out what might have spooked the animal when, all of a sudden, he looked up into the sky.

He was not sure that he wasn't home in bed, dreaming.

His voice caught in his throat, and the horse buckled beneath him, kicking up dust.

Overhead, the trees bent inward as, above them, a tremendous dark object, shaped like a cigar, floated overhead. The boy had never, in his entire life, seen anything like it. It was enormous, and suddenly his ears seemed to catch a bizarre swishing sound as the object moved slowly into the distance. The boy would describe the sound as "a stick being swished overhead."

The horse remained in a frightened state for some time after. Years later, the boy would recount his story exactly as he had always told it.

Lincoln, Nebraska

"Get Thee Behind Me, Satan!"

John Keel relates, in his excellent book *The Complete Guide to Mysterious Beings*, that fellow Ufologist Gray Barker unearthed a strange newspaper clipping from 1922. The clipping was from the *Lincoln, Nebraska Daily Star*. The witness was anonymous.

A man was astounded to see a large circular object land in one of his fields. Furthermore, he was terrified to see an eight-foot-tall being, in the shape of a man, emerge from the craft. A deeply religious man, he interpreted this strange encounter in the only way that he could: this was a visitation from the Devil himself! He began to mutter prayers and biblical verses, telling the strange entity to, "Get thee behind me, Satan!" He turned his back on the creature, and saw another circular craft emerge from the clouds and hover nearby. From this craft emerged sounds like someone quoting Biblical passages, and the man felt that the intent of the occupants of the second craft was to protect him from the hostile intentions of the eight-foot-tall creature.

The creature seemed to lose interest in harming the man, possibly because of the appearance of the second craft, and took off for the woods. The man then claimed to have tracked the creature to where his ship landed; the creature apparently left hoof-marks in the ground.

The creature, at one point, must have passed through a barbed-wire fence, as it was left hot, and the wire appeared to have been cut through with something like a welding torch.

Hubbell, Nebraska

February 22, 1922

Keel goes on to relate another account, also from Nebraska, which is similar to the preceding. Apparently, it is from a letter that was "buried in the Air Force UFO files in Dayton, Ohio."[43]

A Mr. William C. Lamb was out hunting that Wednesday, when at approximately 5 a.m., his attention was first directed to a high-pitched sound, and he saw a "dark object" pass overhead. The object landed close to him, and the man, terrified, went to hide behind a tree.

Out of the object stepped the most astonishing being he had ever seen. It was a "magnificent flying creature" that "landed like an airplane," and it passed directly by the tree where Mr. Lamb was hiding. In a burst of courage, he attempted to follow it, but said that he lost track of the creature.

A most curious account, to be sure.

> Winged entities are, from time to time, associated with UFOs (though mostly in older accounts). One such entity is the West Virginia beastie known as the "Mothman," which John Keel documented in the Fortean classic, *The Mothman Prophecies*.

Mount Pleasant, Iowa

June 3, 1920

A man named Clark, who had just gotten married that year, was working his father's farm when he decided, upon a whim, to go fishing. He grabbed his pole and took off. He claimed he was about six miles northeast of town at the time.

It was approximately ten in the morning when Clark, looking up from his fishing rod, espied something strange coming down from the sky not far away from him. The object landed about fifteen feet from where he sat, and he described it, later, as looking like an aluminum milk can.

Intrigued, Clark watched the weird, egg-shaped little object hover over the grass for a short period of time, before finally working up the nerve to approach it. He said that doing so took every bit of his courage, as he was unaccountably afraid that the object, whatever it was, might be lethal. He noticed that the grass beneath the object seemed to be flattened out, but that the object left no burns or scorch marks in the grass.

It was also, as is often the case, completely silent.

The object suddenly shot up, without turning around, and sped off into the distance, leaving Clark just another bewildered witness. Although, because of the small size of the object, Clark thought it unlikely that it was occupied by actual beings, he did state that, "I didn't know what to believe about it at the time, and I still don't. I've concluded that it wasn't anything from Earth."

A UFO Crash in Missouri?

Cape Girardeau, 1941

As noted, it has long been the contention of conspiracy theorists that the United States government is either hiding what it knows about UFOs and the existence of extraterrestrial life, or even more fantastically, hiding the "smoking gun" evidence of extraterrestrial life in the form of a crashed UFO and possibly bodies that have been retrieved. The most famous account of a crashed UFO being recovered by the government is, of course, the incident at Roswell, New Mexico in 1947. Few people know, however, that there are other accounts of crashed UFOs, some going back as far as the 1890s.

One such account that has recently come to our attention is the strange, bewildering deathbed confession of an elderly cleric, who related the following story to his daughter. It was then related by her, to researcher Leo Stringfield.

William Huffman was an evangelist and minister of Red Star Baptist Church. One night in 1941, he remembered getting a strange call from a government agency, requesting that he be picked up to go and minister to some "plane crash victims." Apparently, the crash had just occurred, and the victims were on the edge of death. Rev. Huffman readily agreed to go out to the site, and was soon in a car with, what he assumed, were men from the government. They drove him fifteen to twenty miles out into the country, to the site of the disaster.

He wasn't surprised, when they finally arrived, to see a number of policeman, firemen, and what he assumed were FBI agents hovering around the scene. What he was surprised to see was the wreckage itself, as it did not correspond to any wreckage of an airplane he had ever seen before in his life.

It was rounded, shiny metallic, having no seams or edges, and was broken up, which allowed Huffman to see inside. Inside, he claimed that he saw a number of dials and gauges, small seats, and, most impressively, a ring of strange "hieroglyphics" around the wall, which put him in mind of Egyptian hieroglyphics.

More astonishing than this, though, were the three occupants of the craft, one of which was still barely alive. Huffman described them as small, with the "frame of a child," and as having large heads, oval eyes, slits for mouths, small holes where the nose should be, and being completely hairless. He also described them as wearing what appeared to be shiny, crinkly aluminum suits.

They apparently had long arms and long, skinny fingers.

Huffman administered last rites to the strange being (although discerning readers must surely be asking themselves why the military took the risk of calling him in at all), and two of the uniformed personnel propped up the little entity between them. A picture was snapped, and that is where the story, from the viewpoint of UFO researchers becomes even more tantalizing.

Sadly, this photograph has yet to be located, but what has been unearthed about this strange, unsettling case are records from the local fire department, records dating back to the incident that confirm that the local firefighters were sworn to secrecy about the crash and that all material at the sight was retrieved by authorized agencies. Also, the brother of the then county sheriff attests to the fact that the crash happened, as well as having heard accounts at the time of "little men in a spaceship."

Huffman was sworn to secrecy, being told: "This didn't happen; you didn't see this; this is national security; it is never to be talked about again." However, he reportedly told his immediate family, being highly agitated about what he had seen, and then later told his wife. She told the full details of the incident to her granddaughter in 1984, while she lay dying of cancer.

Charlette, Huffman's granddaughter, is unique among UFO witnesses in that she claims to have actually seen the photograph, which was lost when her father loaned the picture of the dead entity to a friend. All efforts to retrieve the photo have subsequently failed.

Charlette's sister has confirmed her story in a sworn affidavit. Below are some quotes from an interview she gave concerning the incident:

> She said that grandfather was called out in the spring of 1941 in the evening around 9:00-9:30, that someone had been called out to a plane crash outside of town and would he be willing to go to minister to people there, which he did.
>
> Upon arrival it was a very different situation. It was not a conventional aircraft, as we know it. He described it as a saucer that was metallic in color, no seams, did not look like anything he had seen. It had been broken open in one portion, and so he could walk up and see that.... In looking in, he saw a small metal chair, gauges, and dials, and things he had never seen. However, what impressed him most was around the inside there were inscriptions and writings, which he said he did not recognize, but were similar to Egyptian hieroglyphics....There were three entities, or non-human people, lying on the ground. Two were just outside the saucer, and a third one was further out. His understanding

was that perhaps that third one was not dead on impact. There had been mention of a ball of fire, yet there was fire around the crash site, but none of the entities had been burned and so father did pray over them, giving them last rites...[44]

This particular case is still under investigation.

Rapid City, South Dakota
August 13, 1953

The following account comes to us from Edward Ruppelt, who headed Project Blue Book for two years. His book, *The Report on Unidentified Flying Objects*, is valuable reading.

Ruppelt received a call at 2 a.m. on the 13th of August by Max Futch, advising him that ATIC (Air Technical Intelligence Center) had received a wire "carrying a priority just under that reserved for flashing the word the U.S. has been attacked."

Ruppelt caught a flight from Dayton out to Rapid City immediately. The story he was able to piece together went something like this:

On the night of the 12th, Air Defense Command radar station at Ellsworth AFB had received a call from the Ground Observer Corps filter center, alerting them to the fact that a spotter at Black Hawk had reported "an extremely bright light" in the northeast. The radar had been scanning toward the west due to a jet fighter making some practice patrols, but it was quickly moved to the northeast quadrant, where it indeed detected an object exactly where the lady had said it would be.

The target was described by the warrant officer as "well defined, solid, and bright."

The object was at 16,000 feet and moving very slowly. The warrant officer picked up the phone and was connected to the spotter, who was still watching the UFO. Suddenly, she informed him that the object had begun moving. The object apparently was starting to move southwest, toward Rapid City.

Two men were sent outside to view the object, which they described as a large bluish-white light. All three parties were now watching the object and communicating back and forth about it, and the UFO, which had been just moments ago moving toward Rapid City, suddenly turned back to its original position.

The F-84 pilot who had been on patrol was quickly called and informed that he should get ready to intercept the UFO. The pilot was guided in to where the UFO was located.

It was still at 16,000 feet, and when the pilot closed in within three miles of it, the object began to move. The pilot, controller, and spotter were all in communication, watching the UFO at the same time.

The UFO began to pick up speed, brighten, and head north, with the F-84 still about three miles behind it. The jet could never get much closer, as the

UFO seemed to have some sort of "automatic warning radar linked to its power supply." Every time the pilot tried to close in, the object would brighten, speed up, and climb away. Finally, checking his fuel gauge, the pilot realized that he would have to return to base. He turned around and headed back, with the UFO following him at about ten to fifteen miles behind.

Another fighter jet was scrambled, and the pilot saw the light right away. Still, there was no catching up to it, as it maintained a comfortable distance the whole time. Every time the pilot attempted to close in, the object would move up and away at great speed.

The pilot found himself not believing what he was seeing, and turned out his lights to make sure the object he was chasing wasn't merely a reflection. But the object was as bright as ever, even with the pilot's lights off. He compared it to three stars—and found that the object was not a star, as it moved in relation to them. Finally, he flipped on his radar-ranging gunsight, and, to his amazement, a red blip appeared on his screen. Whatever that thing was out there, it was a solid object.

The pilot later reported that, at this realization, he was "scared."

Ruppelt writes, "When I talked to him, he readily admitted that he'd been scared. He'd met MD 109s, FW 190s, and ME 262s over Germany and he'd met MIG-15s over Korea, but the large, bright, bluish-white light had scared him—he asked the controller if he could break off the intercept."[45]

The object didn't follow the fighter back, but instead headed for the direction of Fargo. When Fargo was contacted, they at first reported no UFO in their vicinity. However, a few minutes later, a call back informed Rapid City that spotter posts in the area had apparently seen a fast-moving, large, bluish-white light.

Ruppelt summarizes: "This was an unknown…one of the best."

Michigan

November 23, 1953

Lieutenant Felix Moncla, like Captain Mantell a few years before him, died chasing a UFO. That fact cannot be argued with.

An unknown target was picked up at Truax AFB, and an F-89C Scorpion jet was scrambled from Kinross Field. The jet chased the UFO at 500 miles per hour, but the object abruptly changed course. What's more, the pilot, Moncla, was having trouble locking in on the thing with radar. The pilot managed to chase the thing for thirty minutes, finally coming out over Lake Superior. He began to gain ground on the UFO, and it was then that the tragedy occurred.

Ground control saw the two radar blips, that of Lieutenant Moncla's Scorpion and that of the UFO, merge into a single blip. They believed, at first, that he had flown over or under the UFO, and that, eventually, they would see two blips again. Of course, it was not to be. The radar return disappeared, and ground control called Search and Rescue.

Despite their best efforts, Search and Rescue found nothing. Lieutenant Moncla and his radar operator, R. Wilson, were pronounced dead, and the investigation began. The official explanation was that Moncla had suffered "vertigo...and crashed into the lake." Alternative theories were just as unconvincing.

Bismark, North Dakota

1953

A truly incredible sighting, one verified by trained Air Force fighter pilots and investigated in a secret report by none other than Dr. J. Allen Hynek, was the 1953 Bismark incident. It was witnessed by more than forty-five mystified townspeople.

The first witness, at approximately 8:05 in the evening, looked up to see a red glowing object making "sweeping movements." This intelligence was quickly related to the North Dakota Air Defense Filter Center, where a Sergeant Harry and others tracked the mysterious object, which would "remain stationary—then hop up several degrees very quickly—almost instantaneously," and which was also said to "Stop...move to the left, and then swerve down in a sort of slanting motion, repeating these maneuvers several times."

According to Sergeant Harry, the general consensus among his colleagues was that: "Somebody was watching us."

How much stranger was it then, when it was discovered that, before being sighted in Bismark, two F-84s over Blackhawk, South Dakota had visual contact with the strange craft for twenty to thirty seconds. Both jets and UFOs were tracked on radar.

The pilot who established visual contact claimed: "It's brighter than the brightest star I've ever seen!"

Robert Emenegger, in his book *UFOs: Past, Present and Future,* gives a description of what happened next:

> Lietenant Needham, the second pilot, spotted one of the objects at 15,000 feet. It was below him to his right. The object moves spasmodically up and down, changing colors from white to green. In pursuit, Lieutenant Needham climbed to 26,000 feet and changed course to 360 degrees. After being steady on 360 degrees for a short time, Needham's radar lock-on-light on the A-4 gun-sight came on and remained on. The object was ahead of him. It increased its speed and moved rapidly ahead and up.[46]

The F-84 and the UFOs were being tracked by radar, which indicated that the UFOs were five to ten miles ahead of the jet. The chase was finally abandoned, but that was not then end of the story.

At 1:09 a.m., an Air Force Globemaster C-124 flew over Bismark and established visual contact with the UFOs, which changed color in a mysterious wave, from red to green and back, as if signaling to each other.

Dr. Hynek would later state:

> The entire incident, in my opinion, has too much of an Alice-in-Wonderland flavor for comfort.

Ann Arbor, Michigan
Story of a Contactee

Richard Miller was a man with a curious hobby: he wanted to contact "outer space" visitors via short-wave radio. He was apparently successful at this, as in 1954, he reportedly was told to travel to a certain location in Ann Arbor to meet his extraterrestrial contact. After journeying to the isolated location and waiting for about fifteen minutes, Richard was amazed to see a "flying saucer," straight from the movies, come down from the sky and land near him. Approaching the object warily, he saw a door slide open, and a man in a brown, one-piece suit beckon him inside.

Here he found himself standing in a circular hallway. Of course, most other folks would have found themselves terrified (or at least somewhat nervous), but Richard insisted later that the young man "radiated friendliness," and that this put Richard at ease. He was taken to the control room to meet the commander of the strange ship (the name of which, incidentally, was the *Phoenix*).

The commander, whose name was "Soltec," informed Richard that their planet, "Centurus," was in the Alpha Centauri system, and, furthermore, that they belonged to the "Universal Confederation" of 680 advanced planets, all members due to their advanced spiritual evolution. Richard was informed that mankind would have to awaken to higher spiritual values before the "Sons of Light," the beings otherwise known as "angels" could appear and the "kingdom of your God" reign on Earth.

Richard was informed that the only thing standing in the way of this was a conspiracy of silence on the part of world governments, who didn't want to lose their base of power in the coming New Age. These governments were actively resisting the influence of the space brothers, and those world leaders and top-scientists who had already been contacted were all part of the conspiracy. Thus, the space brothers were now contacting average people, like Richard, in the hopes that, if they could convert enough people into believing in them, they could force the balance of power against the government conspiracy, and bring about change.

Soltec went on to tell Richard of a war the Atlanteans had fought with their neighbors, the Lemurians, a nuclear war that resulted in the destruction of Atlantis. Soltec warned Richard in the strongest possible terms that the use of nuclear energy was evil, saying: "Do they not realize that by destroying matter, they are opposing the will of the Creator?"

Soltec also took credit for deflecting atomic particles away from the Earth, noting that the planet was currently moving through a cloud of such particles, and that they could only be deflected by orbiting spaceships in the atmosphere.

Richard channeled such messages for twenty years, producing many books and audio recordings.

Branch Hill, Ohio

March, 1955

Mr. R.H. was driving along on his way to Loveland when he spotted three individuals at the side of the road. He slowed his car down to get a better look, when he realized, to his horror, that the three individuals were not human.

They each had frog-like faces, with slits for mouths, bulging eyes, and weird, "painted-on" hair. Each wore a tight-fitting grey suit that bulged on the right side, a bulge that proceeded from the shoulder downward. Mr. R.H. described them as having bodies that seemed "lop-sided." They had tiny arms, and, though he could not see their legs, he estimated their size to be somewhere in the vicinity of three feet tall. One of the little creatures had a wand-like device that seemed to emit a blue shower of sparks. Mr. R.H. tried to get closer, but was warned away by the strange entities. He proceeded to the local sheriff to file a report.

Glenwood City, Wisconsin

1960

In 1960, a group of three women were driving home from church when they spotted a strange, cylindrical object flying at low altitude from the back window of the car. Getting out, one of the women produced a pair of binoculars.

"I've never seen anything like it!"

Her companion took the binoculars from her and looked for herself. Indeed, it was the strangest vehicle either of them had ever seen! It didn't seem to have any wings!

What's more, she swore that she could see people behind the windows of the craft, and they seemed to be motioning as if they were in some sort of distress.

The two women were perplexed, but soon got back in the car and told the driver to follow the craft. It was rough going for awhile, as they were pretty far out into the country, but, soon, they caught sight of the object as it hovered over a local sports field. They pulled their car up to the field, slowly, and turned off the engine. They debated for a moment over what to do; their fear and their curiosity seemed to be at war.

The object was a perfect, hovering cylinder. It had a row of windows on the side, behind which dim shapes could be seen moving. The women stood some distance from the object, not daring to get any closer.

Suddenly, it rose in the air, silently, and zoomed away at a terrific speed. The women stood there in amazement. Whatever it had been had departed as quickly as it had come, but it left all of them believers.

Eagle River, Wisconsin

Joe and the Space Pancakes

It was April 18, 1961. Joe Simonton was a sixty-year-old chicken farmer from Eagle River, Wisconsin, a man, no doubt, possessed of the kind of level-headed common sense that forbids the existence of such fangled things as flying saucers. So when an object that looked like "two washbowls turned face to face" appeared in the sky over his house. He stood up and took notice.

The object settled down in his yard, hovering a few inches off the ground, and Simonton approached the object cautiously, although he claimed later that he had "no fear." A hatch opened up in the top of the object, and Simonton could see inside.

Inside were three little men, each about five feet tall, with dark hair and skin and wearing dark blue knit outfits and turtlenecks. They each also wore a knit helmet. They had no beards, and Simonton never specified what sort of shoes they wore. If any.

The interior of the craft looked to be a dull black, like wrought iron, and he noticed that one of the little men was cooking on what appeared to be a sort of flameless grill, while the other man sat at the controls. The third man then popped out of the hatch and handed him a silver jug with two handles, making a drinking motion to indicate to Simonton that he wanted water. Simonton dutifully filled the jug and brought it back to the little man.

Simonton then noticed that the man cooking had stacked a number of small "cookies" on the side of his grill, and he motioned to the leader of the little men that he wanted one of them. He was given four.

The hatch then closed, Simonton heard a sound like "knobby tires on a wet pavement," and the craft took off at a 45-degree angle, leaving the chicken farmer scratching his head. He took the cookies, and eventually they ended up in a laboratory, subjected to analysis by people interested on whether or not they really were "space cookies."

They turned out to be made of common, everyday ingredients. Simonton was much ridiculed for his story, and later stated, "if it happened again, I don't think I'd tell anybody about it." Understandable. Nobody believed him.

Poor ol' Joe.

Minot, North Dakota

November, 1961

This CE3 report comes to us courtesy of the book *The UFO Experience* by Dr. J. Allen Hynek.

The event took place after midnight. Four individuals, all described as "family men," two of which held security clearances for work related to the military, observed an unusual object land in an open field during inclement weather that included sleet and rain. The men, concerned that the object might be a small plane in need of assistance, stopped their car by the edge of the road and got out. They quickly hopped the fence, and made their way to the craft, but were astounded when they got there to see, not a downed airplane, but a mysterious landed vehicle, surrounded by "humanoids" (there is no description given). One of the humanoids approached the men, seemingly waving them away in a violent manner, when one of the men panicked and pulled his firearm. He shot the humanoid, who fell over. The men fled from the field back to their car.

It was the very next day, and the men had told no one of their unusual experience. Regardless, one of the men reported that, while at work, he was called out and "led into the presence of men he had never seen before." These men asked to be taken to his home, so he did just that, whereupon they examined articles of his clothing, paying particular attention to his boots. They left without further inspection, and nothing more was ever heard from them. Perhaps, they were agents of the Men in Black?

Cedar Falls, Iowa

August 1965

D.G. heard a whining sound while he was sitting on the porch with his father and sister. Looking up, he saw a strange object, one that looked like two pie plates glued end to end, descending from the clouds. The object seemed to settle behind a nearby hill, so D.G. ran to examine it. He found the object easily enough, and as he looked at it, he noticed a little "man" standing outside the object, near a tree. D.G. ran forward, but tripped and looked down to catch his footing. When he looked up again, the little man had disappeared. He heard the whining sound again, saw a blur and a flash, and watched as the object took to the air, flying away at an incredible rate of speed.

Later, when investigating the old quarry just over the hill, where the object had landed, a circular "burned spot" was found, about twenty feet in diameter. It was a definite ring, with the grass on the outside of the charred area being green, while the soil on the inside was very hard. Three indentations, one inch deep and twelve inches long, were found just inside the circle. These were thought to be the impressions of landing gear. When reporting the matter to authorities later, the family was treated with disdain.

Gallipolis, Ohio
1966

The subject of animal mutilations, particularly the mutilation of cattle and other livestock, is one that is closely related to the subject of UFOs, as mentioned earlier. John Keel relates to us the following accounts in his *Complete Guide to Mysterious Beings*.

A German Shepherd dog was found off of Georges Creek Road, with its bones crushed and "no blood in evidence." The grass around the animal's body was pressed flat in a circular pattern that was approximately twenty feet in diameter. There were no signs that the animal had been attacked by predators.

Georges Creek Road was the center of much UFO activity at that time.

Keel relates the story of a Mrs. Taylor, who claimed that she had seen a reddish-orange light appear in front of her car, at telephone pole height, on the night of December 9, 1966. Mrs. Taylor claimed she watched the light bob up and down and shoot beams of light at the road. "It was the size of a helicopter," she stated, "but it was no helicopter!"

She followed the mysterious light for about a mile, until, reaching a local power station, the object suddenly shot up into the air and was gone. Mrs. Taylor was with her children, one of whom expressed great fear at the presence of the object.

Keel further relates the story of an anonymous woman from the same area, who owned cattle and who claimed to be very familiar not only with the presence of UFOs, but also their strange, cattle-mutilating occupants, who, she claimed were "tall men in white coveralls," who could "certainly run and jump." This woman claimed that she had seen them "leap over high fences from a standing start."

She furthermore claimed that she had seen UFOs "like a lantern on the end of a stick," or, to put it in other words, large luminous balls, around her house. She claimed that an elderly couple that lived in the area had first made her aware of the UFOs, and that sightings went back as far as thirty years.

She also stated that the presumed occupants of these UFOs, the aforementioned "tall, skinny, white coverall men," had begun rustling her cattle some years earlier. She claimed that these clandestine cattle killers were "stupid" concerning what they took, bypassing choice steak cuts in favor of the brains and other organs that were, essentially, worthless. As per usual, there was no blood in evidence at any of these mutilation sites.

She and her children also confirmed, as is often the case with those experiencing alien harassment, problems with the telephone. She privately stated she felt the phone was being tapped.

This woman had furthermore experienced "bedroom visitations," one of which came in the form of a strange episode one evening. She was alone in the house, asleep, when she suddenly awoke and found she could not move. She then felt a wave of heat move over her, as she heard the kitchen door open. She saw a tall, skinny figure walk across the kitchen and go out another door.

That particular door, claims Keel, led to nowhere but a steep drop.

Washtenau County, Michigan

1966

The Michigan UFO sightings of 1966 introduced the world to the notion that "swamp gas" could possibly be responsible for many UFO sightings. This notion was first put forward by J. Allen Hynek, the renowned UFO researcher who went on to be a great believer in the reality of the phenomenon. At the time, Dr. Hynek was scientific advisor to the Air Force on UFOs; he later came to regret mentioning his "swamp gas" theory.

The incidents began auspiciously with a close encounter by farmer Frank Mannor and his son, Ronald, who saw a mysterious object settle down in a swampy area.

The two intrepid men went to investigate for themselves the landed object, which they found to have a "quilted" surface, to be round and disc-shaped at the bottom, going toward a tapering cone at the top, and to be adorned with two bluish-green lights that turned to red intermittently. The object would sometimes become heavily illuminated in a yellowish light that covered it brightly. They saw no occupants, but watched the object until it lifted with a sound "like a rifle bullet when it ricochets off something." It disappeared overhead.

This, however, was not the end of the Michigan UFO flap of 1966. Next, a police officer named Hunawell confirmed the sighting, as he was parked near Quigley and Brand Roads at the time. He said he saw the object floating approximately 1,000 feet over nearby trees before being joined by two others. The strange craft then flew away in formation.

Of course, different reports give us a different perspective of the event.

Vicksburg, Michigan

March 31, 1966

A close encounter with a flying saucer was experienced by a man just trying to get home from work. Hungarian-born Jeno Udvardy was coming up the crest of a hill in Vicksburg when he found his attention arrested by some lights on the road. He slowed down, thinking at first that it might be an ambulance or emergency vehicle.

It was then that he realized that the lights were *not* part of any conventional vehicle, but were attached to a disc-shaped object hovering just off the road, and only ten feet ahead of him. The object was blocking his path.

The lights were blindingly bright, making it difficult for Udvardy to make out any detail. He suddenly felt the car moved by what he described as a great gust of wind, and, looking behind him, he saw what he at first took to be another UFO. Instead, he quickly realized it was the first UFO, and that the object had moved from the front of his car, to behind it.

What was worse, his car wouldn't start. Udvardy stuck his head out the window, and could hear a low humming sound. The UFO stayed in position for a few minutes, then slowly rose and flew away. Later, shaken to his core, Udvardy reported the incident to the Kalamazoo Sheriff 's office. Unsurprisingly, he was met with great skepticism.

Ravenna, Ohio

April 17, 1966

One of the most intriguing scenes from the incredible 1977 blockbuster *Close Encounters of the Third Kind* is a UFO chase by police across Indiana state lines into Ohio. The scene ends with one of the cop cars chasing the two glowing UFOs right off a cliff.

The incident, though it is the stuff of major Hollywood productions, is based on truth, as a dramatic close encounter and a resultant chase happened eleven years earlier, in Portage County, to two policemen who could never have dreamed such a thing could happen to them.

Deputy Sherriff Dale Spaur and Mounted Deputy Wilbur "Barney" Neff were called out to investigate an abandoned car when Spaur says, "When I looked in this wooded area behind us, I saw this thing. At this time it was coming up... to about tree top level. I'd say about 100 feet. It started moving toward us..."[47]

His partner was still looking at the car, so Spaur motioned for him to look over his shoulder. Both men then turned to watch the object come up over the tree top, and bathe the area in brilliant light.

They became aware of a hum, like a "transformer" building up, but beyond that, were unaware of any sound. Both men looked down at their hands, as if to check that they weren't burning, and then looked up to see the object directly above them. Out of fear, both went for their squad car.

The UFO began to move east, about 250 feet away, and Spaur picked up the microphone to radio dispatch. The object was tremendously bright, he notes. "It'd make your eyes water," he said.

He reached dispatch. Off-duty Sergeant Schoenfelt told them to follow the object and keep it under observation, while they worked to get photographers out to the area. Spaur and Neff did just that.

The men turned south on Route 183, then east on Route 224. The object was to their right, brightly illuminating the surrounding area, when it suddenly shot north, putting it to their left. The men accelerated to a speed close to 100 miles per hour. As daylight began to approach, the two men could see that they were indisputably chasing a metallic object with a sort of vertical rear projection. At one point, when they took a wrong turn, the object stopped and came back to their position.

The men were keeping up a steady stream of radio chatter as they pursued the object, and Officer Wayne Huston of East Palestine, near the Pennsylvania border, positioned himself to where he knew Neff and Spaur would be passing by. It was not long before he saw the sheriff's car and the UFO fly by.

He quickly joined in the pursuit. At this time, in Conway, Pennsylvania, Spaur and Neff spotted a parked police car and stopped to appeal for aid in the pursuit, as their cruiser was almost out of gas. The officer in the parked car radioed for dispatch, and radio chatter was heard about the scrambling of jets to chase the UFO.

The UFO stopped and hovered. Then, all of a sudden, it zoomed upward and away.

Spaur said:

> When they started talking about fighter planes, it was just as if that thing heard every word that was said. It went PSSSSSHHEW, straight up, and I mean when it went up, friend, it didn't play no games, it went straight up."[48]

The Air Force tried to write the incident off as misidentification of a satellite or Venus, and Major Hector Quintinilla of Project Blue Book argued with the witnesses, refusing to change the identification; he flatly denied there had ever been any plans to scramble jets.

The witnesses pointed out that they had seen Venus and the moon that night, and that the object they had chased across state lines, at speeds in excess of 100 miles per hour, bore no resemblance to either one. A massive report was prepared by the National Investigations Committee on Aerial Phenomena, written by William B. Weitzel, and was delivered to the University of Colorado UFO Project, headed up by Dr. E.U. Condon.

Predictably, the Condon Committee never mentioned the report in their own report.

Bagley, Minnesota

April 22, 1966

The following report was discovered after a random search of some old UFO files, found on the website of Minnesota MUFON. After reading the report, I thought it interesting enough for inclusion here.

On the night in question, a "flying saucer" flew down main street in Bagley, "jumped a school bus," and settled down at the edge of town, where four small, dwarf-like beings got out of the craft and seemed to begin working on it. They then got back in the craft and took off. I have no further information about this sighting, nor do I know precisely how many witnesses there were. However, I do have the testimony of a man named "Rocky," who wrote the incredible account of the Bagley CE3 (or Close Encounter of the Third Kind) from the viewpoint of someone actually flying the saucer.

According to Rocky, he had been invited aboard the craft and flown to Russia. He describes his experience thusly:

> There was no pilot seat, buttons, or any visible controls, or portals to see out. The center of the craft was an empty space allowing access to horizontal receptacles (inside the wall of the ship), which are the only life support on the ship. Once inside, the ship telepathically connects to your mind, your body becomes the ship, and the ship becomes an extension of your mind. Visually everything 360 degrees around the ship is part of your vision; you have to focus your mind up, down, forward to see in one direction. You can reach out with your arms to feel anything outside the craft (you can reach out to planets and feel them). To move, you only have to think it, in any direction. I also remember learning to land from space on a planet.[49]

Astonishing stuff. Rocky claims that, when first brought aboard the ship, he was directed to lie down in a compartment beneath some coils, where he suddenly discovered that he was "one with the ship," that he could control it, and that the ship was conscious. After that, he took the vehicle to Russia, where he believes he teleported down to Moscow on a beam of light, and where "someone like me" helped cure him of the nightmares he had been having since the age of three.

He then took the UFO back to Bagley, his hometown, where he flew over Main Street and jumped the school bus, presumably just to get attention. He then landed the craft at the edge of town, and snuck out before the "greys" (whom he describes as being "drones") could catch him. It was then that, he claims, he started a forest fire for mysterious reasons, but that it was okay since some friendly forest fire fighters happened by and stifled the incipient blaze.

Rocky claimed that the "greys" were in fact created by the ship as robot-like servants, and that the ship itself was alive and had a consciousness all its own.

Ashland, Nebraska

December 3, 1967

Officer Herbert Schirmer was making his usual rounds; he had checked out the Ashland Sales Barn and a number of gas stations before heading through the intersection of Highway 6 and 63, and noticing some red lights in the distance.

At first, Schirmer took them to be the lights of a stalled truck, and he went to investigate. Upon coming nearer the object, however, he came upon the startling realization that, whatever else it may be, the object directly ahead of him was no stalled pickup.

It was an oval-shaped, metallic object, with a shiny surface that looked like polished aluminum. It had oval portholes, from which the red light seemed to be emanating, and a structure beneath it that looked like landing gear. Schirmer was amazed to see the object hover in the air approximately eight feet above the road.

Suddenly, flames shot out from under the object, and it rose in the air, passing almost directly over his patrol car before disappearing. Schirmer drove back to the station, noting with some amazement that it was now 3 a.m. He estimated that he had first seen the object around 2:20, and thought the entire encounter couldn't have taken more than ten minutes. In his logbook, he wrote:

> Saw a flying saucer at the junction of highways 6 and 63. Believe it or not!

Schirmer was unable to forget his curious encounter though, and developed some bizarre symptoms: a red welt on his neck, headaches and nausea, and an inability to concentrate all plagued him. His UFO sighting was reported to the notorious Condon Committee, which at the time was still investigating sightings.

He was asked to make a trip to Boulder, Colorado, where he was put under hypnosis by Dr. R. Leo Sprinkle. Under hypnosis, Schirmer revealed an expanded version of the events of that night.

Schirmer remembered that when he had come upon the UFO, his car had died and his radio quit. Panicked, Schirmer had wanted to draw his gun, but a white object had emerged from the craft and spoke to him telepathically, preventing him from doing so.

He also remembered that the beings claimed to be friendly, that they hailed from "bases on Venus," and that they drew energy from electrical power lines. Predictably, the Condon Committee was unimpressed by this new information, stating:

> Evaluation of psychological assessment tests, the lack of any evidence, and interviews with the patrolman, left project staff with no confidence that the trooper's reported UFO experience was physically real.

Dr. Sprinkle, however, believed that Schirmer believed that what he was telling was the truth.

Schirmer was promoted to Ashland Police Chief, but resigned after only two months, claiming that his UFO experience was making him unable to concentrate. At this time, according to Schirmer, he was ridiculed by townsfolk, his wife left him, and his car was "dynamited."

Future hypnosis sessions revealed the whole story of his unique encounter, the details of which were told in two books: *Gods, Demons, and Space Chariots* and *Gods and Devils from Outer Space*.

Schirmer claims that he tried to follow the UFO, which sat down in a field. He tried to radio for backup, but found that his vehicle and radio were dead. Suddenly, a door opened in the object, and three beings emerged. They shot a green gas at his cruiser, and pointed a ray at him which caused paralysis.

Schirmer then recalls being grabbed around the neck by one of the beings, and asked if he was willing "to shoot at a space ship." When Schirmer answered that he would not, the being invited him aboard the craft. Schirmer recalls that the being was small, perhaps just under five feet tall, and wore a tight fitting silvery suit with a hood, an object that looked like an antenna over the ear, and a weird insignia of a winged serpent on the breast. They had thin, narrow faces, slit-like mouths, and eyes that slanted upward. Their skin was a kind of pale gray.

Schirmer gave details about the ship, and about images he was asked to view on a screen. The leader of the aliens explained to him that they came from a distant galaxy, but that they had bases on Venus, and beneath the Earth[50] and ocean. The Leader explained that, while Schirmer was hearing him speak, he was also receiving information telepathically, directly to his brain. The Leader stated that, to a certain degree, they operated without a pattern while on Earth, in an effort to confuse people.[51]

(Keel has much to say about the UFO occupants and their propensity for purposely confusing people.)

Schirmer affirmed that there would be many more contacts in the future.

"They have no pattern for contacting people. It is by pure chance so the government cannot determine any patterns about them," Schirmer stated while under hypnosis.

Edina, Missouri

January 8, 1969

Mrs. Adeline Davis was tending a sick child. Periodically, she got up to make temperature checks, but she was lying down in her own room when the incident occurred. She was forced awake by some compulsion, and looking out the window, got the surprise of her life when she saw, just outside, an entity floating in a strange vehicle.

The entity was about six feet away from Mrs. Davis, and seemed to be busy at a control panel. Whatever he was doing was hidden from Mrs. Davis, but, suddenly, the strange entity looked up, and a startled expression crossed his face. It was as if he didn't expect to be "caught in the act" by anyone. However, the being went back to his work, bending back over the control panel, and then reaching up for something. Mrs. Davis could not tell what he was reaching for, but, whatever it was, he never seemed to get it.

Mrs. Davis described pinching herself, hitting herself, and going into the bathroom to splash water on her face, all to make sure she wasn't dreaming. When she returned to the bedroom and sat on the bed, she could still see the entity outside the window.

He looked at Mrs. Davis again, and the object he was piloting seemed to back away from the window. The object was army green, had a light extending from the bottom, and had tinted windows.

Mrs. Davis again went to the bathroom to splash water on herself, returning to find that the object, which had landing gear, was moving upward slowly, the landing gear being somewhere between three to five feet off the ground. The object slowly moved away, finally disappearing behind the corner of the house, and it was noted later that it had pushed back tree branches.

Mrs. Davis was, incredibly, unfazed by this incident, but noted that the electricity in the house had gone off during the encounter. Neighbors were questioned later as to whether or not their electricity had gone out for this short period of time, but no one reported in the affirmative.

Mrs. Davis described the occupant as looking like a normal man in a military fatigue cap, with dark clothing, a dark jacket open at the front, a scarf, and an upturned collar. She did say his eyes were strange, that they seemed "slanted and widespread", and that the pupils seemed "fuzzy." Mrs. Davis apparently enjoyed a good night's sleep after her encounter.

Garrison, Iowa

July 13, 1969

Pat Barr was headed to bed when she heard something that sounded "like a low-flying jet." Going to the window, she was astounded to see an object that looked like two saucers stuck end to end, with a glowing ring of lights in the center. It was hovering over a nearby bean field. Calling her cousin, Kathy, to the window, the girls watched as the object took off at an astounding rate of speed. After it departed, the girls noticed that the field over which it had hovered was glowing red.

The next day, Mr. Barr, though skeptical of the girls' story, went to investigate the field for himself. To his astonishment, he found a bare, circular patch in the field that looked as if it had been scorched by lightning. The area was approximately forty feet in diameter, and was eventually photographed from the air.

Analysis of the soil and beans yielded little in the way of results. While Mr. Barr said he would hesitate to attribute a cause to the strange, burned patch of ground, Pat Barr stated that she felt it was an "air-flying object from outer space."

Delphos, Kansas

November 2, 1971

UFOs are sometimes known for leaving "traces" where they appear: broken branches, burnt soil, dead grass, etc. These traces, which often classify a sighting as a CE2 (or Close Encounter of the Second Kind) are analogous, in the interpretation of some researchers such as Vallee, with the "fairy rings" of olden times.

In Delphos, Kansas in 1971, a UFO was sighted by a young man, and left such tell-tale evidence of its appearance in its wake.

Ron Johnson, 16, was out tending the family sheep with his dog when he heard a sound that he described as "like a washing machine which vibrates." He looked up to see a mushroom-shaped object hovering off the ground. The object was approximately fifteen feet away, hidden among the trees, and he estimated its diameter between six to eight feet.

Astounded, he tried to get a better look at the craft, but was prevented in doing so by the sheer brilliance of its light, which seemed to grow as the craft rose. Ron claims he was temporarily blinded, but, after regaining his sight, he quickly ran back to the house to fetch his parents. They came out of the house frankly puzzled, but just in time to see the object depart. They were amazed to discover, however, that the object had left some evidence behind; namely, a ring of bright glowing soil where it had, apparently, touched down.

This soil was "strange, like a slick crust," and felt as if it was "crystallized." Touching it, Ron's mother felt her fingers go numb, as if she had just been administered an anesthetic. There was glowing material on some of the nearby trees, as well.

After taking a little while to calm down, the family retired for the night. They were amazed to discover the next day, however, that the ring was still there. The rainwater of the previous evening had left the ground both inside and outside the ring wet, but the ring itself was dry to the touch.

A month later, when snow finally fell upon the ground, it melted both inside and outside the ring, but, as for the ring itself, the snow on it did not melt, and further investigation proved that water would not penetrate the soil of the ring.

Thaddia Smith, of the *Delphos Republican* later reported:

> The circle was still very distinct and plain to see. The soil was dried and crusted. The circle or ring was approximately 8 feet across, the center of the ring and the outside area were still muddy from recent rains. The area of the ring that was dried was about a foot across and was very light in color.
>
> The object had crushed a dead tree to the ground either when it landed or took off, and from appearance had broken a limb of a live tree when it landed. The broken limb was most unusual, it would snap and break as though it had been dead for quite some time, yet it was green under the bark, and the upper area still had green leaves clinging to its branches.
>
> However the lower area looked as though it had been blistered and had a whitish cast.[52]

Sherrif Enlow, Harlan Enlow, and Kansas State Highway Patrolman Kenneth Yager investigated, noting that they found a "doughnut-shaped circle" with a hole in the middle of it, and mud on the outside of the ring. The sheriff noted discolored trees and broken limbs, as well as a slight discoloration.

Soil from the ring was sent for scientific analysis. The findings concluded the "whitish" substance of the ring was:

> vegetal in nature and belonged to an organism of the order of Actinomycetales, which is an intermediate organism between bacteria and fungus... family actinomycete, genus Nocardia... [and is] often found together with a fungus of the order Basidomycetes, which may flouresce under certain conditions... one possible interpretation is that high energy stimulation triggered the spectacular growth of the Nocardia and of an existing fungus, and caused the latter to flouresce.[53]

Lester Ensbarger, a neighbor, advised the Sheriff Enlow that he had also seen a strange light descending near his property in Delphos, thus corroborating Ron's story.

> **Author Note:** Vallée notes in Dimensions that the witness Ronnie suffered ill-effects due to this encounter, including red, burning eyes, and nightmares of "spacemen" looking through his window. He further notes that the animals in the area became completely quiet during this encounter, as is often noted.

Iowa

June 6, 1972

"Mr. T," a farmer, was working in the fields that afternoon when his attention was diverted by a flash of light in the sky. He at first assumed this to be an airplane, but, upon further inspection, decided that the craft he was looking at was no ordinary plane. It was an egg-shaped device, moving as swiftly as a jet, but slowing down to a crawl as it clearly intended to land.

The object landed about 100 yards from Mr. T, who, in his surprise, didn't attempt to get any closer. The object settled down on three legs, and a hatch opened up, depositing a number of "little men" in what appeared to be one-piece suits. The men, which Mr. T estimated to be about five feet tall, "messed around in the corn" for a little bit, before hopping back inside their flying machine.

The machine then emitted a blue jet of flame, the landing gear retracted, and the object rose with a rumble, taking off into the distance at an enormous rate of speed. Mr. T later made as detailed a drawing of the little men as he could, but did not, he admitted, get to see much detail.

Mansfield, Ohio

The Coyne Incident: October 18, 1973

One of the most convincing aspects of the UFO phenomenon, for those who actually take the time to research or study the reports, is the wealth of sightings and incidents involving knowledgeable, responsible professionals, including soldiers, policemen, airline pilots, astronauts, and military personnel. These reports are often detailed and striking insofar as they are made by people with nothing to gain (and, often, quite a substantial lot to lose) by making up wild stories.

The following account is a classic in the Ufological literature. It happened near Mansfield, Ohio in 1973.

Army Reserve helicopter pilot Captain Lawrence Coyne was a member of the 316 Medical Detachment stationed at Cleveland's Hopkins Airport. He was returning from a flight to Columbus on October 18th when, at approximately 11:10 p.m., he spotted a "big, gray, metallic-looking" object near where the Air National Guard had a squadron of jet fighters based.

A newspaper account from the time claims that Coyne checked, and that none of the unit's F-100 Super Saber jets were in the air. Coyne and his crew were cruising at 2,500 feet when the object, which was at first perceived as a red illumination, was spotted by crew chief Sgt. Robert Yanacsek.

"The light was traveling in excess of 600 knots," Coyne said. "It came from the horizon to our aircraft in about 10 seconds. We were on a collision course."

The craft seemed to be headed right for the helicopter.

"At 1,700 feet I braced myself for the impact with the other craft. It was coming from our right side. I was scared. There had been so little time to respond. The thing was terrifically fast."

However, luckily for the crew, there was no crash.

"We looked up and saw it stopped right over us," Coyne said. "It had a big, gray metallic-looking hull about 60 feet long. It was shaped like an airfoil or a streamlined fat cigar. There was a red light on the front. The leading edge glowed red a short distance back from the nose. There was a center dome. A green light at the rear reflected on the hull."

The green light apparently "swiveled like a spotlight," and bathed the cabin of the Huey in green light. It was at this time that something else shocking occurred.

Coyne claimed that, despite the controls of the craft being set for a 20-degree dive, the helicopter climbed from a 1,700-3,500-foot altitude within seconds with "no g-forces or other noticeable strains."

After returning control of the helicopter to the crew, the UFO moved off to the west and was gone. Coyne complained, "I had to file an official report in detail to the army on this thing."

The "Coyne Incident" is considered one of the most reliable UFO reports ever made.

Hartford, Indiana

The Donathan CE3: October 22, 1973

Author Note: I covered the following story in my previous book *Indiana Ghost Folklore*, but it is such a good story, it is worth repeating.

Mr. and Mrs. Dewayne Donathan of Hartford were driving, at approximately 9:45 p.m., down Indiana State Road 26. They had just been to see Mrs. Donathan's mother, and Mr. Donathan was in the passenger seat holding the baby. They were close to their home when, rounding a curve, their headlights suddenly fell upon a strange scene.

About thirty feet distant were two small figures wearing what appeared to be bright, reflective costumes. Mrs. Donathan at first took the small figures to be children (they were around four feet tall) but, as soon as she got a better look at their appearance, decided that children they most definitely were not.

The little beings looked "confused" and proceeded to "hop in the air." Mrs. Donathan told an APRO (Aerial Phenomenon Research Organization) investigator, "Their feet would come up slow, one at a time, and their arms would flop funny. They moved slower than humans and their feet and arms would go up funny. Their feet came off the ground easy and they were bright silver in color."

Mrs. Donathan, realizing she was seeing something highly unusual, panicked, floored the accelerator, and swerved the car around the little beings, driving for some distance past their own house before finally coming to a stop. She was persuaded by her husband to let him take the wheel, and they went back to where they'd had the sighting. The figures, who had, it was observed, moved off the road in a "slow, clumsy" manner, were nowhere to be seen. However, the couple did see "bright red flashes" of light in the north.

The couple then took themselves to Hartford City and to the sheriff's office, where Deputy Sheriff Ed Townsend, his friend Gary Flatter, and an unidentified state policeman all agreed to go out and hunt for the "little men." Flatter and Townsend went in Townsend's patrol car, and the state policeman went alone.

A "high frequency sound" was heard at the intersection where the Donathans had their encounter, but seemed to be confined to that one spot. After a while of fruitless searching, the men decided to return to Hartford City, but Flatter and the state policeman decided to go back out. Both men drove back to the intersection where the beings had been spotted. Again, they noticed the same "high frequency sound." The two split up, the state policeman driving east, while Flatter drove the back roads of the area. It was then that Mr. Flatter found what he was looking for.

Standing in a field were the two entities. Mr. Flatter could see them in his headlights, but the glare off their silvery suits was very intense, so Mr. Flatter backed up his truck to a distance of approximately seventy-five feet. He tried his spotlight on them, which got them to turn around, but found the glare from their suits to be too much and turned it off. He described them as having egg-shaped heads, wearing "gas masks" with a hose that went down to the chest, and having long arms that just ended. He could not see any hands. He saw no ears or facial features (perhaps this was because of the masks?), and the feet were "rectangular, box-like" and had shoes that were around two inches thick.

The beings moved "much slower" than do normal humans, hopping up in the air and coming down slowly three times before, Mr. Flatter claims, they went up and disappeared into the darkness. Mr. Flatter then saw some red "tracer-like" flashes of light, and the encounter was over.

One wonders who those little beings were, where they came from, and why they were there.

Frederic, Wisconsin

December 2, 1974

A most strange encounter was experienced by farmer William Bosak, who, returning home one evening in the fog, happened upon a strange object in a nearby field, with a curving front made of glass.

The object, which was bullet-shaped, revealed a weird occupant standing inside with his arms raised. The occupant, whom Bosak described as looking "frightened," had ears that stuck out from its head "like a calf's ears," hairy arms, a furry chest, and seemed to be dressed in something "like a diver's suit." It had large, terrified eyes, but Bosak did not stick around to examine anymore. He floored the accelerator, and hurried home. He was, reportedly, too frightened to leave his house at night for some time after the incident.

Fargo, North Dakota

1975 UFO Abduction

Tales of alien abduction are endemic in our culture, whether they be the product of overheated imaginations driven by Hollywood films, or the harrowing accounts of real-life people who find themselves caught in a strange and bewildering situation. Although it has become vogue, in recent years, to scoff at such claims, that does nothing to discount the stories of sincere experiencers, many of whom consider what happened to them to be a legitimate, life-changing experience. The following account is taken from a woman named "Sandy," who in 1975, along with her boyfriend and another friend, had a terrifying experience that changed the course of her life, and what she thought of as her place in the larger scope of what we believe to be reality. Here is her story.

It was 4 a.m. in Fargo North Dakota, and Stacy awoke with her daughter and her boyfriend, angrily turning off the alarm and rolling over in bed to catch a few more winks of sleep before she absolutely had to be up to take the real estate exam that she had scheduled for that day. She finally forced herself out of bed, went into the kitchen for coffee, and made breakfast as her two weary fellow travelers made their grumbling way up and about.

It was a little while later that they set off for Bismark, but the day promised to be a nice one, and Stacy thought she could make it there in a fairly short amount of time.

It was while traveling Interstate 94 that the real strangeness began. A low rumbling seemed to, suddenly, pervade the car, and Stacy could not, for the life of her, figure out where the sound was coming from. The other two thought that this was strange, too, but ignored it until they saw a bright flash out of the window.

Suddenly, there were several strange, glowing objects rushing toward the car from sky, each surrounded by smoke. There was one object that seemed larger than the others, and somehow the three passengers in the car got the idea that the other UFOs had emerged from this larger one. The three objects paced the car for a time before coming to hover over a nearby stand of trees.

It was at this time that the car stalled, and the three passengers came to feel as if they were, somehow, "frozen" for a short period of time. They watched the UFOs ascend and disappear, and then go on their way, although they noted it was strange that they all seemed to be sitting in the backseat when the UFOs departed. They had somehow lost an hour, too.

It was the following year that Stacy and her daughter underwent regressive hypnosis. What was revealed was a story that was so incredible as to defy belief.

Stacy recalled being "floated" into the UFO (one wonders if this was directly through the windshield), and her daughter recalled the same thing. Once inside the mysterious craft, she was put upon a table, and a tall "robot-like" being with frightening eyes rubbed a clear liquid over her body, before inserting an instrument into her nose. She said the pain and aggravation this caused her was intense. A number of other unspecified medical experiments seemed to be performed upon her person before she and her daughter were finally returned to the car. Later, all memory of this incident was erased from their minds.

Marshall County
Near the North Dakota Border

It was August 22, 1979, and Deputy Sheriff Val Johnson was on patrol at about 1:40 a.m., when he noticed a light out of the side window of his patrol car. Noting that it was too bright to be a vehicle and that, furthermore, it was not on a road, Deputy Sheriff Johnson decided to investigate. He thought, perhaps, it might be a small plane.

He turned onto another road in an attempt to get closer to the light. The light, however, suddenly shot toward him at a terrific speed, overtaking his police car from an estimated mile and a half away.

Blinded, Deputy Sheriff Johnson heard glass breaking, and blacked out. When he came to, it was approximately 2:19 a.m., and the car had stalled and "skidded" across the highway. The Deputy was in a mild state of shock, as attested to later by the doctor who examined him, and he had what seemed to be "mild welder's burn": his eyes were extremely irritated, and he was sensitive to any bright light.[54]

The damage done to the patrol car was peculiar: The inside headlight on the driver's side was smashed, but not the one to its immediate left. There was a flat-bottomed circular dent on the left side of the front hood, about a half-inch in diameter, close to the windshield.

There was a crack in the windshield on the driver's side, that ran from top to bottom, with four apparent impacts. The electric clock was running fourteen minutes slow, as was Johnson's wristwatch. The shaft of the roof antenna was bent over at a sixty-degree angle, starting about six inches above its base. The trunk antenna was bent over at ninety degrees, but only near the top. No damage occurred to the car's regular antenna on the front hood. Essentially, all the damage to the car occurred on the left, or driver's side.

Investigations occurred immediately, both by the sheriff's department and by investigators from the Center for UFO Studies. The police determined that Johnson's car traveled about 950 feet after the first damage occurred.[55]

An investigation was carried out by the Sheriff's department, as well as the Center for UFO Studies, and portions of the car were sent to experts from Ford Motors for analysis. A windshield expert named Meridian French stated:

> I can only conclude…that all cracks were from mechanical forces of unknown origin.

Hoax, collision with another vehicle or plane, and any naturally occurring cause were also ruled out. Deputy Sheriff Johnson's eyes quickly healed, but the incident remains unexplained.

Marion, Indiana

1990

The most fascinating UFO encounter out of Indiana that I can think of is the one that happened to me twenty years ago, when walking in the early evening with a relative of mine.

We had started out from my relative's apartment, talking eagerly of many different subjects, and leaving my mother to wait for us to return.

We had been walking for awhile, minding our own business, when we suddenly realized that the streets were eerily dead. Across the street from my relative's apartment complex was a disused radio station and a large field with an antenna reaching into the sky. As we walked in front of the apartment complex, about to turn in and go home, my relative commented, "Hey, what's that over there?"

I turned and glanced over to where my relative was looking.

"It's a helicopter," I said offhandedly.

"But…it isn't making any noise."

I suddenly realized that she was right, and we both turned to fully face the object. It was hovering just over the field: a dark, cigar-shaped object with two lights at either end of it. It was completely silent.

Suddenly, it rose up into the sky, and we could see the enormity of it as it departed. It was immense, dark, and lit not only by the two bright lights at either end, but by a peculiar, lightning-like strobe effect on top.

The object rose above us, seemed to slow for a moment, then exploded into a brilliant crimson or violet light, at which time it shot into the distance until it was nothing more than a point of light, lost among the stars.

"What in the world was that?" My relative asked, bewildered.

"That," I suddenly quipped, "was someone that was a little off-course. Like about seventy million light years."

But I was not really in the mood for joking. The thing that we had just seen was really astounding, terrifying, and I wanted to get inside and get out from under all those stars as quickly as possible. We went back to the apartment, and were immediately accosted by my mother for being gone so long.

We told her what we had seen, but she didn't seem to really believe us. I looked at the clock. It seemed that we hadn't really been gone so long. Somewhere or other, we had lost some time. I was still a teenager at the time, so I found the whole thing to be perplexing.

I searched my memory, decades later, for more information about that night, and the only other thing I can come up with besides the UFO sighting is the strange memory of two men in a black van who slowed down as they passed us. One of the men leaned out and asked us, "Hey, do you want to go for a ride?"

I have read accounts, of course, of the mysterious "Men in Black," said to often follow and harass UFO witnesses even years after their strange encounters. These bizarre agents are said sometimes to be government spooks in black sunglasses and dark suits, driving new cars (in the past it was usually a Lincoln convertible) and wearing black fedoras. Sometimes, they are said to be aliens themselves, as in the accounts that John Keel gives of them in *The Mothman Prophecies*, where they are said to have "Oriental" eyes, heavily suntanned skin (alternately, in some accounts they are said to be very pale), and to speak in weird, halting English that sounds slightly robotic. Stories of the Men in Black include them following witnesses and disappearing into thin air, threatening calamity to UFO witnesses if they reveal what they know, and asking the meaning behind even common expressions when they show up to interview people. Men in Black are said to be menacing, strange, and utterly abnormal.

In short, they are horror movie zombies from some techno nightmare of secret agents and alien visitation. One wonders if they are not the revivified dead.

Did the Men in Black drive a van past me and my relative, and offer us a "ride," minutes before we saw an extraordinary UFO rise above a field and flash away? I don't know. I do know, however, that the second most interesting close encounter I have had involved a black van, as well.

Van Buren, Indiana

Summer of 1990

My friend, Matt, responded to a general email I sent to acquaintances, asking them to fill me in on any UFO sightings they might have had. Here is his response[56] to the list of questions I sent him:

When and where did you see the UFO? Do you remember the time of day?

> Van Buren, during summer vacation '89/'90, the kind of beautiful summer day that is followed by a beautiful clear summer night; it had just gotten dark. We were leaving my grandparent's house where we'd just finished a family supper to go home. I was getting into the car when I noticed a bright object in the sky, so I looked up.

Can you describe what the object looked like? Did it make any sound?

> What I saw was I believe spherical, and glowing a bluish-white light. It was very bright but the intensity of the light changed, becoming brighter and dimmer at random—or at least not at any pattern that I could discern during the short time I witnessed it. It came from the northeast and was traveling southwest. It was very fast but there was no noise at all. It appeared to be just a glowing ball of light that rotated and spun on its axis in all different directions while maintaining on its course. It was so fast that it took no time at all for it to fly over us and disappear over the tree line, and then it was gone. We then got into the car and drove home talking about it and wondering what it could be. Alien ship? Experimental aircraft? Grissom AFB was not far from us and it was not an uncommon occurrence as a child to see A-10 Thunderbolt IIs streaking across the sky. Although these were flying the (almost exact) opposite course of southwest to northeast. And they were very loud.

Was it moving fast or slow? Could you *guesstimate* how fast it might have been traveling?

> If I had to gauge speed, I would clock it at somewhere around the speed of a very fast helicopter. But again there was no noise.

How high up was it, would you say?

> As for distance in height, it's hard to guess, as I do not know the true size of the object, and, as I said, it was a clear night, so I didn't have clouds to give perspective. My guess is 200-300 feet or a little higher than a twenty- or so -story building.

Did you experience any bizarre electrical malfunctions? Did the car stall or the radio quit working?

No electronics were functioning during the entire time of the sighting and the car was off, so we didn't experience anything like that.

Did you experience any "missing time"?

No missing time that I know of.

What are your final thoughts on the experience?

I do not know to this day what I saw, and as the area in question was rural farm country and not heavily populated, we do not know of anyone else who saw the object. What I *do* know is that I have no explanation for the lack of noise, given the proximity and speed of said object.

Plymouth, Minnesota

November 27, 1990

The following is the story of "Jade," a young man who believes he was abducted by UFO occupants.

"Jade" was a fairly normal, sixteen-year-old boy who had just had a stormy fight with his parents. He left the house that cold November day wearing jeans, a T-shirt, and moccasins, and proceeded to walk about glumly, perhaps musing on the occasionally rocky relationship with his mom and dad. Jade, who had dressed inappropriately for the weather, soon found himself cold.

He started to head home, but thought better of it. Then, a strange thing happened. He began to feel tingly all over, and warm, and suddenly it was as if a light bulb had gone off in his brain. He rushed home, confronted his parents in a state of joy and proclaimed that he knew he had "the answer."

(Jade incidentally, had been unaccountably interested in UFOs all his life.)

It was a year later that Jade began to have flashbacks. These were invariably of a dark object hovering over him, with a light shining down. (When asked by a Roman Catholic youth group leader the first time he "felt God," Jade gave the date of his strange encounter.)

A talented artist, Jade began to keep a sketchbook of his flashbacks. He began to have vivid dreams of a close encounter with a dark, spherical object. In one of the dreams, Jade remembered being aboard the object.

The investigator from MUFON made a detailed composite of the alleged encounter. The following is based on that report.

Jade found himself in a run down area with old buildings. Above him, a dark body shined a light down, and the next thing he knew, he was in a room. The place seemed dark, and Jade was apparently paralyzed. He felt himself being pulled backward into another room, as if a pair of arms were around his chest.

He was laid out on a table that looked very much like a restaurant countertop, with drawers and cabinets, and above him an "inverted cone" of light shone down. In this light, Jade felt he could see a mysterious black object that looked "like a mobile"; the object seemed to be silhouetted against the light.

The surface of the table he was lying on was cold. He remembers that it was almost "contoured" so that an unconscious person could be sat inside it without the examiner having to worry about their body slipping. The room itself was circular, dark blue or black, and contained a "mechanical arm" that was rectangular, with a beveled edge.

The mechanical arm was attached to a post, from which protruded two prongs, though neither of them looked sharp. Jake was aware that this post, which was cylindrical in shape, was being wheeled toward him, but most of his attention was drawn to the two entities that seemed to be standing on either side of him. He remembered that they had the most expressive eyes, eyes that looked normal, as if oriental, and tremendous dark black pupils. The entities communicated with Jade telepathically.

"Who are you?" asked one of the entities.

"Why are you so depressed?" inquired another.

Jake, for his part, couldn't communicate with the entities at all. He must have been under too much shock to have even been able to spit out a coherent answer.

The entities had "flared heads" that protruded from the temples, and yellowish, "flesh-colored" skin. They had thumbs, and wore v-neck jumpsuits of some sort of gray, metallic-looking material. He could remember no ears or mouth, no nose, or apparently any other facial features; he did draw creatures with cheekbones that the investigator claimed were "more prominent" than those of an average Grey.

At one point Jade recalls the entities were "looking into him." Then, at another point in the examination, they seemed to completely ignore him, and disagree or argue over something between themselves. Jade examined the room, finding it (as mentioned before) circular, with a number of "pillars" ringed about. He got the impression of walls outside the room, and a number of hallways leading to other places in the craft. He also spotted a possible third entity in the act of putting a mysterious cylinder into a hole in the wall near a control panel. He saw a window, through which he could see the city outside.

Jade has no memory of actually leaving the craft.

Illinois Police Sighting

January, 5, 2000

The sighting of a massive, triangular-shaped UFO by several police officers in Illinois has become one of the most famous UFO events in modern times.

It is now the subject of a special documentary using computer technology to accurately and realistically recreate what the officers reported seeing.

Events first begin on the night of January 4, 2000, when an unidentified witness reported seeing an object at around 10:30 over the Chicago suburb of Lake Forest. The object, he claimed, was "bigger than a Boeing 747," was triangular-shaped, moved with no sound and with a peculiar slowness over his house, and was lit on the underside of it by about 500 lights. In short, it must have really been something to see.

The UFO was headed in a southwesterly direction. The witness later said, "It was just a very surreal experience."

Melvern Noll of Highland next saw the object at approximately 4 a.m. the next morning. He claimed that the object was as "big as a two or three-story house." He stated that the object had a circular ring of lights on the bottom, windows at the back and side, and that, to him at least, it looked like a rectangular box. He could hear no sound, and intimated that the sight of the object was something he will never forget.

Next, police officer Ed Barton was contacted by dispatch and told to "look out for a UFO," a directive he initially thought to be a joke. It was no joke. The Lebanon, Illinois policeman looked for and found the object, close to Summerfield, and turned on his emergency light. He began to follow the object, driving towards Summerfield.

While Officer Barton was heading toward Summerfield, another witness saw the object, which he described as being "twice the size of a C-5 cargo plane," and that the shape was that of a "boomerang." He said the object moved very slowly, and that it gave off a sound, like a "high-tuned V8 engine". The object was, he estimated, 900 feet high and 800 feet away, moving toward Lebanon.

Officer Barton pulled over and shut off his lights and engine to get a better visual and aural sense of the object. The lights on the object were intense, brighter than any aircraft landing lights, and included a red light on the bottom, in the center of the object. The light in front sent down a shaft of light that, curiously enough, did not actually light the ground beneath it. Officer Barton could see multicolored light running along the back of the object as well. The thing was a strange, brilliant spectacle in the night sky.

Officer Barton reached into his squad car to radio dispatch what he was seeing. When he next looked at the object, it was, unaccountably, already an estimated six miles away, near Shiloh.

This was at 4:23 a.m.

Officer David Martin, driving down Lebanon Avenue in nearby Shiloh, radioed in that he "saw something," but that he had no idea what it was. It seemed to be a triangular-shaped craft, he reported, as "big as a football field," moving silently along with three white lights and a widely-spaced red and green blinking light. The object did not appear to be flat at the bottom, but instead seemed to have "an irregular surface," which was compared later to the surface of a battleship. Just as Officer Martin got out of his car to get a better look at the object, it suddenly shot away at an incredible speed, with "no sound whatsoever."

The object is reported next some miles away near Belleville.

It was 4:28 when Millstadt Officer Craig Stevens, who was parked and listening to the radio chatter about the UFO, first spotted the object. He radioed into dispatch at 4:39, and the dispatcher on the end thought that he was joking. Officer Stevens reported that he was not joking. As if mystified, he said, "It's huge."

He described an arrowhead-shaped craft with a "strobing" red light at the back, and a bank of white lights "on the aft side." Officer Stevens added to the description given by other witnesses, as he claimed he could hear a strange buzzing coming from the craft, like the sound of an "electrical transformer," and that a strange optical effect made it seem as if the stars above the craft were reflected on the underside of it.

He described the surface of the craft in the same manner as others, noting that it was "irregular" and not smooth or seamless.

Warren, Michigan

March 22, 2001

"It seemed as though heaven spilled a bucket of fireflies," said one terrified witness to a UFO event that occurred at 8:10 p.m. The witness saw a "wave" of lights traveling west that began to break up into separate "V formations." The objects moved with the speed of a "passenger jet," and the witness could hear the roar of jets north of them, probably coming from Selfridge National Guard Air Base. The witness' neighbor, who reportedly thought "the world was ending," saw the UFOs and reported that they slowed with the approach of a police helicopter from behind him. The neighbor reported the UFOs as moving at a constant, slow speed, at varying heights, until with the passing of the police helicopter, they united in a "nice little row" and took off at "light speed."

Washington, Missouri

March 29, 2001

The witness was with his young daughter, driving down Jefferson Street at approximately 3:30 in the afternoon. The child pointed out the window and said, "What's that? It's really shiny."

The witness then noticed the object and pulled over to get a better look at it. The object he described was "square from a frontal view, but thin from a side view," and that it contained "four circular shapes…like dinner plates placed side by side…to fill up the square." He described the front of the object as "chrome-like" and "extremely shiny," and the back part of the object as "flat and black with no markings." He said the object was "on end, and slowly spinning horizontally," so when it was looked at, the observer would see the "shiny side of the square…

then the thin side…then the black—a pattern of thick and thins." The object was apparently spinning slowly, and traveled north at 125 feet, heading downtown, then turning west to head towards Busch Creek. The witness estimated the craft at a little over five feet, and the speed at approximately 10-25 miles per hour. The "thinner" side of the object was perhaps one foot thick, he said.

An attempt to follow the object was unsuccessful.

Westville, Indiana

April 4, 2001

A retired Chicago school teacher who lives on a farm in Westville made a report of an object that passed almost directly over her at 11:30 p.m., moving in a straight line in a westward direction. The object was eventually obscured by distant trees. The witness stated:

> The light was like a motorcycle headlight—single, not double as an airplane's. There was no accompanying jet noise or airplane motor noise—only a soft "hum," like a furnace running, or wind through trees. This craft did not have red and green running lights. I saw four distinct lights arranged in a diamond shape (or a triangle with a tail). There was also the suggestion of a few smaller lights around the back of the craft. The front and rear lights were cream colored, while the sidelights were amber and chartreuse. It was traveling rapidly—from initial sighting to the point where I lost it in the trees. It took less than 30 seconds to cover 3/4 of a mile. The sky around my farm usually has many moving lights—all attached to regular aircraft. The speed of this craft astonished me, making me realize that it was not one of the "regulars."[57]

Canton, Ohio

April 7, 2001

The witnesses were picnicking when one of them looked to the sky at about 7 p.m. They noticed an object that looked "like a triangular-shaped craft" with "spinning red lights" They claimed the craft was "surrounded by smoke, like from an engine." The witnesses claimed that there were four lights spinning. The stars, they noted, had not yet come out.

St. Louis, Missouri

April 5, 2001

Two witnesses, one of them a child, saw a bright object "as big as two or three full moons" flying over their home at 9:56 p.m. The witness, who lives near an airport, said the light was "brighter than any airplane I'd ever seen." The witness then called the son to help identify the craft, and by the time he got outside, it was "right over us." The object was described as very large, with an oval-shaped light in front, very bright, and several other lights forming what appeared to be "a triangular-shaped craft." None of the lights were flashing, and, as the object was overhead, the witnesses noticed a red light in the center. As the object flew overhead, the witnesses claimed they could hear a "soft humming" sound[58] emanating from the UFO. They further described a sort of misty haze around the object "probably due to the bright light." The object headed in a northwest direction. The sighting lasted for approximately three minutes, and the witnesses were later adamant that what they had seen was no conventional aircraft.

Riverview, Michigan

April 11, 2001

Three teenage girls were swinging on some playground equipment when they saw ten "saucers" flying approximately 100-300 feet from the ground. Noting that they were an orange color and that they constantly "switched places with each other," the girls, one of whom described herself as scared "of aliens and UFOs in the extreme," had been playing when one of them pointed to the sky and said, "Look!"

DePere, Wisconsin

April 11, 2001

The witnesses said they observed a disc "outlined with red lights" flying south to north, less than 300 feet above them. They said that the disc made a "hair-pin" 180 degree turn, and then headed south. The witnesses claimed that the exterior of the craft was dark. They said they could "feel its presence" as it approached them, and feel its "presence diminish" as it flew off into the distance. The time was night.

Middlefield, Ohio

April 13, 2001

The encounter occurred at approximately 11:37 p.m. while the witness was driving westbound on State Road 87 by the Geauga and Trumbull County Line. The witness reported that a "bright beam of light" appeared between the witnesses' car and another, and that, consequently, both cars lost power. The car was dead for three minutes. Then the light simply disappeared, and the cars started back up again. The witness reported that the radio and clock presets were lost, and that, afterward, they "didn't want to seem to be reset."

Evansville, Indiana

April 13, 2001

An anonymous witness reported seeing a "fleet of plates all gray" moving through the sky northward, at approximately 2:37 a.m., describing them as silent. The witness also said they were covered in reddish lights that "turned green when they left." The witness likewise said that the objects were covered in "fins" that went down to the center of them in a spiral that "constantly opened and closed." The sighting lasted for about twenty seconds, and one of the objects occasionally dropped "a few hundred feet" and made a sound "like a jet."

East Lansing, Michigan

April 13, 2001

The witness was reportedly just walking around his home town when he saw a group of three saucer-shaped craft fly overhead in a triangular formation. This was at approximately 10:30 at night. The witness reported that he has seen these same silent, saucer-shaped craft many times in East Lansing, and that, often they fly so fast "it seems impossible."

Rothschild, Wisconsin

April 13, 2001

An object described as having four bright lights and hovering 100 feet off the ground was spotted by two witnesses, who said the strange object took off at a phenomenal speed as soon as they approached. This was as 12 a.m. Another witness, who was driving through the area at the same time, reported the same object, noting that the four bright lights resembled "stadium lights." The object they saw was hovering over some trees, and as they turned the corner, it took off at a rapid pace. The witnesses claimed they tried to follow it, but that it disappeared "too quickly."

Gaylord, Michigan

April 14, 2001

The witnesses were relaxing in their hot tub at 10:15 p.m., when one of them pointed to the sky and inquired, "Is that Cassiopeia?" The other witness then corrected the first, and noticed what they thought was simply a shooting star. The witness then realized that, unlike a shooting star, the object didn't fade. Then a cluster of four objects and a cluster of three, all in a "V" formation, moving slowly, east to west, flew over the rooftop of the witness' house. According to the witness there was no sound, and "the lights never dimmed." The witness stood up in the hot tub to try and get a better view.

St. Louis, Missouri

April 21, 2001

At approximately 8:10 p.m., the witness was looking out of the window of a building when an object like a bright light was seen approaching. The object "looked strange" with "three to five lights on the front of the craft." The lights did not blink, and the object made no sound. As the object flew overhead, the witness could make out a "circular outline." The object disappeared behind the building. The witness reports that the weather was cloudy and that there was an approaching thunderstorm. It was also claimed that the object was flying lower than a commercial aircraft, and was "a bit smaller." The witness did not believe he had seen any conventional aircraft.

Iowa

Highway 283, Five Miles South of Norton, Kansas

A most unusual account comes to us from Kansas, where a family driving along the highway. The father, the driver, noticed a number of blue lights in the northwest. The car, which had run out of gas, was pulled over to the side of the road, and, in a perplexed state, the driver flashed his high beams at the mysterious blue lights. There was one large light, and a number of smaller lights "leap-frogging" over the larger one. Suddenly, there was a bright flash of light near the car.

The family, which included three adults, one child, and a dog, were shocked to see, in a nearby field, three solitary entities dressed in white robes. These entities were bluish in cast, and appeared to approach the car slowly. The family was terrified, and attempted to use a cell phone to call the local sheriff. The call was dropped, and it was ten minutes before the dispatcher could send someone out to the family. By that time, the entities had disappeared, but the family was in a highly agitated state. Of course, the sheriff disbelieved their story.

Eagle Butte, South Dakota

March 5, 2011

One of the strangest recent cases that I have learned about from South Dakota concerns a man who was driving home from his job as security officer. The conventional wisdom of what a UFO alien looks like is challenged by the vivid description of the beings in this report. You decide.

Joe Alvarez was tired. He swung his bag of work supplies over his shoulder, unlocked his car door, and got in, starting up the car and heading out of the parking lot with a yawn. The night was crystal clear, the stars stretched out in front of him as he began the hour long drive back home.

It was a long commute, but for his job as a security guard at a local casino, it was more than worth it. Besides, he had gotten use to the long miles on the road, back and forth, every night. He was a cautious driver, and had never had any problems.

It was only a few minutes into his drive, however, when Joe began to notice something strange. A number of curious red balls of light began to circle around his car. They were some distance from it, and they were about the size of softballs. Joe sped up, suddenly feeling nervous; he didn't understand what this phenomenon was, and, moreover, he didn't like it.

Just then, the car seemed to lose speed. It was as if the power was, somehow, being sucked out of it. The speed of the vehicle slowed down to a crawl, as Joe put his foot on the gas in a vain attempt to get the car to accelerate. It was no use.

The red balls of light continued to spin around the car, mystifying the driver, who turned off onto where the highway led into a gravel drive, outside a "windblock experiment station." It was then that the 100-200 balls slowly vanished, leaving Joe as perplexed as before. However, if he thought that he was in for an uneventful ride home the rest of the way, he was sorely mistaken.

Joe spied two figures at the side of the road. They both seemed oddly peculiar, freakish even, and he noted with growing alarm that they both seemed to be...glowing. Joe claimed that he suddenly got a "tingly" feeling all over, like goose bumps. Suddenly, one of the strange beings was on top of his car.

Joe said that the strange being reached in through the windshield. It touched his face, and then ran its long, skinny fingers down his back. He later wrote that the head of the being was oblong, that it had a wide mouth and long skinny arms, but that, in contradiction of almost every piece of conventional wisdom about what an alien is supposed to look like, the being had a tremendously long nose and "human shaped eyes." The being glowed from within "like a light bulb," and apparently Joe felt he could see through it. He also claimed that it had a tremendous mouth.

The other being at the side of the road was even more horrifying. Though Joe only got a fleeting glimpse of it, he claimed that it looked like it was squatting as it walked, was "wrinkly," and had a face that was "horrifying...like a beast." Apparently this creature vanished into thin air after only a few moments, as Joe never saw it again.

Incredibly, Joe drove on with the strange being seemingly roosting on the top of the car. It eventually vanished, but Joe didn't return home until two o'clock in the morning. When he finally did get home, he rushed inside, telling his panicked wife that, "It touched me! It touched me!"

Joe was hot and feverish, and, although there were no marks upon his body, Joe realized that he was missing a large block of time on his way home. It usually took him only an hour to get home. Tonight, it had taken him several hours.

An Unprecedented Wave of Sightings in Missouri
2011

Margie Kay, Assistant State Director for Missouri MUFON, was kind enough to send us her report of the situation in her home state in 2011. There was, apparently, an unprecedented wave of UFO activity in that state, so much so that Linda Moulton Howe was compelled to comment on it on a recent episode of the *Coast to Coast AM* radio program. What follows is a summary of her report.

A large number of reports (47) remained unidentified. These reports were primarily of orb-shaped objects, alternating in color from blue to black spheres, as well as large objects with atypical lights, and diamond and triangular-shaped objects. Some of these objects have descended to within 500 feet of the ground; others took off at a high rate of speed, which is a typical characteristic of UFOs.

Whiteman AFB was training B-2 Bombers in that area, and this could possibly explain some sightings, even those in which no sound was heard coming from the object, as it was explained by Air Force personnel that witnesses to the exercises wouldn't necessarily hear any sound unless directly under the planes, or standing in their wake. However, the test flights cannot logically explain *all* sightings. There were also strange radar reports returned, indicating a stationary object at 38,000 feet; MUFON is analyzing such reports.

The EAA Flying Team may have been responsible for some UFO reports. There were seven planes flying in formation, with red and green lights and strobe lights that are atypical of conventional aircraft. Apparently, they flew over areas of Lee's Summitt, Raytown, and Kansas City. This was your basic stunt flying, in preparation for a display planned for a football game on October 31st.

Margie suggests in her report that MUFON might want to put a video of the stunt flyers on their website, so that people could tell the difference, and not confuse the planes with genuine UFOs.

The media jumped on the bandwagon, with local news and papers covering the sightings heavily. Margie received a heavy volume of calls, and rumors began to circulate to the effect that the UFO sightings were either *all* caused by the stunt flying team, or were genuine unknowns. There were a number of striking reports, some including lighted, disc-shaped craft, such as:

- the saucer craft that hovered above the Raytown water tower, then took off at "light speed."
- the woman who saw a disc-shaped UFO hovering as she was leaving her hairdresser one evening.
- the witnesses who saw a diamond-shaped craft with white and blue lights at tree-top level, on I-435 at the I-70 exit. The craft turned and took off at a high rate of speed, leaving the witnesses astounded.

There were many more such reports, too. Margie details some of the strangest ones, such as the large UFO that was witnessed by some thirty people. The object was originally spotted while waiting at an intersection at Hwy 291 and Todd George Road in Lee's Summit, on Halloween night, but seemed to follow the witnesses as they drove to a neighborhood to take their children trick-or-treating. The witnesses reported a strange "hum" that seemed to emanate from the object, and later said they felt that the hum may have been something the UFOnauts projected to calm down the large body of witnesses. An even stranger aspect to this particular case is the fact that the witnesses, swearing that the time it should have taken to reach their final destination was only ten minutes, nonetheless arrived their one and a half hours later. The witnesses have become convinced they have experienced the tell-tale "missing time," and wish to be hypnotically regressed.

I could go on endlessly repeating stories, both old and new, but I think that you get the picture. UFOs have been in our skies since at least the late 1890s, and, though the outward characteristics of the phenomenon may have changed (people no longer report long-whiskered "airship inventors"), the essentials of the UFO encounter experience remain the same.

During the course of research for this book, it came to our attention that I knew of someone who was, most likely, an experiencer. I know of this person personally, and know that this individual has had a close-encounter UFO sighting. The individual has, for years, had a propensity for walking around at night (a dangerous hobby), and has told this author that she has recently spotted a "new type of airplane," a type that remains stationary in the air. When told that there were no such planes, she seemed to shrug off the information as unimportant. She likewise told this author that she once witnessed, while walking, a strange animal staring at her from a wooded area, an animal she could not easily identify. I was immediately interested in this, not only because unexplained animals seem to follow in the wake of paranormal phenomena, but because her memory of the incident, of a wild animal of unknown origin just staring her down from a wooded area, seems suspiciously as if it might be a "screen memory": a memory masking a possible abduction by UFO occupants. (UFO witnesses seem to have a strange relationship with hairy men, black dogs, and what John Keel would call "Abominable Swamp Slobs." Likewise, in such famous cases as that of the "Bell Witch" of Tennessee, a "black, dog-like" creature was sighted before the mysterious activity began to occur.)

However, what raised the serious "red flags" in her case was her admission that, many years ago, she had a series of disturbing dreams in which she was attacked in the middle of the night by "reptilian" beings. She would often "dream" that these beings were lying on top of her, suffocating her, in much the same way that people have reported the "night hag" or incubus of legend attacking them in the middle of the night. Of course, reptilians are a type of "alien" or UFOnaut commonly reported now by abductees as being aboard UFO craft, working side-by-side with the Greys and Preying Mantis entities.

(To conspiracy author Icke, reptilians are the literal authors of evil in the world: the workers behind the One Great Conspiracy. He claims they originate from the "lower fourth dimension," drink blood, participate in satanic rituals, shapeshift into politicians and movie stars, etc.)

This author has tried repeatedly to get an in-depth interview with this person, but has been met with little interest. The individual seems to be in a state of denial about the phenomena she has been experiencing, we must assume, all her life. We can only speculate at how many thousands of other individuals are reacting to their UFO experiences in exactly the same manner.

Chapter 7:
The Wheel in the Sky

I have whirled with the earth at the dawning,
When the sky was a vaporous flame;
I have seen the dark universe yawning,
Where the black planets roll without aim—
Where they roll in their horror unheeded, without
knowledge or lustre or name.

~H.P. Lovecraft

I begin this chapter with a quote from the undisputed king of "cosmic horror," the great H.P. Lovecraft, who, in a selection of stories as ghastly as anything ever penned, created an entire "mythos" centered on a race of "extraterrestrial gods." These gods, hideous in appearance, once ruled over man in the dim past, but were driven out, where they wait beyond the stars and beneath the sea to return and with "idiot horror…blow man's dust away."

One of the most hideous of these gods, Great Cthulu, is "dreaming" in his sunken city, waiting only for the time when the "stars are in alignment" to rise up. He is described as a gigantic being with bat wings and a mass of tentacles for a face. Other Lovecraftian monsters, such as the "Shoggoth" that is invoked by Wilbur Whately in *The Dunwich Horror*, are so grotesque that, Lovecraft writes, they are "amorphous" and beyond description.[59]

The Old Ones could be invoked by means of the hideous Necronomicon of the "Mad Arab" Abdul Alhazred, a black grimoire handed down from time immemorial, full of the dark secrets of other dimensions. There are several hoax "Necronomicons" that have circulated over the years, and, according to author "Simon," at least one authentic one.[60]

Lovecraft inspired a slew of imitators, something he encouraged, as he was generous to a fault (he died in poverty in 1937). I mention him here, though, because I find his ideas fascinating (he seems to have thought of "ancient astronauts" long before Charroux or von Däniken came along) and because one particular set of experiences he confessed to having is relevant to the topic of this book.

"Night Gaunts"

When I was 6 or 7, I used to be tormented constantly with a peculiar type of recurrent nightmare in which a monstrous race of entities (called by me "night-gaunts"—I don't know where I got hold of the name) used to snatch me up [and] carry me off... Undoubtedly I derived the [creatures'

> appearance] from the jumbled memory of Dore drawings (largely the illustrations to *Paradise Lost*) which fascinated me in waking hours.
>
> ~H.P. Lovecraft

Lovecraft was a sickly, overly-imaginative child who read frequently at a level far beyond his years. Thus, it is not surprising that he was plagued by nightmares. These nightmares, however, sound suspiciously like the "bedroom visitations" often reported by experiencers, or even outright screen memories for alien abduction.

Lovecraft confessed that he was terrorized at night by the "Night Gaunts": hideous stick-thin demons with no faces, inward curving horns, hooked tails, wings, and long claws. He claimed these bizarre creatures would come into his bedroom to strike terror into his heart, a notion shared by many an abductee, probably.

Of course, whether or not Lovecraft was what we would, today, term an "abductee" is a matter of conjecture. I mention it because I find the correlation between this strange experience and what H.P. Lovecraft went on to write to be striking.

Phillip K. Dick and the "Pink Moment"

Science fiction guru Phillip K. Dick, whose work has inspired such blockbuster films as *Bladerunner, Total Recall*, and *Minority Report*, documented his own strange and hallucinatory experience with "VALIS" or, the "Vast Active Living Intelligence System," an extraterrestrial object he thought was orbiting the Earth and beaming messages to his brain.

Phillip K. Dick was once the hardest working author in science fiction, spending endless hours a day pounding at the typewriter. He churned out novel after novel, many of them brilliant, and kept a grueling schedule that he sometimes facilitated with the use of speed and large doses of vitamins. His obsessions seemed to include memory and the nature of reality, what makes us human, and his novels often transcended the sci-fi ghetto and rose to the level of serious literature.

So it is not surprising, I think, that what happened to him, happened.

Dick was suffering from an impacted wisdom tooth, and so he called to have more pain medication brought to him. The pain medication arrived, and was delivered by a woman wearing what Dick referred to later as an "ichthys fish" as a necklace. This was the fish symbol used by early Christians, when they were forced to hide in the catacombs due to Roman persecution. The necklace caught a gleam of sunlight, and it was then that Dick felt himself…transported. The following is in his own words:

> In that instant, as I stared at the gleaming fish sign and heard her words, I suddenly experienced what I later learned is called

> anamnesis—a Greek word meaning, literally, "loss of forgetfulness." I remembered who I was and where I was. In an instant, in the twinkling of an eye, it all came back to me. And not only could I remember it but I could see it. The girl was a secret Christian and so was I. We lived in fear of detection by the Romans. We had to communicate with cryptic signs. She had just told me all this, and it was true. For a short time, as hard as this is to believe or explain, I saw fading into view the black, prison-like contours of hateful Rome. But, of much more importance, I remembered Jesus, who had just recently been with us, and had gone temporarily away, and would very soon return. My emotion was one of joy. We were secretly preparing to welcome Him back. It would not be long. And the Romans did not know. They thought He was dead, forever dead. That was our great secret, our joyous knowledge. Despite all appearances, Christ was going to return, and our delight and anticipation were boundless.[61]

Dick went up to his bed and collapsed in utter exhaustion. It was then that he experienced what he came to call his "pink moment": he was hit by an "information-rich" beam of light that began transmitting right into his head. This was probably sent from VALIS, the extraterrestrial satellite he believed was orbiting the Earth. According to my friend, John, who studies magic and occultism to a degree greater than I could ever hope to, Dick's experience of being "flooded with information" due to being struck by this "living" beam of pink light is very much in line with the ideas of Gnosticism and, also, very close to what is experienced by some of those who have UFO encounters, particular those who "channel" space brothers.

(My friend, John, also compared Dick's experience to those of shamans who believe that a fluid-like substance that imparts knowledge. This is called "super-fluid" or "magic mirror" that can be obtained or called up by the initiated.)

Afterwards, Dick began to believe a number of bizarre things, including that Nixon was actually Nero, and that the world we are currently living in is just an alternate dimension of ancient Rome. He also complained of people burglarizing his home, and must have grown increasingly paranoid. This appears to be a function of the phenomenon, as it has been documented by authors such as Vallée , Keel, and Gray Barker.

The "psychic component" to UFO experiences is explored heavily by Vallee in *Dimensions*, where he asserts that a great deal of "psi phenomena" (psychic powers and occurrences) manifest themselves around close encounter witnesses. He gives the example of precognition and psychic "dreams," wherein an individual might dream beforehand that they are going to see a UFO, and then do shortly thereafter. Also, he has stated that poltergeist-like phenomena are sometimes reported by UFO experiencers, and that this is one strong reason to doubt the ETH (Extraterrestrial Hypothesis). (After all, why would a visitation by extraterrestrial "explorers" lend itself to such weird after effects? There must be, Vallée reasons, something else occurring.)

Dick went on to write the trilogy *Valis* based on his unusual experience, and also the mammoth journal that was eventually published as *Exegesis*. Although

I'm not so sure I would ever want to visit the world that Dick was living in, I sure wouldn't mind taking a firsthand look.

Dick died in 1982.

"The He-Man Alien Hatin' Club"

I must confess (and serious writers aren't supposed to be so forthcoming about their personal failings), but, at this point, I am feeling a little burnt-out on the subject of UFOs and extraterrestrials. Perhaps this sort of admission doesn't belong in a book like this, or maybe that's exactly where it belongs. But I am starting to find the whole subject to be somewhat overwhelming. I have pounded out 53,000 words in just over three weeks, and Dear Reader, methinks me is due for a long vacation.

I have spent nearly every day, hours a day, reading UFO stories and books and scanning the Internet, and I have been trying, with little success to make contact with folks of a like mind, who might want to talk to me about their various experiences and insights into this so puzzling and perplexing phenomenon. So far, with one notable exception, I am batting zero.

As of 5:10 pm December 5, 2011, nobody wants to talk to me. My email box is emptier than my checking account. My phone didn't ring at all yesterday, and so I am bearing the burden of "uforia" all by my lonesome. And, Dear Reader, it is a lonely, sullen place where I am at right now.

Because the subject is so unremittingly bizarre, grim, and fraught with paranoia, it is a real stressor to become involved in. I'd swear it never made anyone any happier. John Keel once warned parents to keep their kids away from UFOs as if he were warning them against letting their kids use heroin, and I can see what he was driving at. Once you let the idea into your mind, it can become an all-consuming fire, a "control mechanism," and you might find yourself thinking and behaving in ways that are completely irrational. And then the fun really starts.

For instance, I keep getting strange beeps on my answering machine. Well, actually, to back up a bit, before that I was getting calls from people who would remain silent and then hang up. Some joker or sex freak, maybe. Maybe some poor slob that just got a wrong number and decided not to say anything. I can't really say who in the hell it was, but I am pretty sure there is a reasonable explanation for it.

Or is there?

I read UFO literature and I start to wonder. I start to feel a little nervous, in fact. I smoke more, I have vivid dreams, I don't sleep as well; I start thinking about the damn things all the time. Sometimes I have panic attacks.

The subject of ghosts doesn't trouble me half so much, and I am nearly oblivious to other forms of frightening phenomena. I am not intensely interested in Bigfoot, Yowie, giant birds, bent spoons, ghosts, goblins, or phantom felines.

These things are interesting, but not nearly as consuming as the subject of UFOs. But, to be blunt, there's a fine line between love and hate.

It may be unfashionable, but I'm starting to hate.

I hate the little grey bastards. Or whatever color they are this week.

I don't care what you say. They cause nothing but problems. They sow confusion wherever they dip their four (five? six?) toes. That's why, even though I've seen them, I choose not to believe in them. Or, at the very least, not to have any definite, formed opinion about them.

I'd hate to think that they are nothing more than extraterrestrial astronauts. If that were the case, then I wouldn't even be curious about them.

As far as I'm concerned, if they are nothing more than "alien astronauts," they can ride those UFOs straight to hell, because they've been flying our friendly skies for decades and have done nothing, nothing, NOTHING…to help us out (except for supposedly warning people of nuclear fallout dangers). Where is the interstellar cure for cancer? How about helping us end famine? What about warning us of impending disaster, or healing sick kids, or doing SOMETHING useful besides flying around, mutilating cattle, pressing messages into wheat fields, and terrifying innocent citizens by dragging them out of bed and into hovering UFOs in the middle of the night? Is this how an advanced race of extraterrestrial scientists and explorers actually behaves?

Psychic channels and contactees have assured us that benevolent "space brothers" seek the "spiritual advancement" of mankind. Of course, even the Devil can quote scripture, and the many cults that have flourished around the banal pronouncements of space brothers have done nothing to better the collective situation of mankind. The world, far from becoming a spiritually advanced utopia fit for entry into the "Galactic Federation," is growing more violent, crazy, and aberrant by the day. Is there any coincidence in the fact that so many "religious miracles" are, when examined, nearly identical to UFO experiences?

Must the Gods be crazy? If, as Charles Fort states, there is a universal mind, must it be sane?

I think that we may be the butt of a colossal cosmic con job. On the other hand, I may just be a mean, narrow-minded man, who is jumping at shadows because, as he grows older, he realizes shadows are all he has left.

Synchronicity

I mentioned the strange beeps on my answering machine mainly because I read about a similar phenomena affecting UFO and paranormal experiencers in the book *The Mothman Prophecies*. I had actually forgotten about it until rereading the book (in preparation for writing this book), but, putting two and two together…

I had been getting the beeps for awhile, and had thought nothing of it. Then I started writing this book, and the beeps appeared again on my phone, and now I felt a little uneasy. Again, could just be coincidence. I'll tell you about something that happened just today though, and let me know what you think about it.

I was talking to one of the witnesses interviewed for this book. We were having a fairly pleasant conversation when, all of a sudden, we got on to the topic of "poltergeist activity." I asked her if she had ever had anything like that happen to her. She said no, and then I clarified that it could also include electronic disturbances, such as radios or televisions going on the blink for no reason. She was just about to answer when, all of a sudden, I heard a mysterious explosion, and the lights went out. Just as we were discussing such a possibility.

And I wonder.

The lights weren't out for long, and the reason was probably nothing more prosaic than a blown transformer or something…but it was the timing. It was almost like somebody was trying to send me a message.

Dear Reader, since I've been writing this book, I've had some strange dreams, and haven't slept well. I'm struggling to understand something that, finally, may be beyond the grasp of the human mind. I told you that I hate aliens, and I do; their shortcomings as "uninvited visitors" are extensive.

But I also love them. I really do. They are a tantalizing mystery that can never be solved; a glowing, shifting mandala that seems to mirror whatever dreams and nightmares we have about them. They are the Four Living Creatures. They ride the Wheel in the Sky.

The rock band, Journey, has a song whose chorus speaks of a wheel in the sky that keeps on turning. Truly, as we have progressed as a race, this mysterious "other" has been there to perplex and fascinate and madden, to fly the skies and consternate those observing from the ground. Yeah, it keeps on turning, baby.

Dear Reader, we have just a little farther to go. I know it's dark and lonely out here, and it seems that the night will never end. But aren't the stars uncommonly beautiful? Like little jewels in the heavens? Now, fasten your seat belts, because we have a lot to do and little time to do it. Grab your dancing shoes, turn on "The Purple People Eater," and climb aboard, because this flight travels at light speed, and we're gonna rock n' roll!

Aliens or...Something Else?

I began this chapter with some examples of brilliant writers who were seemingly troubled by alien contact. Lovecraft was tormented by "Night Gaunts", and Dick was contacted by "Valis." The phenomenon these individuals experienced would lead one to believe that the phenomenon manifests itself to the brilliant, creative, and unstable…also, that it chooses those who are bound, by dint of their special gifts and abilities, to influence the expectations of the larger society around them. In other words, I don't think it was an accident that Lovecraft and Dick had these sorts of experiences. Instead, it seems to me that the UFO phenomenon, as attested to by folks who have studied it for fifty years or better, is *not* an extraterrestrial phenomenon. Rather, it is something so unusual that mankind has never quite come to terms with it. It is inter-dimensional, paranormal, or the result of a highly-advanced intelligence that, for whatever reason, manifests itself at the edge of technological advancement, pretending to dominate the air or outer space, manifesting itself in whatever form is expected by those witnessing it. Perhaps, like Keel posited in Operation Trojan Horse, it has a lifespan that approaches immortality, and is as far beyond our ability to comprehend it as we are to a nest of tree-frogs. So, for untold ages it attempts communication, creating temporary anomalies as message boards, unintentionally influencing our science, religion, and technology. Perhaps, as has been suggested, it is many different inter-dimensional entities, always shifting its disguise, from angel, to demon, to fairy, to airship inventor, to space alien in a couple of thousand years. Perhaps Earth is the Ultraterrestrial laboratory, where humans as diverse as Joseph Smith and Phillip K. Dick are each given their "conversion moments," all the better to move the species along on whatever religious or mystical program they intend.

Or maybe, it's all just a projection of our unconscious mind, a kind of hiccup from the recesses of the human psyche, as Jung suggested in his book *Flying Saucers*. It could be that none of these things are true; perhaps they really are just damnably elusive space visitors, who have been here for many thousands of years, for some reason as yet unfathomable. Here are some cases to think about.

Dayton, Texas

The Cash/Landrum Case

One of the most frightening UFO stories we know of is that of Betty Cash and Vickie Landrum. We can briefly touch on it here, as evidence that UFOs are real, physical objects.

Betty and Vickie were traveling with Vickie's 7-year-old grandson Colby through a pine forest, headed toward Dayton, Texas on the night of December 29, 1980. At about 9 p.m, Betty looked up and saw an intense light in the sky ahead. The light seemed to be emanating from a "fiery object" in the sky. The object descended and hovered right above the road, emitting bursts of "flame," and making the ground around it intensely hot.

The three witnesses were terrified, but each got out of the car to examine the object, which was making a sound "like a flame thrower" as it hovered. Each of the witnesses varied in their description of the object, with Betty Cash recalling a "bright light with no shape," while the others seemed to recall the object as rounded at the top and pointed at the bottom. Vickie's grandson Colby said it was "diamond shaped." As well as the flame thrower sounds, there was a "roaring and bleeping" that seemed to last throughout the encounter.

The little boy began to grow hysterical, and he and his grandmother climbed back in the car while Betty Cash continued to stare upward at the object, mesmerized. The other two began to yell that they wanted to get away, so Betty finally grasped the door handle. The handle was too hot to touch.

Her wedding ring was burned into her finger, and the heat coming down from the UFO was, by now, intense. Betty got into the car and the object started to move away, but, before it did, the witnesses on the ground noticed military Chinook helicopters circling it. They decided to follow the object for awhile, but, after stopping two more times, realized that they'd had enough for the night. They went home.

Once they got home, though, they quickly realized that everything was *not* alright. The three began to suffer from symptoms of radiation sickness; Colby was sunburned and had irritation in his eyes. His grandmother, Vickie, suffered similar eye irritation and hair loss. Betty Cash, who was exposed most directly and for the longest time to the object's rays, developed nausea, vomiting, diarrhea, hair loss, blisters on her scalp, and other horrific symptoms. She was finally admitted to Parkway General Hospital in Houston. She was treated as a burn victim, but the doctors there were at a loss to diagnose, exactly, what was wrong with her.

She was released for a short time, but soon found herself back in hospital, as her symptoms quickly returned. Her medical bills were in excess of ten thousand dollars by the time she developed breast cancer.

She became, to put it mildly, a very sick woman, and she was certain that it was the encounter with the UFO that had done it to her.

The two women remembered that the UFO had been surrounded by military helicopters, and so accordingly they blamed a government experiment for their condition. They took the unprecedented step of suing the government for making them ill, only to find that the U.S. Government didn't recognize the UFO phenomenon. The case dragged out in court until 1986, finally being dismissed by a judge due to the "expert" testimony of members of NASA, the Air Force, Army, and Navy, all of whom testified that the U.S. Government did not possess such an aerial device.[62]

This case is reminiscent of that of Steven Michalak in Canada. He was out hiking in Lake Ontario, in 1967, when he came upon a landed, disc-like vehicle. Approaching it, the vehicle let out a blast of fire which burned a strange pattern into his chest. Michalak later experienced symptoms of radiation sickness, and met with great skepticism from government authorities despite his condition.

(Now, combine the above with the mysterious deaths of workers at Area 51, and you have the perfect subject for a new book. Call it: *When UFOs Kill.*)

Southwest and Midwest

Cattle Mutilations and Crop Circles

Speaking of killer UFOs, it might not be remiss to touch upon one phenomena that is quite closely related to the whole UFO mystery: that of "cattle mutilations."

John Keel, in his book *The Complete Guide to Mysterious Beings*, tells us that not only cattle, but chickens and pigs, as well as dogs, have also been found mutilated, and that UFOs are often sighted before the carcasses of mutilated animals are discovered. Of course, the idea of "alien mutilators" hearkens back to the "hoax" (if indeed it was) perpetrated in 1897 by Alexander Hamilton, but can the charge be so easily dismissed?

The animals that are found mutilated generally have been completely drained of blood. The flesh is sometimes stripped from the face; the tongue, eyes, and anus removed, the genitals and abdominal cavity cleaned out with "surgical precision." There are no footprints leading up to or away from the animal (although, in the case of "Lady," a horse that was allegedly a victim of the unknown mutilators, there were mysterious "gouge marks" located nearby).

The animals are often captured and mutilated while grazing in remote locations where, otherwise, they would not be accessible to anyone who happened to be driving by. Prior to the death of Lady, UFOs had been reported pretty steadily in the area.

In some locations where mutilations have occurred, people have been witnesses to flyovers by mysterious black helicopters with no identifiable markings. Thus, speculation that the government was behind the mutilations, possibly as some sort of secret warfare experiment, soon surfaced. The causes of the mutilations were incidental to angry ranchers in the Southwest and Midwest, however, who began to organize posses to try and put an end to the killings.

Law enforcement, at one point, blamed satanic cultists, but nobody in the early years of the mutilation wave really knew what was going on. Linda Moulton Howe, an award-winning documentary filmmaker, produced a show called *Strange Harvest*, in which an alleged abductee recounted, under regressive hypnosis, her horrifying experiences aboard a craft.

Recalling that she was driving along the Texas highway when she encountered a UFO, she described a bright beam sucking a writhing animal up into it. She next described standing inside a room, presumably aboard the UFO, while alien beings mutilated the animal, claiming all the while they were doing it "for the betterment" of mankind. According to the testimony elicited under hypnosis, the genitals and organs were pierced with needles.[63]

The woman began to panic when she realized her daughter was in the craft with her, and was also being "examined." Although the daughter was unharmed, Keel tells us of a case in Brazil where a man, Telemaco Xavier, was reported missing after a UFO wave that took place in 1962. The same wave saw the disappearance of a number of local livestock, and three plantation workers testified that they had seen a lone man walking down a remote road when an object emitting sparks "swooped" down upon him. They reported that three men leapt from the object when it landed, and dragged this man away. Keel notes that no one is certain this was, in fact, Telemaco Xavier, but that the coincidence with the missing man is striking and leads one to naturally wonder: Are there ever "human mutilations"?[64]

Jacques Vallee notes that the "little people" of fairy lore also chased and abducted animals, and some ufologists, including Keel, speculate that the animal mutilations are needed by the UFOnauts to create "flesh and blood" bodies, or robots, perhaps as a way of manifesting in our "reality." Charles Fort began documenting mutilations of sheep (sheep exsanguinated by invisible "vampires" who left puncture marks in their flesh) in the 1920s, and further documented falls of flesh-like substances from the sky. Does all of this lead to the same conclusion?

It should be noted that the UFOnauts and associated mysterious entities are absolutely obsessed with sexual liaisons with human beings. The old-fashioned incubi and succubae of Medieval folklore were forced to "borrow" the body of a corpse, it was said, to perform such sexual assaults. Or, alternately, they were said to construct temporary bodies from other materials.

Could this be the reason that our alien mutilators sliced and diced their way through an estimated ten thousand head of cattle by 1994? Is it that the intelligence behind UFO manifestations needs the genetic material to construct for itself "temporary anomalies," bodies to serve as vehicles for its own will? Nothing else seems to so succinctly explain the mutilations, when considered in the light of UFO phenomena. After all, if it is just an "experiment" being carried out by "space alien scientists," why the need for so many victims? Couldn't an advanced race, capable of interstellar travel, learn everything they wanted to know after just one mutilation? (The same objection is offered for the sheer number of alleged UFO abductions.)

On the other hand, it *could* also be the result of a "clandestine" government operation; the unmarked black helicopters seem to bear this out. If so, we are about as likely to discover the truth of it as we are if it is an "intergalactic conspiracy."

Of course, if the government and the Greys are working in tandem, as is suggested by the conspiracy literature of Cooper, Branton, and others, then that could well explain the presence of black helicopters and UFOs at the mutilation sights.

Mutilations, unfortunately, are not confined to the United States, but have been reported in South America and Europe as well.

A far less grizzly, but no less fascinating phenomenon that has come to worldwide attention in the last couple of decades is the mystifying "crop circles" that have appeared regularly, every year, around the world. These giant pictographs, which were first found pressed into wheat fields in England in the early eighties, originally only approximated the shape of landed UFOs. Unlike the "saucer nests," however, the crops themselves were not scorched or burnt, but simply pressed down into an unusual formation. These elaborate designs (and they seem to grow more startling every year), have been found in fields all across the world, seeming to negate the claims made by some (including two notable British pranksters) that they are entirely the work of con artists.

I will state that, based on the huge, elaborate nature of many of the crop formations I have seen, I find it highly unlikely that any human agency could have created *all* the circles. Yet the debate rages on, with claims and counterclaims made in favor of hoaxes and natural phenomena, extraterrestrials and shadowy supernatural agencies. Strange "earthlights" are often seen around the fields where circles form (and circles are said to form overnight), and the idea that these arcane symbols are the UFOnauts attempting to communicate with us has made deep inroads in the public psyche. The Mel Gibson alien invasion flick *Signs* used crop circles as a plot device, and now they are considered to be as much a part of Ufology as stories of abductions or close encounter tales.

While I concede the "crop artwork" to be cryptic and beautiful, I find the subject rather leaves me cold. I don't, particularly see the connection with UFOs, although I admit I haven't studied the phenomenon enough to make an informed comment.

It has been suggested that, perhaps, if we are dealing with actual extraterrestrial visitors, they are using the crop formations as a coded message to humanity; the formations are often staggering in the scope of their design, and some are said to even correspond roughly to the musical scale. Skeptics maintain that it is all nothing more than the work of bored pranksters pressing down crops with boards and rope, doing these elaborate and mind-boggling jobs under cover of darkness.

(I'm sure I don't believe that, at any rate.)

Bob Lazar and Area 51

Bob Lazar is a painfully geeky guy with an incredible story. Those who are looking for real, live "space alien visitors" should pay close attention to what he says: after all, according to Bob, he's worked on actual flying saucers.

His story first came to light in a television interview with George Knapp back in the eighties. Bob claimed that from 1988-89 he worked as a physicist at a facility called "S-4," which is a part of the super-secret government base known popularly as "Area 51," a place that, officially, does not even exist. There is one long dirt road going into Area 51, and signs posted reveal that guards are authorized to use "deadly force" to keep out the unwary.

Area 51, also known as Groom Lake, is the sight of much persistent fascination for sky watchers and those who keep tabs on high technology. Classified government projects and secret test flights have been performed there, and one commentator basically nailed it when he said that Area 51 was the place where the government went "when it wants to be alone." Of course, conspiracy theorists and UFO buffs have invested the place with an almost mythic significance, and it is believed by many to be the place where crashed UFO technology is reverse-engineered to build new forms of stealth aircraft and weapons systems.

At one time, sky watchers were known to gather at the only spot they legally could to watch for UFOs that allegedly belong to the U.S. Government: a place overlooking the base called "Freedom Ridge." Unfortunately for these enthusiasts, however, the Clinton Administration closed off all the surrounding area for fifty miles back in the mid-nineties, thereby putting an end to the spectators' sport.

Lazar claimed that he worked on nine different model discs, craft he originally believed to have been of earthly manufacture until he actually got to go inside one. Once inside one of the American UFOs, he quickly realized that the craft itself must have been of extraterrestrial manufacture, as the seats, passageways, controls, and other accoutrements were all seemingly designed for "little" pilots. Lazar gave details of the propulsion system of the UFOs, as well as detailed sketches, and, furthermore, told of a peculiar briefing in which he was informed that the "Zeta Reticulans" had been involved in mankind's evolution for the past 100,000 years.

Lazar claimed to hold degrees from the California Institute of Technology and the Massachusetts Institute of Technology, but Ufologist Stanton Friedman was only able to verify that he took physics courses at a junior college. Lazar claims that the government, to retaliate for his having gone public, deleted his background records so as to strip him of his credibility. One newspaper article, dating from the time Lazar and a friend (described as a researcher from NASA) designed and built a rocket-powered car, *does* describe Lazar as a "physicist."

Ufologist John Lear has backed up part of Lazar's claims on a radio broadcast, where he recounted a time when Lazar drove him out to a restricted area near Area 51 to watch a "flying saucer test flight." Lear basically stated that, had Lazar not been employed by the base at the time, he would never have been allowed to get so close.

Some believe Bob Lazar. Some don't.

Budd Hopkins and The Abduction Explosion

This is a difficult chapter to write, in light of the fact that, I myself, have had a close encounter. The very notion of alien abductions—that you can be taken at any time of the day or night, forced aboard a UFO, given a horrifying medical examination, and then returned with your memory wiped clean—is the stuff of paranoid nightmares. Yet, in the past couple of decades, it has come to represent to people the very nexus of what the UFO phenomenon is all about. If you ask anyone, anywhere, to draw a picture of what an "alien" is supposed to look like, they will invariably draw a picture of a classic "Grey," influenced, to a great degree, by the image fostered by Hollywood and the mass media.

Ironically, the image of the Grey is not new. Aliester Crowley is said to have invoked, during one of his magical rituals, an entity he called "Lam," a portrait of which looks remarkably like a Grey alien. In an old book called *From India to the Planet Mars*, a female medium documents her time with grey "Martians," and a science fiction scholar has traced the popular image back to publications of the last century.

Certain cave paintings, as studied by von Däniken and others, suggest robed visitors with tiny chins, huge domed heads, and huge, expressive, insect-like eyes. Could these have been the Greys of thousands of years ago? Is this now generally-accepted image of an alien some sort of deep-seated psychological projection? Is it all in our heads?

Not if you're Budd Hopkins, acclaimed New York artist and UFO abduction researcher. Budd (now deceased) has documented many, many cases of alien abduction, and, during the eighties, was one of the men most responsible for cementing the idea of alien abduction in the public consciousness.

To Hopkins, the aliens are menacing extraterrestrial exploiters, members of a dying race that are coming here for one purpose and one purpose only: to breed "hybrid" offspring to take back with them to the home world. Hopkins's abductees are often women who feel they've been impregnated with such hybrid children, only to have them stolen later at another abduction.

This remarkable scenario seems to hearken back to the fairy folklore of the changeling, and those who know the history of UFO abduction accounts will no doubt be reminded of the story of Antonio Villas Boas, who supposedly had sex with an extraterrestrial that later pointed at her (presumably pregnant) belly, and then pointed to the ceiling—to the stars.

Others will remember that Betty Hill had a long needle-like object inserted in her navel, which some take as an interstellar pregnancy test.

Hopkins elicits the stories of the alleged abductee encounters while they are under hypnosis. His first book, *Missing Time*, documented several cases, but it was his book *Intruders*, the story of an abductee from Indianapolis, that really brought him notoriety.

The book centers on the alleged encounters of "Kathy," a painfully normal Midwestern woman whose entire family, it seems, has a history of alien encounters. That they cannot quite remember the details of these encounters, or have their memories hidden by "screen memories," becomes an integral part of the book, as does the idea that abduction is an intergenerational occurrence. Kathy experiences some of the paranormal phenomenon associated with UFO close encounters (for instance, strange telephone messages), and is also "implanted" with one of the alien devices that are thought by some to roughly approximate the "tracking chips" wildlife researchers implant in captured Elk. Kathy reveals under hypnosis that her alien abductors are the classic Greys, and, furthermore, that she is the mother of a "hybrid" daughter that must be out there, somewhere.

Hopkins next wrote the book *Witnessed* to document an incredible abduction episode that supposedly took place in Manhattan. The subject of the abduction was allegedly floated from her high-rise apartment building into a hovering UFO, while below, two policeman, acting as security guards for a foreign dignitary, watched in stunned amazement. The abduction was supposedly witnessed by this unnamed dignitary.

Intruders was eventually filmed for television. Hopkins has been criticized in the past because of his reliance on regressive hypnosis, which, according to some professionals, is completely unreliable, and can foster false memories of an event. If this is so, we may rightly regard a good percentage of what Hopkins's abductees recall as fantasy. But must we dismiss all their claims?

One man who certainly didn't was Harvard professor Dr. John Mack, whose book *Abduction* recounted the experiences of several Americans who claimed alien abduction. Mack, who was tragically killed in London several years ago, was an award-winning author and researcher, who felt the claims of abductees must be taken seriously. His status as a Harvard professor no doubt lent legitimacy to those who wanted to prove abductions were real, tangible experiences.

But are they? Jenny Randles, in *The Complete Book of UFOs*, states:

> In six cases, independent observers saw the witness during the period when they felt they were on board the UFO. None of these witnesses had been inside a UFO when testimony suggested they ought to be! In fact, these people were just where they were before the experience began.[65]

Randles describes alleged abductees who enter altered states of consciousness, interact with alien beings who are not there, and generally behave as if they are having a hallucinatory experience. Not good for those who want to prove alien abduction as a real, tangible experience that happens in the physical world.

Folklorist Eddie Bullard did a study of hundreds of abduction cases, trying to prove that abductions are a form of modern folklore, comparable to the folk legends of old. He succeeded in demonstrating a pattern in the abduction narratives that seemed to prove his point.

But what of evidence that suggests the abductions are "real"? What of the strange scars and scoop marks, the X-rays of "implants," and the related UFO and paranormal occurrences that seem to manifest around these people?

We have to confess, on this particular facet of the UFO question, the jury is still out.

For those not entirely familiar with the cliché abduction experience, it goes something like this:

The victim is often driving, but can also be alone in their bedroom when the abduction occurs. They may see a UFO in the distance, perhaps landed, and the car may stall; or they may awake to find themselves paralyzed, with "dark forms" moving around their bed.

These forms may be hooded, or may not be, but inevitably the victim will be taken against their will and perhaps floated from their car or (even more fantastically) through a window or wall, into the UFO. There, they will be subjected to a painful, often humiliating "medical examination" by beings described as thin, with long fingers, large heads, thin, slit-like mouths, vestigial nostrils, and huge, almond-shaped black eyes. The beings are said not to talk audibly, but communicate by telepathy, and have some sort of hypnotic control over the abductee. Sperm may be taken from males, blood drawn, skin scraped, but after the medical examination, the abductee is usually lead on a tour of the ship. Then, they may be shown some images of the fate of the world, of pollution, of the devastation wrought by man's bad treatment of the environment. In some cases, women claim to have been shown "hybrid" (half-alien, half-human) children, or to have been forced to hold hybrid babies.

The abductee will then be reassured that what they have undergone is for the "betterment" of humanity, and will then be returned to their car or bedroom (or wherever the abduction occurred). They will awaken with no memory or only a vague memory that something has happened to them; they may have unexplained scars or scoop-marks, and some abductees have related waking up with their clothes fitted on backwards. They may experience a nosebleed or some other discomfort from an "implant" (usually a BB-like object) placed in the nasal cavity or some other part of the body. They will, of course, wonder what has happened to them during their puzzling instance of "missing time."

They may have a "screen memory" of an animal, maybe an owl or a wolf, staring at them. In one wild case, an abductee reported that he had a memory of a naked man approaching his car, wearing a giant cowboy hat.

Abduction memories are frequently recovered with the aid of hypnosis.

Some Possible Alien Races

While we're on the subject of "physical" ETs, we might as well rundown some of the purported "races" of UFO occupants.

There have been as many types of UFO occupants reported as you can possibly imagine. A man named Fred Reagen was supposedly abducted by robotic entities that he compared to "giant stalks of celery." That said, there seem to be five or six types that are reported most often. (Note: some websites or other areas of research list many more.)

These include:

1. Hairy Dwarfs

The name says it all. These entities seem mythological to us, but are frequently reported in South America. They are known to carry little tubes that shoot paralyzing rays. Some of them, the Ikals, are said to fly with "rockets" on their back.

2. Nordics

These are the tall, blond, blue-eyed "Aryans" of the UFO world, a group that was quite popular when contactees still rode "Scout Ships" on interstellar cruises. They are bland, non-threatening, given to mouthing banal religious platitudes, and beam messages to the brain of expensive psychic "channels." They are frequently reported in Europe.

3. Preying Mantises

Hideously ugly insect-like entities that torment abductees. Perceived as loathsome and evil, and for good reason; it does, after all, look like a giant bug.

4. Reptilians

The "demons" of UFO conspiracy folklore, these lizard-like beings figure prominently in the conspiracy theories of David Icke, where they are presented as "shape-shifting, blood drinking, ritual abusers" who, at least in some cases, masquerade as prominent entertainers, heads of state, royalty, etc. They are considered to be monstrously negative, are sometimes said to wear hoods, have glowing red eyes, and probably give off the tell-tale sulfur-like stench reported by Keel and others. They are not nice folks, to put it bluntly.

5. Greys

These are the most culturally popular form of alien, made so by Budd Hopkins' book *Intruders* and the cover of Whitley Strieber's book *Communion*. They are skinny, with large domed heads, grayish skin, long skinny fingers, and slits for mouths. They have two holes where the nose should be and, most importantly, large, insect-like, fathomless black eyes that seem to penetrate the abductee unlucky enough to find themselves on the examining table.

The Greys are the alien primarily reported in America by abductees. They are complex little philosophers, and Whitley Strieber has attributed all manner of strange behavior to them in his series of bestselling books.

We could add to these what Frank Edwards called the "Midgets from Mars," an early type of occupant that was short and stocky, dwarf-like, with an oversized head and normal looking, though oversized eyes. Sometimes these were described as looking "mongoloid" in appearance.

In Asian countries, we understand that miniature (very tiny) UFO occupants have been reported. There are also the many creatures that have appeared wearing "diving suits" or helmets, and a few monsters thrown in the mix. One UFO witness reported beings that looked like floating jelly.

I Wish I Could Have Covered...

Besides Ancient Egypt, topics we perhaps should have touched on include the Martian meteorite that was unearthed by scientists back in the nineties. When bits of this rock were later examined under a microscope, it was found that they contained fossilized life forms. Thus, some people at the time were suggesting that we, at long last, had our first glimpse of E.T., and that, ironically enough, it was a glimpse of a fossilized microbe.

Of course, the scientist that made the momentous pronouncement later retracted it; it was feared that the fossilized microbes might have been the result of earthly contamination, and that they could not, specifically, state that they originated on Mars. It has been some years since I last heard about the supposed Martian fossils. Are they still being studied? I don't know.

Likewise, I would have liked to have had a deeper exploration of the Bible and "flying saucers"; there was simply not enough room to go into it sufficiently (or this volume would have been thousands of pages long). Suffice it to say, the material is out there, readily available, if you want to seek it out.

Ditto "Ancient Astronaut" theories, which totally absorb me once I get started on them. I didn't have the space to more than touch on this, and, for that, I am deeply regretful.

The issue of whether or not the "Majestic-12" documents are to be believed totally bypassed me. The documents in question were slipped anonymously to UFO researchers in the eighties, and contained supposed secret orders signed by Truman to set up a top-secret investigatory committee (composed of people like Dr. Vannevar Bush and arch-skeptic Donald Menzel) to study crashed UFO technology. Some claimed that this was the "smoking gun" that proved that the Roswell incident was really extraterrestrial. Others pointed to the document as forgeries, noting that Truman's signature looked as if it had been "lifted" from another document. I have no firm opinion either way, but hope for the best for anyone who can prove or disprove the legitimacy of these papers.

Conspiracy theories missed me almost entirely, as we give them virtually no credence. I do like the theories of David Icke to a certain extent (his books are really incredible reads), but his idea that shape-shifting, blood-drinking reptilians from "the lower fourth dimension" are masquerading as political figures and television stars in an effort to bring about some sort of Orwellian state strikes me as a little…mind boggling? Too much? His metaphysical ideas—that reality is simply an "illusion," that we are all "Universal Oneness," and that we only have to realize the "virtual reality" nature of the apparent video game we all live in—are much more to my liking. After all, we have always been too short, too fat, too bald, not sexy enough…must be those damn shape-shifting reptilians and their mind-control devices at work again.

Moving on, I regret we didn't get to Hollow Earth, "Dr." Shaver, Deros, the Gulf Breeze sightings, the Phoenix Lights, Tesla, UFO sightings by astronauts, Martian "radio transmissions," the Tunguska explosion, and a million other subjects. As I said, if I tried to cover everything, I'd be here until UFOs landed on the Capitol Mall.

One little item I would like to touch on, just for fun (you'll indulge me, won't you?) is Morris K. Jessup and "The Philadelphia Experiment," mainly because it demonstrates just how an "urban legend" gets started. Here goes.

Morris K. Jessup was a brilliant man and an early writer on UFOs. He floated the ancient astronaut hypothesis long before Erich von Däniken, and his book *The Case for the UFO* was considered groundbreaking for its time. Jessup, however, was beset by personal and financial difficulties, and, much as many other individuals cursed with a beautiful mind, was plagued by depression. He finally succumbed to his inner-demons in 1959, committing suicide by carbon-monoxide poisoning. He left a note.

Just before his suicide, Jessup had received a bizarre missive from a man calling himself "Carlos Allende." Mr. Allende had apparently read Jessup's book and liked it very much. Mr. Allende went on to give some bizarre details about an "experiment" the military had conducted in October of 1943.

This experiment was supposedly using Einstein's Unified Field Theory to make a ship…invisible. This would of course be a boon to the war-time Navy. The ship was alleged to have been "teleported" from a dock in Philadelphia to one in Virginia and back again. This, apparently, drove the crew insane, as the first thing they did was ransack a bar (!). "THE EXPERIMENT WAS A COMPLETE SUCCESS…THE MEN WERE COMPLETE FAILURES," Allende wrote in his original letter.

Jessup all but forgot about the missive, though, until called in by officers of the ONR (Office of Naval Research) about a copy of *The Case for the UFO* that had been sent to them with some strange annotations. These writings in the margins of the book revealed insights into UFOs, gravity, and other subjects, supposedly written by three different people, in three different colors of ink. The ONR officers were so intrigued they eventually printed a small run of the new "annotated" *Case for the UFO,* with the two original letters sent by "Carlos Allende" covering the "Philadelphia Experiment."

It took until 1962 for this special edition of Jessup's book to leak out, but once it did, the UFO writers and enthusiasts embraced the strange tale. William Moore even wrote an entire book, *The Philadelphia Experiment: Project Invisibility*, based on the story. This was later made into a movie.

The story of the Philadelphia Experiment became stranger and stranger, like a game of "telephone" gone mad, and eventually the account included alien beings from another dimension and sailors being "fused" into the sides of the ship. For years, a man named Al Bielek lectured on it, making astonishing claims that, quite frankly, boggle the mind. (Bielek claimed, for instance, to have actually been aboard the ship when it teleported, or was rendered invisible, or something.)

Sadly, despite the fantastic tales it spawned, the "Philadelphia Experiment" never happened. The truth was far more simple than the many apocryphal stories would suggest.

The mysterious "Carlos Allende" was revealed to be none other than plain old Carl Allen, a man with mental problems who "just loved to pull people's legs." Apparently, Allen had written the letters to Jessup, and later admitted he wrote the annotations in *Case for the UFO* that the ONR had found so fascinating.[66]

However, like any good urban legend, the story refuses to die. Hell, I read Moore's book myself and half-believed it at the time. Alas, some stories simply are too good to be true.

The Oldest Trick in the Galaxy?

My first thought when I set out to write this last section was: I don't want to.

I really, really don't want to.

Mainly because I hate to admit my ignorance about anything (it's a matter of pride), and, as to the subject of UFOs, I remain as clueless as the next poor slob.

Keep in mind I've been studying this subject for twenty plus years. I've seen the UFOs myself, so you'd think I'd have already jumped on the "little grey man from Zeta Reticuli" bandwagon.

Fortunately, no.

As I write this, just yesterday I saw an article on Yahoo about NASA discovering a planet they are CERTAIN can support life. Are we being prepared for something? Maybe; it seems like I see new articles confirming UFOs and the possibility of "alien" life popping up all the time. Of course, soon someone will shoot down this new discovery with some minor objections, call the whole thing silly, and we will never hear of it again. Maybe.

But we might.

They might be preparing us. By "They" I mean the Establishment who, by now, must surely know that UFOs are real. The various governments, militaries, corporations, and media empires of the world might very well be sitting on a powder keg if caught unawares, so they slowly "prime the pump," letting out just enough information every year to "get people ready" for the day when "THEY" will sail out of the heavens, on worldwide television and the Internet, and the whole world will wonder about them at the same time.

If that day ever comes. But, buddy, you can be sure that those with the money and the power are aware of the problem, and are getting ready for it. The government doesn't want a repeat of the sort of panic Orson Welles induced with his *War of the Worlds* radio broadcast (today, the rioting and violence would probably be a hundred thousand times worse!), so they give a little hint here, a little there…at least, that's one of the theories.

But what if that day never comes? If, as Budd Hopkins believed, they are here simply to replenish their "genetic stock" (albeit, in a "bassackwards," seemingly primitive way), they may never care to introduce themselves formally, in which case, we'll be chasing them forever!

Or, what if they aren't "space visitors" at all? What if they are something far stranger, even more sinister?

What if they originate not from some other planet but, as Martin Sheen's "Mr. X" character said in the movie *Roswell*, "someplace closer…yet much farther away."

John Keel theorized that UFOs (and all paranormal phenomena) originated in the "super spectrum," a force invisible to the naked eye which would manifest itself as intense, bright light. This light would resolve itself into UFOs, extraterrestrial forms, hairy monsters, ghosts, and any other number of bizarre, troubling entities. The fact that the phenomenon manifested itself as both physical and psychological could be explained by the creation of "transmogrifications," or, temporary bodies and vehicles the entity could use to occupy space in the "real world." Hence, the need for cattle mutilations, human abductions, and a ready explanation for why UFOs seemed to often eject "junk" while flying overhead.

Keel thought this one intelligence capable of an infinite variety of tricks and guises, crediting it for religious miracles, sightings of the Blessed Virgin Mary, and other uncanny happenings. He writes:

> They are the phantoms that come crashing out of the bushes late at night. They seem to be part of something else. Something sinister and even hostile to us. This nucleate phenomenon has always existed on this planet and has taken many forms. Some of the Unbelievables we have described may have been transmogrifications or disguises for the central phenomenon. They materialize when lightning courses across the sky or certain magnetic conditions prevail in "window" areas. They are not real or physical in the usual sense of those terms. But they are real enough while they last. They are paraphysical and can assume the forms of one-eyed giants stepping out of magnificent flying machines, or long-fingered Orientals driving around in black Cadillacs which can melt into thin air. Their shenanigans over the past several thousand years have spawned many of our religious and occult beliefs...The demonologists have been studying the same thing as the Ufologists.[67]

Keel goes on to allege that the phenomenon is "reflective," even imitative, and that it conforms to our fears and expectations. In his various writings he gives numerous examples of people who have gone "off the deep end" due to their involvement in UFO research (such as a young man who hallucinated an alligator with antennae following him around), and claims that similar sinister phenomena also plague those who have investigated the Kennedy assassination, or become involved in small political cults. He contends that the force behind the phenomenon feeds off the paranoia of those it ensnares within its clutches, riding them through a labyrinth of fear, hallucination, and confusion until they are emotionally destroyed.

We might, in other words, refer to the "super spectrum" as the Devil. Or, maybe it is God sending us a message that we are simply too daft to pick up on.

The Miracle of Fatima of 1917 seemed to have many of the common traits of UFO encounters, including a burning, sun-like disc throwing off rays of light. Vallée has compared the two, and found them to be identical in many respects. Could it be that religious apparitions and UFO encounters all originate from the same source, and that this source is simply trying to control mankind, for whatever reason, by manipulating the beliefs of various vulnerable groups of witnesses?

I cannot say with any certainty that UFOs and their occupants originate from another dimension any more than I can say with any certainty that they come from such and such a planet or constellation. What I can do is see for myself that the UFO phenomenon does not behave in any rational manner, but instead manifests itself with a level of shocking absurdity, defying the easy categorization of "visitors from space."

Author George C. Andrews, in his book *Extra-Terrestrials Among Us*, gives us a sizable excerpt of Charles Fort's account of the 1904-1905 mass hysteria that swept parts of Britain in the wake of a religious revival. These events included a woman minister who was followed by glowing spheres of light in the sky, the eruption of mob and sectarian violence, the appearance of disheveled men who gibbered piteously and were thought to be insane, poltergeist effects, and the draining of local farm animals for their blood. It is now common stuff to those who delve into such reports, but it seems to suggest that there is some force lurking beyond the range of human sight that manifests as UFOs, all the better to manipulate human longings and spur the apathetic and spiritually lazy into action. Is it just a coincidence that this same force seems to have a predilection for animal blood? What strange creatures lurk beyond the range of visible sight (which is only a fraction of the 0.005 percent of the electromagnetic spectrum)?

The author can speak from experience. He has seen a UFO close-up. The object that the author saw, while wide awake, was not an amorphous blob of light in the sky, but was a solid dark object with two exterior lights at either end and a strobe-like flash on top. It was clearly a flying object, manufactured to be piloted through the skies, if not the stars.

Or perhaps time?

If we are to credit the theories of New Age gurus, all of reality is simply a vast frequency range which consciousness attunes itself to at different levels. Lower vibrational frequencies (those of the average workaday slob) are attuned to very dense, low frequencies, while certain beings who have "ascended" are attuned to higher frequencies. We think of this latter group of folks as the psychically "gifted," the miracle-workers and saints, and the deeply spiritual. Beyond these higher frequency ranges are "spaces between," where lurk various nonhuman entities, with various agendas. To believe someone like David Icke is to believe that these entities of the spaces between are fomenting confusion and negativity so as to keep consciousness divided unto itself; in other words, to keep Joe Sixpack and Sally Soccermom mired in the delusion that this external reality is all that exists; that they are, in fact, *not* simply an aspect of the divine experiencing itself in a variety of different incarnations, but simply carbon-based life forms crawling across a rock in the vastness of space, life forms whose existence on this planet is finite and whose death is an infinity of...nothing. Not what most believe, but what, essentially is behind the "Aliens as Interdimensional Conspirators" angle.

But there may be physical UFOnauts, too. And UFOnauts that come in from other dimensions. We may have flying saucer pilots from some distant future world, come back to warn a more primitive form of themselves that nuclear testing and environmental destruction will bring certain catastrophe to the Earth if not halted immediately. We are intrigued by the claims made by Col. Philip Corso before his death. In his book, *The Day After Roswell*, Colonel Corso, a man with a distinguished military career, admits that his job while working at the Pentagon was to farm crashed UFO technology out to defense industries. Is this true? If so, it suggests that at least some of our UFO visitors are literal, flesh and blood beings, who live and breathe and die like other beings.

We fear that those at the highest echelons of power, the secret cabal responsible for the security and defense of the country, or perhaps some rogue agency within, must know and understand *far* more than what the heavily-controlled mainstream media and population at large could ever guess. It is almost as if there is a parallel world, a valley of nightmares from which the UFO phenomenon festers and originates, waiting to morph again into a new, more viable form, all the better to manipulate and control the vast herds of silent, shuffling humanity, as they go about their humdrum and confused existences.

Hollow Earth. Other planets. Other dimensions. Are we dealing with a "master race" from beyond the stars, an invasion by hybrid "children," birthed in the test tubes aboard alien ships by shockingly inhuman scientists, or some vast intelligence that simply manifests in a variety of bizarre, temporary forms in an eons-long attempt to communicate with man? Is this force hungry for the flesh and blood of mutilated cattle? Does it occasionally mutilate humans? Are the "gods" of yesteryear morphing into the mythological UFOnauts of a confusing, high-tech age, that can no longer abide stories of angels, but who can accept stories of friendly space astronauts and their channeled philosophies? We don't know.

I know that I have seen the UFOs. More than once. As a child, I was lying in the backseat of a car driving from Texas to Indiana. I saw a strange, lighted craft move across the back window. I at first thought it was an airplane, until I suddenly remembered that airplanes aren't perfectly round. I shot up in the backseat, but I didn't say anything to my parents; I didn't think they would believe me anyway.

I went back to sleep. When I woke up again, I suddenly realized that my parents were screaming. I again shot up in the backseat, and I could see the headlights lighting up the long stretch of lonely highway in front of us. Then, ahead, all suddenly fell to darkness. My parents started screaming again. I didn't know what was going on; amazingly, I went back to sleep.

When I woke up again, everything was fine. All my mother will say about the incident now is that the "headlights kept going on and off for no reason" while they were driving. Of course, such electrical interference is common when UFOs hover close by.

Flashing forward a few years, I have gained a steady obsession with science fiction and UFOs. I read the books of Daniel Cohen, became an 8-year-old UFO buff, thought about the subject constantly…and I had a number of strange experiences, too.

I remember waking up at night, while my father was stationed in Central America, and seeing a weird, willowy being "dancing" in my room. It looked like a living plant, or at least, that's what it looked like to me, and it had a large head. I was not afraid, but found the whole weird, wispy dance to be charming. It disappeared gradually in the moonlight. (Note: Author William S. Burroughs, in his book *Junky*, relates a similar story of seeing "little blue men" enter his room as a child, and cavort in a wooden playhouse. He further relates disturbing nightmares of "animal faces" peering in at him from the walls.) I remember waking up one morning, and seeing the dimensions of my room differently. It was as if the walls were converging at non-Euclidean angles. I looked in the doorway.

In the doorway stood a tall, hooded figure that filled me with terror. It was a figure I couldn't actually look at. It may have had bat-like wings. It seemed to flee into nothing at lightning speed, and suddenly my vision returned to normal, and the room returned to normal dimensions. I noticed there was blood on my pillow. Had I had a nosebleed in the middle of the night?

Another night, as I lay trying to sleep, I began to hear something that sounded like ghostly singing, or chanting. I tried to ignore it, tried to explain it away, but just couldn't. I got up and went into my parent's room. I tried to explain to them that I was scared. They thought I was just being a child, and my father got up and went and laid down in my bed, to prove to me that there was nothing to be afraid of. I laid down with my mother. A few minutes later, I remember my father came into the bedroom, carrying his gun. He had a weird look on his face, said he could "feel" something strange…I got to sleep in my parent's bed that night.

A dog I had as a child was killed by a truck. Oddly, several weeks later, I was sleeping when suddenly, upon awakening, I saw my dog come padding slowly into my bedroom. I was delighted to see my dog again, until I remembered that my pet had been killed. As soon as I remembered this, the dog seemed to freeze in suspended animation, and faded into nothing…

A year later, perhaps, we were still in Central America, but we had moved on to a military base by this time, and were somewhat more comfortable. I was riding my bike around the complex one day (there was a huge yard with a sidewalk circling it, ringed by white, two-story housing complexes). Suddenly, as I rode past a particular house, I heard what sounded like the screech of a wildcat. I was intrigued, as the sound seemed to be coming from a particular apartment complex…was there a wildcat in the house? I got off my bike, and walked toward the apartment complex. I noticed that all the windows were dark and closed. No way sound could have been coming from that place, but it was. In fact, the sound seemed to be surrounding the place, as if it was in stereo or something.

Suddenly, the cougar screech changed into a roar. It sounded like an insane man roaring at the top of his lungs. The sound was everywhere, and nowhere. I suddenly knew sharp, intense fear, and ran, leaving my bike behind. Brave thing that I was, I later tried to get a younger, smaller boy to walk down to that apartment complex and get my bike for me. He wouldn't. All he would say about it was that, "It scares me over there." I'm still not sure how I got my bike back.

I obsessed about UFOs on and off for years. Of course, I have already related to you, in an earlier chapter, the amazing close-encounter experience I had as a teenager, the night that I learned, once and for all, that UFOs are real. Before that happened, I had an amazing few months of strange experiences when, going through childhood depression and trauma, I was "visited" in the night by a being similar to the bat-winged, hooded being I saw in Panama, Central America.

I woke up to a tall, hooded being standing over my bed. It had long, claw-like, curling fingers, no face, and what seemed like dully glowing red eyes. It was huge, blacker than the black around it, and I woke up screaming. It dissolved into the dark, but it was not the last time I would see this being. It would return one terrible night months later, when I was lying in bed, dreaming of traveling through a land that was full of death and decay.

I woke up and could not move. Above me, the Hooded Man stood, inspiring a terror I can only describe, as Whitley Strieber has, as "body terror." Its claw-like, black fingers were inches away from my face. I could see through this being, this phantasm, but I could also see it distinctly, see every fold of its billowing cloak, see it as a being "blacker than the dark around it." This night, there was another entity with the Hooded Man. This being had a white, emaciated body, with long skeletal arms and fingers, like a preying mantis. It had a skinny neck, a head that seemed to bob back and forth heavily, and a head that was immense. It had a pointed chin, a slit for a mouth, no nose, and immense, black, insect-like eyes. In other words, it had the classic face of a Grey alien.

I lost my mind for a moment. It was as if I was outside of myself, looking at myself screaming. I bolted upward, screamed, fell back onto the bed, and passed out. I remember my family coming into the room, and the last words I remember hearing were, "Oh, he's just having a nightmare."

The next morning I had a hell of a headache. It took me several hours to remember that anything had happened at all. I also remembered the heavy smell of sulfur in my room that night; many times, UFO entities are accompanied by the smell of sulfur.

I went through years studying UFOs on and off compulsively, almost like a recovering alcoholic, ignoring the topic for long periods, and then "bingeing" on books and films. I remember odd dreams of a tall, robed being in white coming into my room, a being with a small head that looked as if it was wearing some sort of mask (not the first time a UFOnaut has been described as wearing a "mask"). Behind the mask, the being seemed to have incredibly ancient, sad eyes. The being was very tall. I remember sitting up in bed, and looking into a place that seemed all white (the inside of UFOs has been described in a similar way, often). There was a squat green being with immensely long arms waddling toward me, and I began to laugh. "Is that f-&$ing ET?" I remember laughing to myself.

I also remember one night waking up and seeing the entire room lit up, as if it was daylight. Confused, I looked over at the clock and saw that it was still around ten o'clock at night. It sounded like there were a group of bikers outside, circling my house, shining lights into the window. I remember, unaccountably, laying back down in bed and going to sleep.

My mother reported a dream of being taken aboard a UFO during this time period. I have had many dreams of driving with my mother to the "UFO" spot, to wait for the spaceships. My entire family has seen UFOs—everyone.

One other very strange occurrence during the teen years was a day when, after getting out of college classes, I was supposed to go and meet some guys in town for band practice. Instead, I drove back to my home town (which wasn't far away), headed for the local library. I remember for some reason going inside, getting a book off the shelf…and that's the last thing that I remember. The next thing I knew, I was driving home several hours later. Friends had been leaving messages on my machine, wondering where in the hell I had been. And you know what? I have no idea what I was doing during those hours, why I didn't go to band practice, and why I couldn't seem to remember anything after picking up that strange book off of the library shelves. What was I doing? Where had I been, and why had I decided to miss band practice?

Make a long story short: I went to university and met my ex-wife. We had many strange experiences together, and she once told me about the dreams she had where "men in radiation suits" came through the window and took her away. One night, we woke up in her dorm room and found someone on the outside, messing with the door handle. When we looked out the peep hole in the door, there was no one there. We were terrified.

We often had the same dream. One dream involved walking around a strange medical facility, with charts on the wall that showed cross-sections of the human head. As I described this dream to her, she described the same thing to me. We also sometimes woke the next morning with the idea that "something" strange had happened in the night, something involving an animal.

We saw UFOs together. One, a bright ball of light floating over a football field, suddenly illuminated before disappearing behind our apartment building. The next thing we knew, we saw it on the other side of the building, instantaneously, before it floated slowly away. We had spent the previous night, unaccountably, staring out the window at the street. Or, at least that's what we remembered.

We once drove from Marion to Muncie through the backroads of Indiana. Something strange must have happened, because when we got home, we realized it was much later than it should have been. My ex-wife once told me, "I didn't start seeing UFOs until I met you."

When I got divorced, I moved into an old college dorm that was reputedly haunted. I experienced this haunting phenomenon firsthand while upstairs one night, using the restroom. I could swear that I heard a woman moaning behind me, as if in pain. This wasn't some sound coming through the pipes; this was a sound that was in the restroom stall with me. And it wasn't the only time I heard such a thing.

When working as a janitor in an administration building, after hours, I was emptying a garbage can when, suddenly, behind me, I could hear the high, moaning wail of what sounded like a young woman. The administration building had formerly, during the 20s, been a girls' dormitory. I got the hell out of there that night, and went outside to settle my nerves.

I saw a man disappear into thin air (or just about) while working late one night as a computer lab assistant. My ex-wife came into the lab in the early hours of the morning, laughing a little hysterically, and said, "You're not going to believe this, but I think I've just seen a ghost!"

I didn't believe her at first, but she told me she had been in the hallway, bending over at the fountain to get a drink of water. She said there was a man standing right behind her. She bent down to get her drink, and when she glanced back over her shoulder, he had disappeared. The hallway was long, with an exit at either end, and she would have seen him if he had merely walked away.

I didn't know what to believe about this, but put it out of my mind until I had to go to the restroom. I left my ex-wife sitting at a computer, and went out into the hall, into the men's room.

Standing in the men's room was a strange man whom I at first took to be a janitor. He had on work clothes, had short black hair, and a thick moustache. He may or may not have been wearing glasses, but I don't remember now. He was just standing there, and, curiously, I didn't find this odd as I used the urinal, and then bent over the sink to wash my hands. I could see him looking at me, standing behind me, as I glanced into the mirror. He looked at me quizzically, as if he couldn't quite understand what I was. At any rate, he turned to walk out the door, and I followed, directly behind.

He swung the restroom door shut.

I swung it back open.

He had disappeared.

I looked up and down the hall, suddenly waking up a little. All the classroom doors leading off the hall were locked. I hadn't heard him open one of them. He wasn't walking toward an exit. He hadn't teleported into the computer lab.

He was just…gone.

(You may be asking what this ghost stuff has to do with UFOs, but bear with me a moment, and you'll see.)

I went back into the computer lab, sat down, and tried to process what I had just seen. I couldn't. I suddenly had exactly the same feeling as I had had all those years ago, when I had the close-encounter UFO sighting.

Was the man a ghost? The spirit of some former employee who doesn't realize that he is dead, that his shift, in the literal and figurative sense, has ended? I don't know. Perhaps there are "thin places" between dimensions, places where people from "beyond" sometimes turn the wrong corner, and slip in through the cracks.

It was a year or more after this incident that I climbed the stairs of the haunted college dorm I was living in, up to the attic, and found a number of people sitting around playing with a Ouija board. This night, effectively, changed my life.

I won't go into all the details, as they are tiresome now, at this point in my life, but suffice it to say that the intense energy of that night brought me together with those people in a way I had never experienced before. All of us received revelations from the "spirit" of the board, revelations that electrified the atmosphere in that attic room in those wee hours of the morning. Later, we all spilled outside in the darkness to smoke nervously and talk. We had all suddenly discovered a belief in "past lives," and were sure we had known each other before, decades before we just happened to gather together in that attic room.

Soon, we threw the board away, and I began to act as the "channel" for the entity. Now it was almost as if a cult or something was starting, and the entity of course had "special writing" it wanted me, specifically, to "channel" for it.

All of this writing turned out, eventually, to be drivel, but we didn't know that at the time. We explored haunted hotels that year, saw ghosts and shades, felt weird presences, and were all convinced we had stepped into the center of some psychic whirlpool.

Of course, UFOs had to play a part, and sure enough, I began to be obsessed with the topic again. I didn't feel the entity I was communicating with was an actual ghost, or departed spirit; I felt it was, most likely, some sort of high "extraterrestrial" being from another dimension, or a higher plane of existence, and so I began to read voraciously about the subject of UFOs again, refreshing my memory of stuff I hadn't read in many years.

At the same time, I began to have weird feelings and dreams, of floating out of my body and into the ceiling. I lay down one night in frustration, my mind a mess of questions, and closed my eyes. It was at this time that I feel I had my one undeniable religious vision.

I was suddenly transported to another place, a place I took to be earth in the distant past. I could see warlike tribes of cave dwellers cowering on a rocky plain. Suddenly, from the sky, what looks to be a robotic cube drops down, coming to rest upon the soil.

It has an uneven metal surface, and a red light, like an unblinking eye, on the side of it. I get the idea that it communicates with the stone age dwellers, and it must have communicated some really virulent messages, because the next thing I knew, the cave dwelling tribes seemed to be at war with each other. They were carrying clubs, and there was fire and smoke, and violent faces peering out at me.

And then, of course, there was the alien. The Watcher. That's the only way I can describe him. He was undeniably an alien in the conventional sense of the word, with skinny arms, long skinny fingers, tan flesh, a thin body and neck, and a huge head. His eyes, though normal looking, were much larger than average human eyes. As he held out each scroll, I could see that the fierce war I was watching was projected upon it, like a movie.

After each scene ended, he would release the scroll, and it would blow away into darkness, bursting into flame.

He said one cryptic thing which I can still remember:

"Our world is on fire. But there are still trees."

Or something to that effect. Was he warning me against ecological disaster? UFOnauts have been known to do that. Or, was he telling me about the conditions on his own home world, perhaps hinting that this was the reason (ecological devastation) that his people (if people they could truly be called) were so deeply concerned about the fate of our own world.

The final scroll he showed me I felt was the most profound. It was the ancient symbol of the hand with the eye in the center of the palm. It was the last image I saw before the vision ended.

(That symbol, called the "Hamsa" hand, is universal, and is associated with the ancient Egyptian "Watchers"—in other words, it is a holy symbol of the UFOnauts.)

I woke up startled, ready to float out of my skin. I had never experienced anything so bizarre and electrifying, and as I walked out of my room and down the street, I had another vision of millions of people seemingly floating in the air, suspended by nothing. I thought that, perhaps, someday man would be able to fly in much the way he had always fantasized: without aid of a vehicle or machine, but simply as himself, free as a bird. I even thought, just then, that a device that could aid us in the pursuit of this dream was likely to be built at sometime in the future. I still do.

We can cut to the chase here. I started "trancing out" for my college friends quite a bit, and we experienced any and all manner of weirdness. One night, after a séance in which we contacted a spirit that came on like a demon, we went out into the Indiana countryside, driving around, looking for specific geographic features that the spirit said we would find.

Sure enough, we found them.

It was either extremely late or extremely early, depending upon your perspective, so we took a young man home, and I said to my friend, "Hey, there's something else for us to see. We need to drive around a bit more." So we headed back out to the country roads.

It was not long after we headed back out that we turned a corner down a dark country road, cutting between two fields. I looked up, and a glittering bright jewel was coming up over a corn field.

"And there it is," I said, "that's the UFO we were supposed to see."

My friend who was driving suddenly got a very determined look on her face, an expression somewhere between foolhardy bravery and sheer panic. The thing was large, and was coming, slowly, up over the road. If we drove forward, we would be directly under it.

"No! Turn around!" I suddenly said. "I don't want to deal with these entities right now."

I had been reading the *UFO Encyclopedia* by Jerome Clark extensively, and was well-aware of these sorts of encounters. I imagined the thing would land and we would be taken aboard; I wasn't sure if I was ready for that, wide awake, whether or not it had happened before and I couldn't remember it.

We had gone over some old railroad tracks. Now, the interesting part of all of this was the fact that, while we were in the middle of nowhere, we did pass one other vehicle, going the opposite direction. Care to guess what sort of vehicle we passed while in close proximity to this hovering UFO?

Yes, you guessed it: it was the infamous black van.

We managed to turn around. Above us, the thing was a huge, glittering, shimmering amber jewel, a real-life "fire in the sky." We began to drive back out to the main highway. Amazingly, the thing kept pace with us as we went.

I could see it out the passenger side window. A friend of mine later suggested that it was Venus. I examined Venus later with my naked eyes, and can tell you that, whatever it was we saw, it was certainly *not* Venus, or anything else native to the heavens.

The thing followed us back home.

We went inside our haunted college dormitory and talked about the night. At intervals, we would go back outside and stare at the thing as it shimmered in the heavens.

"It's probably a satellite," I suggested.

"It's too big to be a satellite," said my friend, who seemed as mystified as myself.

The whole early morning UFO sighting scenario now seems surreal, like something that happened in a dream of long ago (it was nearly ten years ago). Now I wonder if what I remember happening, really happened. The next day was the first visit I ever made to Chesterfield Spiritualist Camp. I wanted answers, and I felt that the mediums there might, possibly, be able to give them to me.

But I never got any answers, and nearly ten years later, all I have left are shadows, dim memories, puzzling experiences, and lingering doubts about what I remember versus what might have actually happened. And it seems to me that this is one of the central problems of the UFO enigma.

I can't say for certain I've ever been aboard a UFO; I can't remember, although, just based on the number of UFO experiences I've had, I've believed for many months now that there might be a distinct possibility that this, indeed, occurred, at one time or another. If so, then I am left with the hideous proposition that my life is not my own, that my memories are false, screen memories, implants; that my humdrum reality and my sense of self are not what they seem. Because I know the phenomenon is real (having seen the craft with my own eyes, close up), I must entertain the possibility that contact occurs, that possibly even abductions occur. And since these memories are buried in the mind of the experiencer, then they might also be buried in *my* mind, as well.

I have no way of reliably getting at those memories, if there are indeed any to get at. I know this subject inside and out, so hypnosis would probably only bring up fantasy and confabulation…or would it? I don't know. I don't know a great many things.

I sat one night in dread of them.

I sat at the kitchen table of my mother's apartment, and thought about ancient astronauts, the Great Pyramid, Betty and Barney Hill, Roswell, Strieber, the Men in Black, Mothman, Indrid Cold, and felt it all swirling around in my mind like a gigantic whirlwind threatening to engulf me. I would drop off to sleep and see the UFO I witnessed years ago, as if I was seeing it again, reliving the moment; I thought about the drive up from Texas; about the Hooded Man and the "Preying Mantis"; about sleep paralysis; false memories; amnesia drugs; Nephilim; Heaven; Hell; and other realities.

I wondered for a few days if I might be having a paranoid breakdown. I started to feel tense, and I jumped when the phone rang. I honestly started to think about UFOs from the time I woke up to the time I went to sleep. I felt eyes on me constantly, and I feared the night time, and the sky.

All I can ask, at this point, is: What are we dealing with here? Is it the oldest trick in the galaxy? Is an alien race harvesting us, our souls, our genetic material, in preparation for something, some new evolutionary step? If so, they've been at this game for many thousands of years. (Assuming, of course, there is only *one* group of them. There could have been many over the millennia.)

Perhaps there are many groups of them, *have been* many groups of them, since before the Great Pyramid was erected, since before the "oceans drank Atlantis," and perhaps each of them has had a different agenda, a different way of viewing their interaction with humankind as a developing species. Would we, in our ascent from primitive man to Space Age Man, understand their strange, secretive ways, especially if they decided to take a "hands off" approach, merely observing, contacting random people, spreading the message of a new faith, warning us about nuclear devastation and the destruction of the environment.

We would (as we have always been) be dazzled by their strange technology (a technology they, seemingly, have always possessed), and we would chronicle their odd, infrequent appearances. We wouldn't understand them though; couldn't begin to grasp them. Two cultures, two species, light years apart in development, trying to find common ground—perhaps it's impossible.

Of course, there is evidence to suggest (mainly from the machinations of the hidden government) that some UFOs and their occupants are indeed extraterrestrials from another planet, that they have crashed inadvertently on our own world a number of times, and that this technology has been reverse-engineered to help build modern weapons and missile defense systems. Very well, then: UFOs must be extraterrestrials from another planet.

After all, didn't they help build the pyramids?

But that scenario doesn't cover all the weirdness that floats through this very arcane subject. It doesn't explain the sightings of mysterious creatures, the Men in Black who seem to be More Than Human, the psychic and poltergeist effects from UFO sightings, the sheer absurdity of the whole thing. (UFOnauts who behave like ghosts, walk through walls, etc.)

It doesn't explain the religious aspects, that go way back to the Bible and beyond.

Of course, there is another layer to the UFO phenomenon, a paranoid, conspiracy-fueled layer of the cake that states that abductions, kidnappings, human experimentation, slavery, invasions, etc., are all occurring at the hands of sinister Grey or Reptilian aliens, who control the government, media, and various other institutions. These beings are said to come from the "lower fifth dimension," the Hollow Earth, bases on the Moon. The religious go even further, equating the UFOnauts with the original "fallen angels," the Nephilim, with the serpent in the story of Eden, with an ages-old plot to corrupt humanity and control us by breeding with us. And those demons and fairies of old just loved to cohabitate with human women, as do UFO abductors today.

Is it the oldest trick in the galaxy, to control Humankind and breed us out like cattle, for whatever purposes? Is it the machinations of sinister Greys and Reptilians? Is our government in cahoots with them, at some secret level? Or, are they the simple watchful denizens of another planet, simply keeping an eye on the store until the time is required of them, as in the channeled predictions from so many "Space Brothers," to arrive in their fleet of ships and save us from catastrophic Earth changes and global upheavals? Or, as a third alternative, are they the denizens of some dimension close to our own, some alternate Earth that could be affected, just as surely as we are affected, by our propensity to wage war and destroy the ecosystem? Perhaps they are, as Jacques Vallée has posited, simply the agents of a control system we cannot, with our limited minds, yet grasp.

Or perhaps they are simply *one* mind, *one* consciousness, manifesting itself in bizarre and striking patterns (crop circles, cattle mutilations, weird lights in the sky), in a ceaseless attempt to communicate with its inferiors, in much the same way we must seem pretty bizarre to insects and lower life forms...John Keel believed this, and I can't say he was entirely off the mark.

Perhaps it is all of them, some combination of things that is so unlikely, so mathematically improbable, that the sheer fact of its existence in our reality would blow our minds. Perhaps we have extraterrestrials, inner-terrestrials, ultra-terrestrials, ad infinitum...perhaps life exists in such strange, obscure forms, in so many weird crevices of what we consider to be "real" that the sheer scope of it is enough to crash the finely-tuned computer we call the human brain. Just watching the excellent French documentary *Microcosmos*, which deals with insect life, should be enough to convince anyone that life is varied, strange, brilliant, breathtaking—not more bizarre than we imagine, but more bizarre than we can imagine.

So what have I learned?

Answer: Nothing.

There is no "final secret," I think, to unraveling this mystery. The human mind is finite, but the UFO question touches on the *Infinite*, unseating our deepest, most cherished notions of what is real and unreal, possible and impossible, reality and myth.

There is a line from a song in the film *Microcosmos*, a high, haunting line sung by a child. "Open your eyes," it says, "before you die." That's what I've been trying to do with this book, to open my eyes before it is too late, to come out of the closet of denial I've been in for over twenty years, and to finally, in much the same way that Whitley Strieber has, face the alien, "other" that has been with me, in one form or another, since I was a child.

Do UFOs come from other planets?

Are they from other dimensions?

Are they angels?

Are they demons?

I don't know.

And, what's more, I don't think it really matters.

They're here.

They're real.

And they have their vision of the future, much as we have our own.

Now, the question is: Whose vision will it be?

Some Celebrated UFO Cases

> **Author Note:** the following is a short run-through of a handful of notable cases. It is by no means complete, and I am sure that there are some notable cases I've managed to forget about. The interested student is invited to explore, to the best of his/her ability, the extensive history of the UFO phenomena, and, as always, draw what conclusions he or she may. The following are cases that I, personally, finds interesting, for one reason or another.

The Aurora Texas UFO Crash of 1897

One of the strangest UFO accounts of all time is the controversial event that happened in Aurora, Texas in 1897. The story must count as the first tale of a UFO crash ever recorded, and, whether it be fake or not, is as compelling as the most interesting science fiction.

One of the most startling facts about the case is the 1973 grave robbery. In the local cemetery, a single stone with an engraving of a UFO upon it was stolen, and someone had used an instrument, perhaps a metal rod, to fish in the ground for supposed buried particles of metal debris. The grave contained, supposedly, the remains of the extraterrestrial pilot that crash landed in Aurora.

It was around April 17, 1897, according to the account, when one of the mysterious "airships" that had been making the news from coast to coast soared down from the skies over Aurora at around six in the morning. The craft was seemingly having some problems, because it soon crashed into a windmill on the property belonging to a Judge Proctor. The craft flew to pieces, scattering debris over a wide field, and ejecting the body of its sole occupant, described only as a little man and "not of this world." Apparently, some paper with strange hieroglyphics was also found, and this was thought by witnesses to be the ship's log. While the newspaper account states that a local authority on astronomy, a Mr. T.J. Weems with the Signal Service, gave his learned opinion that the strange visitor was from Mars (in other words, the usual suspect at the time), his true origin must certainly remain forever unknown. That is, supposing the story is even true.

The citizens of Aurora were good enough to hold an impromptu funeral for the little space voyager, and many were said to have collected debris from the crash site. The ship itself is reported to have appeared to be a curious mixture of aluminum and silver, and to have "weighed several tons." All in all, a yarn worthy for an episode of *The Twilight Zone*.

Sadly, though, as good as this story is, in all probability, it is nothing more than a tall tale or hoax, passed down generation to generation, and offering a tantalizing possibility to UFO researchers eager for stories of crashed discs.

A man who was 11 years old at the time was located, and he basically said that he could remember nothing about a crash, that Mr. T.J. Weems was really the local blacksmith, and that there never was a windmill on Judge Proctor's farm. In the opinion of this august personage, the whole thing had been a hoax, dreamed up by local reporter F.E. Hayden to help his ailing community after the railroad company decided to pass it up.

In 1973, an investigator named Bill Case reopened the case, and wrote a series of sensational articles about it that had people popping out of the woodwork, claiming that they had either seen the crash as young children, or heard about it from their parents. Dr. J. Allen Hynek, the renowned professor at Northwestern University and the director of CUFOS (Center for UFO Studies) urged residents of Aurora to "search their attics and basements" in the hope of finding evidence of the crash that had long been stowed away by dead witnesses.

A search of the supposed crash site itself with a metal detector revealed nothing unusual.

A most comical situation finally developed involving the town cemetery. Tourists, poking around in the cemetery in an effort to find the "spaceman's grave," were damaging the monuments and creating quite a mess. The Aurora Cemetery Association responded by banning all investigation. The struggle between UFO groups and the City of Aurora would reach comic levels when they finally entered into a battle over whether or not to exhume the body of the alleged spaceman for study!

Most researchers today feel the entire story is simply a little old-fashioned sci-fi.

Captain Thomas Mantell

The following "report of unusual incident" was entered in the Air Force records:

> At approximately 1400E, 7 January 1947, Kentucky State Police reported to Ft. Knox Military Police they had sighted an unusual aircraft or object flying through air, circular in appearance, approximately 250-300 feet in diameter, moving westward at "a pretty good clip." This in turn was reported to the Commanding Officer, Godman Field, Ft. Knox, Kentucky, who called Godman Tower and asked them to have Flight Service check with Flight Test at Wright Field to see if they had any experimental aircraft in that area.

The object had actually been sighted by Godman Tower forty minutes before being reported by the State Police. A number of personnel had sighted a disc-shaped object, and Base Commanding Officer Colonel Hix looked at it through binoculars, noting, "It's very white and looks like an umbrella. I just don't know what it is. Through the binocs is appears to have a red border at the bottom at times...and a red border at the top at times."

Four P-51s, en route from Marietta, Georgia to Standiford Field in Louisville, were alerted by Godman Tower and asked to take a look at the strange object. The leader of this squadron of P-51s was none other than veteran pilot Captain Thomas Mantell—Mantell was a WWII veteran of Normandy and the Rhine crossing, who operated his own flying school. He was considered an exemplary pilot by all who knew him.

One of the four P-51s broke away, but the other three found the object and went further toward it. Mantell pushed ahead of the others, radioing in at one point: "It's above me...it appears metallic and to be tremendous in size...I'm going to 20,000 feet." Mantell was not equipped with oxygen.

The other planes dared not risk it, and started down, but Mantell apparently continued to climb, chasing the UFO upward. At 3:15 p.m., Godman Tower lost sight of both Mantell and the UFO, and could hear nothing over the intercom but the strain of his engine as his plane continued to climb.

A few minutes later, the phone rang. The call informed Godman Tower that Captain Mantell's plane had been found crashed, and he had been killed. He left behind a wife and two small children.

The conventional explanation for this tragedy is that Captain Mantell blacked out at 30,000 feet, causing his plane to go into a nosedive and crash. As for the UFO, the Air Force originally touted the absurd notion that Mantell died while chasing Venus, a notion completely discredited by the erratic course the object was following. A military man later signed an affidavit claiming he had sighted the object through a telescope, and that it was "man-made" but of an unknown origin. He claimed it had a cone shape, was "red with a green tail", and was surrounded by "burning gas" or something which gave off a great light.

Alternately, the Air Force suggested Mantell died chasing a Navy Skyhook balloon.

The Chiles-Whitted Affair

The Chiles-Whitted case is exceptional because of the two high caliber witnesses.

The story begins July 24, 1948, when a cylindrical object giving off a "phosphorescent glow" was spotted over Robins Air Force Base in Georgia. Forty minutes later a pilot in Virginia spotted a similar object heading in a southwesterly direction.

Eastern Airlines pilots Captain C.S. Chiles and First Officer J.B. Whitted were flying #576 from Houston to Atlanta when they suddenly sighted an object coming toward them. The night was bright with moonlight, and both men got an excellent look at the object, which they described as "cigar-like" with double rows of windows, very brightly lit from the inside, with a blue glow beneath.

They claimed that the object streaked past them at 700 miles an hour, and that it had no wings supporting it. It was, they said, approximately 100 feet in length.

There was no noise or turbulence from the object as it passed on the right side of the plane. Unbeknownst to the pilots at the time of the sighting, the strange aircraft was also witnessed by the only passenger aboard the flight that was still awake, Clarence McKelvie. Mr. McKelvie later wrote a letter describing what he had seen:

> The male steward said to me, "I noticed you watching out the window." I told him there was something flashing—it looked like a cigar with a cherry flame going out the back. There was a row of windows and going in that direction fast. It made no noise. I heard nothing because of the sound of the plane. It disappeared very quickly…it was on the right side of the plane. Going off the horizon. It disappeared, or we went past it.
>
> The steward asked if I would talk to the pilot. Yes. The pilot came back and took down verbatim. He didn't say anything—he was shook. He said he had flown all during the war, and "this is the strangest experience I ever had." He was shaking all the time.
>
> Oh, I was interrogated by groups—Air Force Intelligence of Wright Patterson and Hynek's group. I was asked, "Do you think it was a flying saucer?" I don't know—I was looking at it on edge. If I had been looking above or below, but I was looking directly. Couldn't tell. Scared me to death.[68]

The Air Force initially tried to pooh-pooh the Chiles-Whitted sighting as being only the misidentification of a meteor, although unofficially they seem to have had great interest in it, as evidenced by an Air Intelligence report that states the object was clearly "not of a domestic origin." Perhaps a bit of an understatement.

The same report goes on in great technical detail, speculating about the feasibility of the design of the UFO, and mentioning the "ghost rockets" of Sweden, Denmark, Norway, and Holland. The report dismisses natural explanations for the sighting, and treats the account given by Chiles-Whitted as a very serious matter.

The Maury Island UFO Mystery

The Maury Island Incident is very weird, even by UFO standards, involving flying donuts and including at least one link to the Kennedy assassination. We will try to be succinct.

On June 21, 1947, a fisherman named Harold Dahl was floating off the bay area east of Maury Island, an almost completely deserted area of Puget Sound. With him were his son, a Mr. Crisman, and a dog. It was not long before six "flying doughnuts" appeared in the sky, each, save for one, rotating upon its axis. Dahl and the others were glued to the sight, but Dahl suddenly began to think of a possible crash, and took the boat away after allegedly snapping a few photographs. His timing was prescient, for it was not a few moments later that the immobile UFO suddenly exploded, raining down a wealth of smoking fragments.

The falling debris supposedly hurt Dahl's son and killed his dog, and a great amount of wreckage had collected in the boat.

It was not long after the reporting of this incident that Ray Palmer, the editor of the science fiction pulp magazine *Amazing Stories*, hired none other than Kenneth Arnold, whose sighting of nine UFOs flying in formation over Mt. Rainier, Washington earlier in the year had helped usher in the "flying saucer" craze, to go to Tacoma and check the story out. Arnold agreed, and found a rather strange situation awaiting for him when he got there.

For instance, somebody unknown to him had already made reservations for him at a hotel, and Arnold very quickly came to the conclusion that he was under some sort of surveillance. What's more, he found himself unimpressed, upon first meeting Dahl and Crisman, with the story that he was being fed. He didn't think the UFO "wreckage" to be anything more than lava rock, and it wasn't until he read of a similar case[69] of flying saucers ejecting material that he became excited by the Maury Island incident. He states:

> Right there and then I became inwardly excited about the fragments I had seen the night before. I wanted some immediately and even though our meetings had been entirely in the talking stage I put a great more credence in Dahl's and Crisman's stories of their experiences. I seemed all of a sudden to wake up and want to get to doing things. I told Dahl I would like to see the photographs he had taken, even if they were bad, and asked Crisman for some of the white metal as well as other fragments he had stored in his garage.

Arnold was to be disappointed, as the photos never materialized. Arnold called in his friend Captain Smith, and convinced him to come to Tacoma and interrogate Dahl and Crisman, which he agreed to do. Both Arnold and Smith felt that their presence in Tacoma was being monitored by someone; they received a number of anonymous calls at their hotel room, and the press had gotten wind that they were there.

The military sent two investigators, Brown and Davidson, to Tacoma, and both men had asked Arnold to report to them if he found out anything interesting. Arnold asked both of the men to proceed with their own interrogation of Dahl and Crisman, as it was thought that the prospect of being grilled by military intelligence might shake the two men if they were not telling the truth. Brown and Davidson, after hearing a description of the case from Arnold and Smith, found themselves unimpressed with the weight of the evidence for the encounter, and decided, oddly, that they had to take the next possible flight home. Arnold pressed them to stay, but the military investigators would not hear of it.

They may or may not have taken some of the strange debris from the flying doughnuts back to Washington with them for testing. If they did so, they must have done so reluctantly.

Their flight incidentally crashed. Both Davidson and Brown were killed.

Maury Island turned out to be a bust, and while one of the initial witnesses disappeared, another confessed that the whole thing was a colossal con. Arnold found himself stuck with egg on his face. Or, perhaps that was the intention of the hoaxers all along.

It turns out that one of the witnesses, Crisman, was a shady character with possible ties to military intelligence. New Orleans District Attorney Jim Garrison subpoenaed him during the trial of Clay Shaw for the "conspiracy" to kill JFK. Garrison had found Crisman's name in the Warren report. Of course, Crisman's previous connection to a famous UFO case has made some conspiracy buffs sit up and take notice.

Any discussion of possible intersecting points between the JFK assassination and UFOs[70] is far, far beyond the scope of the present volume.

The Hopkinsville Demons

A truly frightening encounter with UFO entities happened to a family having a reunion in rural Kentucky on the night of August 21, 1955. The incident, which has all the earmarks of a bad horror movie, is one that is often discussed in UFO books you may encounter, so it deserves inclusion here.

The Sutton family lived in Christian County, on the outskirts of a little town called Kelly, near the bigger city of Hopkinsville. "Lucky" Sutton was entertaining his distant relation from Pennsylvania, a Mr. Billy Ray Taylor. At one point, Billy Ray decided he was thirsty, and went out to the well for some water, as the Sutton's, like many rural Kentucky families at the time, had no indoor plumbing.

While Billy was outside gathering water at the well, he saw something that astounded him. A large, shiny object appeared to come down from the sky, landing in a nearby gully, and Billy Ray lost no time in dropping his water pail and running back into the house to report to the others what he had seen.

At first he was met with much understandable skepticism, but it was not long before the family began to get uneasy. Outside, their dog began to howl unaccountably, and the men grabbed their shotguns and raced out, willing to shoot first and ask questions later.

As soon as they got out on the porch they saw a sight that horrified them. There was a creature the likes of which they had never seen before advancing on them. The creature was short, top heavy, with long dangling arms and claw-like hands. The creature furthermore had large, bug eyes, a large head, protrusions on the forehead, and most grotesquely, ears like an elephant. It was greenish in cast, and had a long slit for a mouth.

The arms were raised in a gesture as if to surrender, but one of the men shot at it, hitting it but not noticeably injuring it. The little creature then did a sort of back flip and ran off into the trees, leaving the men puzzled.

Alarmed, the men went back into the house, but no sooner had they stepped inside than another of the creatures appeared at the window. One of the men fired, blasting a hole through the screen, and the creature disappeared. The men ran back out onto the porch to see if they had killed it, when, suddenly, a clawed hand reached down from the roof and attempted to grab one of them.

Again, the men shot at the creature, but the little entity merely floated down from the roof and scurried away.

They ran back inside, and the creatures continued to play an unnerving game of "now you see me, now you don't," appearing at the windows again and again, and receiving shotgun blasts in exchange. The family seemed to be under siege, and spent the night in a terrific emotional strain, before they finally risked running outside, jumping into two vehicles, and heading out to the police station in nearby Hopkinsville. The police, naturally, were initially skeptical, but finally the Sutton clan convinced Sheriff Russell Greenwell that they were not playing a joke on him. He and a number of other men went out to the Sutton place and investigated. They found no aliens, but they did find a number of bullet holes in the windows and walls of the Sutton home, and were convinced that, indeed, something strange had occurred to throw the family into such a state of abject terror.

A careful canvassing of the neighborhood revealed that the neighbors had heard the shots, and that some of them had seen strange lights in the sky that night.

The police finally left at about 2:15 a.m., and no sooner had they gone than the little creatures returned, appearing again at the windows, as if out of curiosity. More shots were fired, and the same weird siege continued, finally breaking off at just about daybreak.

When informed of this, the Sheriff decided, the next day, to call in Air Force personnel. The police and the Air Force investigators took turns interviewing the Suttons.

Of course, the stereotype of this sort of thing is that the "dumb hillbillies" were making up a story to get their name in the papers, or perhaps even make money, but in the case of the "Hopkinsville Demons" nothing could be further from the truth. All the primary witnesses were interviewed separately, and all told the same story, even producing separate drawings of the creatures. All of them stuck rigidly to their stories, even years later, and none of them ever attempted to make a red cent from their frightening experience. Why would they go to the trouble of staging an elaborate hoax, blowing shotgun holes in the walls of their home (which they had to take the time and expense to repair), if they didn't plan on trying to cash in on the hoax?

The case was accepted by researchers Isabel Davis and Dr. J Allen Hynek as a genuine experience.

Antonio Villas Boas

An obscure UFO event from Brazil would prove to be one of the first modern accounts of abduction, and predates the Betty and Barney Hill incident by four years. However, for various reasons, the incident, which was investigated by renowned UFO researcher Dr. Olavo T. Fontes, was not widely reported until 1966. It involves the encounter of a farmer named Antonio Villas Boas in the state of Minas Gerais, on October 15, 1957.

Villas Boas was out riding his tractor late in the evening when he suddenly noticed a very bright light overhead. Interested, but as yet unafraid, he continued working as the light seemed to grow in intensity. Suddenly, the light transformed itself into a saucer-like vehicle, which came to rest in the field not far from where Villa Boas was situated. He then claimed that four dwarfs dressed in one-piece gray uniforms and helmets (and wearing what appeared to be breathing apparatuses) accosted him, pulling him, with great strength, off of his tractor and into the strange vehicle.

Blood was taken from him, and he was suddenly thrust into a small chamber. In the chamber was a couch, and suddenly a noxious smoke, like "burning oil cloth" began to pour out of vents in the ceiling. Villas Boas claims that this smoke made him sick to his stomach, but that after a few moments he was able to adjust to it.

It was then that a nude woman entered the chamber.

She was described as small, with high cheekbones and large, elongated eyes, and thin lips. She had a very pointed chin. She looked, for all the world, like a beautiful, pale hybrid between the dwarf-like aliens that had first dragged him aboard their ship, and man.

When she spoke, it was in a rough, barking sort of language Villas Boas could not understand.

The two of them had sex.

Villas Boas claimed that it was wonderful, and that they had sex twice. Later, he claimed that the strange woman patted her stomach and pointed skyward, indicating that, to his mind, she would take his unborn child with her, back amongst the stars.

Villas Boas was given a tour of the ship. At one point, he saw a strange device that looked like a clock with no hands. He attempted to take the item with him as proof, an act that seemed to anger his captors. He was finally released.

Dr. Fontes claims Villas Boas later came down with symptoms of radiation sickness. As John Keel points out, as preposterous as this story seems to be, it is consistent with many of the accounts that would come shortly thereafter.

Papua, New Guinea, 1959

The sighting of an unidentified aerial object by the Rev. William Booth Gill and thirty-seven other witnesses at a mission school in Papua, New Guinea, is a classic in UFO literature. The witnesses all signed sworn statements, and Rev. Gill was known in particular as thoroughly reliable. No one involved was expected to have hallucinations, or make up a story as a hoax.

Jim and Coral Lorenzen give us the rundown on this very important case in their book, *Encounters with UFO Occupants*.

During a time of incredible UFO activity in the area, Father Gill, an Anglican priest and a graduate of Brisbane University, was running the mission at Boainai, when on the 26th and 27th of June, 1959, he and thirty other witnesses had an encounter with something very unusual.

At 6:45 the evening of the 26th, a bright light was spotted from the northwest, and someone called Father Gill to come and look at it. At 6:50 he called others to witness the object too, as it had approached quickly, and seemed to be manned. Three beings in silver suits had appeared from a hatch in the top of the object, and they began to move around a sort of deck that went the length of the disc-shaped craft. The beings are described as wearing "silver suits" that seemed highly reflective.

For the next few minutes the men would appear, disappear, and reappear in different combinations. Father Gill and the other witnesses remained looking at the strange object until it was joined, later, by three other objects that came out of the clouds. The other objects were not as large as the first, and lacked the strange "deck" on top that the humanoids had walked around. They were small, classic disc-shaped UFOs.

At one point, the "men" on board shined down a "thin blue spotlight."

The objects left at about 9:50 p.m.

The next night, the UFOs were back, making an appearance again at 6 p.m. A mission worker sighted the craft, and called over Father Gill, who in turn called other witnesses over. The object was joined by two of the smaller discs, and again the "glowing men" were seen on the deck of the UFO, apparently raising their arms as if adjusting something that could not be seen by the witnesses below. Father Gill and another man identified as Ananias waved their arms impulsively.

To their astonishment, the humanoids aboard the craft waved their arms back!

It was now dark, so Father Gill called for a flashlight, and began to flash a series of short dashes to the hovering object. It "wavered" in the sky, and for awhile seemed to get closer to where the witnesses were trying to signal. Then it stopped, seemed to get no closer, and the two "men" on top seemed to go back to their work. They disappeared below deck, reappeared, and continued the weird actions they had previously been engaged in; the blue spotlight came on twice, very briefly.

The men disappeared below deck.

The witnesses went in to dinner. When they came out, the UFO with the deck was still visible, but had obviously receded into the distance. Father Gill went in to attend evensong, and at 7:45, when the witnesses returned, the UFOs were gone.

Father Gill made copious notes of the encounter; he originally thought it must have been a secret device of the U.S. Air Force. He was quickly disabused of that notion, and found himself genuinely puzzled to the end of his days.[71]

According to Dr. Hynek, in his book *The UFO Experience*:

> The British Air Ministry did not take Father Gill's sighting seriously, and almost with relief they gave me their report on it; it had apparently been cluttering up their files.

Betty and Barney Hill

Betty and Barney Hill were a racially-mixed couple from New Hampshire, who had a very strange incident befall them one night while driving home from a short vacation in Canada. That incident, related in the book *The Interrupted Journey* by John Fuller, would come to be the first of a long, long series of (modern) accounts of alien abduction. Their story is this:

On the night of September 19, 1961, while driving down a deserted highway back from Montreal, and traveling through an area of New Hampshire called the White Mountains, the Hills, along with their pet dachshund, Delsey, noticed a bright light following their car. This was about ten o'clock that night.

The dog began to grow restless, so Betty asked Barney to pull the car over to the side of the road so she could walk her for a little bit. Barney agreed, thinking it would be a good opportunity to get a look at the strange light in the sky that seemed to be pacing their car. He had a pair of binoculars with him. He, at first, thought that it might be some kind of passenger plane that was in trouble.

They got back in the car and drove onward. Unaccountably, about twelve o'clock, Barney stopped the car again, near a White Mountains landmark called "the Old Man of the Mountains," and got back out, looking at the object through his binoculars again. Now he could make out more details; the thing looked like a plane without wings. It was alternating flashing lights, and had what looked like a row of windows on it. Barney suddenly began to panic, hopped back in the car, and sped away.

It was a short time later that they saw a road sign, indicating that they had driven thirty-five miles, and were now close to being back home in Portsmouth. Betty looked at her watch, but could tell that something was not quite right. They had driven about thirty-five miles, but, for some reason, it was now two hours later than what it should have been. Somehow, it had taken them two hours to drive thirty-five miles. In other words, there was two hours of time out on the road that were unaccounted for.

The Hills didn't speak much on their way home, but when they got back, they went directly to bed. They were both exhausted, and Barney seemed to stay exhausted. He grew tense and irritable, had trouble sleeping at night and was tired during the day. What was worse, Betty began having terrible nightmares about being kidnapped by strange-looking creatures with enormous noses and dark suits, who surrounded their car out on the highway. Barney began to see a doctor, who urged him to see a specialist in mental problems.

Barney at first resisted, but eventually both he and Betty ended up with Dr. Benjamin Simon, a renowned psychiatrist who was an expert in hypnosis. Dr. Simon hypnotized the Hills, taking them back to the night of their troubling encounter. What followed would make the couple famous around the world.

Betty and Barney Hill, under hypnosis, both claimed that they had driven off onto a side road, after seeing what they thought was a vehicle on fire in the trees. However, what they saw glowing through the trees was not a burning car, but a landed UFO. Lights flashed brilliantly on the outside of the object, and Barney thought he could see a row of windows with "people" moving on the other side of it. He ran back to the car, got inside, and prepared to drive away at full speed when, suddenly, the Hills heard a strange beeping sound.

The car was suddenly surrounded by strange creatures, with larger than average heads and strange large, "cat-like" eyes that seemed to wrap around the sides of their heads. They were dressed, apparently, in dark jackets, but otherwise Betty always claimed that they looked "just like we do." Barney had to be dragged into the craft, but Betty went quietly, led by one of the strange occupants.

Once inside, the Hills were separated, and a variety of different devices were applied to them. Barney said the visitors were apparently very interested or perplexed by his false teeth, and Betty claimed that one of the visitors inserted a long needle in her navel. When she asked why he did this the alien replied, "It's a pregnancy test." It is interesting to note that this was years before the development of amniocentesis, so if Betty somehow subconsciously invented this detail, how did she know?

The Hills were told that they would remember nothing of their ordeal, a fact that would become the hallmark of the whole abduction phenomenon. Before she left, Betty spied what she took to be a star map on the wall. She asked the presumed leader of the aliens where they came from; he pointed to a cluster of stars on the map.

They were eventually returned to their car, where they heard the weird beeping again, and found themselves driving away as if nothing had happened. Barney stopped the car again, got out with his binoculars, and watched the craft depart, apparently never suspecting that he had actually been aboard. They then resumed their journey.

Barney Hill died a few years later, but Betty continued to be active in UFO circles for decades afterward. The Hills never attempted to capitalize on their strange experience, and were it not for the intervention of author John Fuller, author of *Incident at Exeter*, the story might have been buried from the larger public. In an interesting addendum, the "star map" that Betty had purportedly seen on the ship was later redrawn from memory. Astronomer Marjorie Fish was so intrigued by the Hills' story, she carefully examined the map to see if she could locate the star system it depicted. After exhaustive research she finally found a match; she determined that the aliens came from a planet somewhere in the vicinity of Zeta Reticuli.

Lonnie Zamora

A close encounter that has received much attention is the case of Soccoro, New Mexico policeman Lonnie Zamora. It was April 24, 1964, and Officer Zamora was in hot pursuit of a speeding car at approximately 5:45 p.m. He was traveling through the desert when, all of a sudden, he saw a bright blue flash and heard what sounded like a loud explosion. Pulling over near a gully, Officer Zamora got out of his patrol car to investigate; he thought, perhaps, that a nearby dynamite shack had exploded.

What he saw instead astonished him. There was an egg-shaped object standing on three legs, like landing gear. On the side of the object was a weird red symbol. But what was even weirder were the two men in white coveralls who were standing outside the unusual craft. The men seemed startled by Zamora's presence. They quickly went up the ramp and through a doorway back into the craft, and Zamora heard another loud bang.

There was an intense fire beneath the craft as it lifted, flying away quickly into the distance. Zamora had taken cover behind his squad car.

New Mexico state trooper M.S. Chavez was the next man on the scene, and both confirmed four indentations in the soil, scorched vegetation, and what might have been the footprints of the two UfOnauts. Later, the place was crawling with investigators who independently confirmed these findings.

Dr. Hynek investigated for Blue Book, who reluctantly entered the strange sighting as an "unidentified." It was the only combination landing, trace, and occupant sighting listed in Blue Book files.

Incident at Exeter

The UFO incident at Exeter, New Hampshire in 1965 began on a September morning (the 3rd), when hitchhiker Norman Muscarello was trying to make his way back from the nearby town of Amesbury, twelve miles away.

There were not many cars on the road, so Norman was mainly hoofing it. It was after midnight, and Muscarello was only about two miles away from his home. That was when he first saw the object.

A huge glowing sphere rose up from behind some trees; it was ringed round about with red lights, and was bigger than a house. Muscarello could not believe his eyes, but how much more shocked he was when the object, which moved silently in an erratic motion, began to come toward him.

He dove into a ditch for cover, but the object flew over him and into a stand of trees. He got up and went to the nearest house, pounding frantically on the door, but received no response. He then proceeded to flag down a motorist, who agreed to give the shaken young man a lift.

At 2:25 a.m., he stumbled into the local police station. The officer on duty, Reginald Toland, at first thought he was drunk, jokingly asking the young man,

"How many beers did you buy today?" Muscarello protested that he was not drunk, telling the officer, "Look, I know you don't believe me. I don't blame you. But you got to send somebody back out there with me!"

Officer Toland was impressed with the apparent sincerity of the young man, and called in a patrol car. The officer in the car, Eugene Bertrand, actually found himself convinced by the young man's story, based on something that happened to him earlier in the evening. He had been patrolling along the outskirts of Exeter earlier in the evening when he came across a car parked at the side of the road. Pulling over to see what the situation was, he found a woman behind the wheel. The woman was fraught with fear, claiming that a huge, glowing object had followed her from Epping, New Hampshire, and hovered over her car, then shot straight up and away. The officer had initially dismissed her as a nut, but now he was not so sure. He agreed to take Muscarello back out to the field where he had seen the object, and the two left together.

Bertrand parked the cruiser by a telephone pole, radioed in to Toland that he did not see anything unusual, and tried to calm Muscarello, who was still visibly upset. The night was moonless, with a vast array of stars shining in the black vault of heaven. The two men got out and Muscarello headed for a stand of trees, Bertrand following him, and then they both crossed a field. Bertrand tried to convince the young man that he had probably just seen a helicopter, but the young man was adamant.

They reached a horse corral, Officer Bertrand flicking his flashlight on. He shot the beam around him, and was about ready to tell the young man it was time to go, when, all of a sudden, they heard the horses whinnying in the coral. Then, dogs began to bark.

"I see it! I see it!" yelled Muscarello, pointing, as the UFO rose from above some trees. Officer Bertrand was too perplexed to react for a moment, then, in a burst of panic, pulled his revolver, putting it back after realizing it was a futile gesture. Both men raced for the squad car.

"My God, I see the damn thing myself!" Bertrand yelled into the radio.

The object rose with the familiar "falling leaf" pattern (wobbling) that has been reported in a great number of UFO cases. It bathed the landscape in red light.

At that moment, Officer David Hunt was listening to the radio, and headed toward the scene to check it out firsthand. He pulled up while the object was still hovering 100 feet above the ground, and approximately 300 feet away.

"I could see those pulsating lights. I could hear those horses kicking out in the barn there. Those dogs were really howling. Then it started moving, slow-like, across the tops of the trees, just above the trees. It was rocking when it did this. A creepy type of look. Airplanes don't do this."

Officer Bertrand stated, "Your mind is telling you this can't be true, and yet you're seeing it. I kept telling Dave, "What is that, Dave? What do you think?" He'd say, "I don't know. I have never seen an aircraft like that before, and I know damn well they haven't changed that much since I was in the service."

Finally, the object moved away toward the ocean, leaving the three men bewildered.

Mothman

The late, great paranormal writer and researcher John Keel lived many strange and bewildering experiences, if his various writings are to be believed, but none of them are as weird and unsettling as what he documents in his groundbreaking book *The Mothman Prophecies*, which was made into a feature film with Richard Gere. That story, which is, in essence, two stories, is as unnerving as any that has ever been told.

The story begins with several sightings of the famed flying weirdo called the "Mothman" by the citizens of Point Pleasant, West Virginia. The entity, which is closely associated, from Keel's research, with the appearance of UFOs in the area, is said to be eight feet tall, with wrinkled gray skin, a huge build, no head, and a pair of red, flaming eyes that burn like coals and hypnotically entrance anyone who looks into them. What's more, this terrifying being is said to have a ten-foot wingspan, to soar upward like a helicopter, and to emit a strange squeaking sound, like a mouse.

This being is only one part of the story, though, as Keel also documents the appearance of strange, gigantic birds in the area, as well as the continual harassment of witnesses to the phenomena by creepy Men in Black. These black-clad agents are described as suntanned, wheezing, and wearing clothes that are either long out of fashion, or that haven't come into fashion yet. The Men in Black are said to drive old cars that look brand new, to take strange medications in the presence of others, and to be essentially clueless about even the most common things. (One Man in Black, for instance, tried to drink Jello. Another didn't seem to know what a ballpoint pen was.)

Point Pleasant, West Virginia began to be troubled by UFO sightings, and the nearby case of one Woodrow Derenberger would add another layer of high strangeness to the mix. Derenberger was driving home from work one evening on Interstate 77 near Parkersburg, when, suddenly, he heard a loud noise in back of his panel truck. Seeing that a sewing machine had fallen, he thought nothing of it, but noticed that another vehicle seemed to be coming up behind him. It quickly passed him and cut in front of him, and then old Woody got the shock of his life.

What he had at first assumed to be another car was not a car at all, but something that looked like "an old-fashioned kerosene lamp chimney, flaring at both ends, narrowing down to a small neck, and then enlarging in a great bulge in the center."[72] The vehicle stopped in the center of the road and landed.

Derenberger came to a screeching halt, and was furthermore amazed when a door slid open in the side of the strange craft, and a man got out. The man looked normal, wore a heavy topcoat and a suit of some weird, greenish material that looked almost like metal, had long hair, a broad grin, and walked with folded arms. He was, claims Keel, said to be "deeply suntanned." (Note: Keel makes a point of this again and again during the course of the book, leading the reader to wonder if the MIB and various UFO entities didn't all spend the summer vacationing in Florida that year.)

The man spoke no English apparently, but communicated to Woodrow through the power of his mind.[73] His name, he said, was "Cold," and he was from a country that was "far less powerful than yours." Mr. Cold furthermore asked about the nearby city, said that, where he came from, such places were called "gatherings," and told Derenberger that he should go to the authorities and report what he had experienced, as Cold would appear later and confirm it all. While he was talking, apparently the craft began to hover forty or fifty feet off the ground of its own accord.

After he was finished, Cold approached his vehicle again, got inside, and it slowly rose into the air and took off. Numerous cars had gone by while this strange event was transpiring, and witnesses would report later that they had either seen Derenberger talking to Cold or had seen his weird vehicle fly away.

When Derenberger returned home, he was frantic with alarm, and his wife encouraged him to go to the police. He dutifully did, and they accepted his story uncritically, asking if he wanted a doctor. Derenberger became, for a short time, a celebrity contactee, and people began to camp out on the lawn in front of his house, waiting for a glimpse of the mysterious Mr. Cold, or his "space ship."

Keel tells us that Cold (whose first name, incidentally, is "Indrid") does, indeed, make another appearance; that he gives Durenberger a pill to cure his stomach ailments; that he takes him on a trip to his home planet of "Lanulos," where everyone is, apparently, a nudist; and that, in his opinion, Cold is nothing more than another manifestation of the strange power of the "super spectrum" to create these weird Men in Black-type characters in an effort to either communicate with or control human beings.

Keel, during the weird, long "Year of the Garuda," (the original title of *The Mothman Prophies* that provided connections to ancient Indian legends) traveled to West Virginia from New York and back again several times. While he was in West Virginia, he investigated the Mothman sightings, interviewed witnesses personally, and, although he never claims to have seen the creature himself, did have many close-up UFO sightings, which he documents. More troubling, perhaps, are the paranoia-inducing "games non-people play" that seemed to plague him while he was there. These include people impersonating him, calling up and harassing his witnesses, and weird phone calls that seem to be electronic beeps and heavy breathing.

Once back in New York, Keel makes contact with a number of "silent contactees," who begin to feed him information concerning airplane crashes and disasters that will happen in the future. Some of this begins to come true, so when one of them relates to him that the Pope [Paul V1] will be assassinated in Turkey and then the "Antichrist will arise in Israel," he sits up and takes notice.

Keel descends into paranoia as his mail is tampered with, he sees bright blue flashes outside his apartment window, and he receives endless phone calls from people quoting Biblical passages and random numbers. Some of the calls are weird electronic beeps and noise, others are from the supposed UFO entity "Mr. Apol," who seems to able to see Keel even when he is alone. Keel says of Mr. Apol that:

> It became apparent that he really did not know who or what he was. He was a prisoner of our time frame. He often confused the past with the future. I gathered that he and all his fellow entities found

> themselves transported backward and forward in time involuntarily, playing out their little games because they were programmed to do so, living—or existing—only so long as they could feed off the energy and minds of mediums and contactees. I could ask him any kind of obscure question and receive an instant and accurate answer, perhaps because my own mind was being tapped just like my telephone. Where was my mother's father born? Cameron Mills, New York, of course. Where had I misplaced my stopwatch? Look in the shoebox in the upper right-hand corner of the bedroom closet (it was there).[74]

One of Keel's contactees makes a prediction that a Naval installation in Point Pleasant is going to explode, and, after a series of failed predictions, Keel finds himself skeptical. A local friend, newspaper reporter Mary Hyre, tells him of a strange dream she had, where she sees Christmas packages floating on the Ohio river. Keel then receives a prediction that a nationwide blackout is going to occur due to an "EMF event" caused by UFOs. While waiting for the blackout, he turns on the nightly news and hears about the tragic occurrence in Point Pleasant: the Silver Bridge, which spans the river from the Ohio side to West Virginia, has collapsed, killing thirty-eight people. This was on December 15, 1967. Keel curses himself for not being able to see through the "smoke and mirrors" and misdirection of the entities' predictions.

Keel, of course, *did not* believe in the "extraterrestrial hypothesis," but instead subscribed to a theory that UFOs and their occupants originated in the "super spectrum" beyond visible sight. In his groundbreaking book *UFOs: Operation Trojan Horse*, he speculates at great length about the nature of this all-powerful intelligence, whom he suspects is ancient, beyond the ken of our abilities to grasp, and has been trying to communicate with us by sending out "manifestations" in the form of paranormal phenomena since time began. He even speculates that the entity may use the blood and organs of mutilated animals (and perhaps people?) to create "temporary bodies," which manifest as UFO occupants and MIB (Men in Black). He uses the example of a scientist trying to communicate with microscopic life forms he may have in a beaker.[75]

Whatever the case, *The Mothman Prophecies* must stand as one of the most unnerving stories ever put into print.

Betty Andreasson

The abduction narrative of Betty Andreasson must qualify as one of the most bizarre ever recorded. It is all the more strange in that it is bristling with ornate, sometimes baroque detail, and adds an almost dream-like quality to an eyewitness account. The regressive hypnosis sessions which brought out these shocking memories are recorded in Raymond Fowler's book *The Andreasson Affair*.

The events of the Andreasson case begin on January 25, 1967, when Betty Andreasson, at home with her large family, first notices a weird pink light outside her kitchen window, which overlooks the rolling backyard of her home in Massachusetts. The light grows more intense, as the electricity begins to flicker and finally goes dim. The light dances kaleidoscopically off the kitchen walls, and her father goes to investigate. Finally, he sees what he takes to be "Halloween freaks" outside the kitchen window.

> These creatures that I saw through the window of Betty's house were just like Halloween freaks. I thought they had put on a funny kind of headdress imitating a moon man. It was funny the way they jumped one after the other—just like grasshoppers. When they saw me looking at them, they stopped...the one in front looked at me and I felt kind of queer. That's all I know.

The creatures are described as moving in a "jerky motion" and leaving a "vapor trail" behind. They moved through the kitchen door into the home, going straight through the wood, and suddenly Betty found that her entire family had been put in a state of suspended animation. She at first completely misunderstood the intentions of her strange visitors, thinking they wanted food, so she produced some meat from the refrigerator, and began to cook it!

The leader of the UFOnauts, whose name was "Quazgaa" said (via telepathy) that they didn't eat that kind of food.

"We cannot eat food unless it is burned," said Quazgaa. So Betty started to oblige, shocking the little beings. Quazgaa then said, "But that's not our kind of food. Our food is tried by fire, knowledge tried by fire. Do you have any food like that?"

Betty, perceiving she knew what he was talking about, went and got her Bible. She gave it to Quazgaa (who is described as a short being with large, almond-like eyes, gray skin that looked like wet clay, three thick, club-like fingers, and a slit for a mouth. In other words, despite the uniform and sash he was said to be wearing, he looked exactly like the conventional idea of an alien.)

He waved his thick little hand over it, and, miraculously, produced a number of other Bibles thicker than the first, which he passed around to his comrades. They then gave Betty a thin blue book that glowed and seemed to be full of diagrams. They asked her if she would come with them, and she agreed.

Betty was floated out her back door and into the yard, which seemed to be covered with mist. Up on the hill she noticed a round vehicle with a dome sitting on some landing gear. The beings made the bottom of the vehicle transparent so she could see the inner workings. To her amazement, the diagrams in the book were a rough correspondence of this engine.

(Betty described and drew the engine for investigators in detail.)

She was whisked through a door in the side of the landed UFO, where she was escorted to a room, told to strip, given a white gown open at the front, and taken to a room for a "medical examination." The little beings had stripped from their uniforms (which bore a weird insignia of a bird on the arm[76]), and were now in tight fitting medical scrubs. The inserted a needle up her nose, which was quite painful, and one in her navel, and then waved a wand that looked like it had a tulip on the end of it over her body, declaring that she was deficient in "light."

After that, a giant eye descended from the ceiling on a robotic arm and ran itself up and down her body. She was then told to get dressed, and taken to a room with a row of what appeared to be glass chairs.

She is eventually enclosed in one of these chairs, with tubes up her nose and a hose in her mouth. A gray liquid begins to fill up the chair, and another liquid, like cough syrup, is forced down her throat. She finds she is in ecstasy, until awakening and being taken by two hooded beings in silver suits down a long, rocky tunnel.[77] There are openings in the sides of the tunnel, but the beings take her to the end of the tunnel, which is bathed in a pulsing red light.

Beyond the red light is an arid, red city with a number of cement buildings and a weird track going down the center of it. The masked, silver-suited beings lead Betty past these buildings; she sees a number of grotesque, hairless, monkey-like creatures with huge eyes on the ends of stalks, climbing all over them.

The weird track leads to a "green membrane," and like Alice through the looking glass, they pass through it into a world where the atmosphere is green. Here Betty sees incredible vegetation and an animal that seems part fish and part bird. She also sees a pyramid with a stone head at the top of it, and a futuristic city with towers and bridges rising into the distance. Apparently, they were now very high up.

The track leads them to a place of great floating crystals, shining with rainbow colors, and they pass through this place, which is very bright. Finally, Betty realizes that the two beings have left her, and she is standing in front of what appears to be a giant bird. Phoenix-like, the bird suddenly bursts into flames, burns into a pile of embers, and emerges again as a giant worm.

Betty feels intense pain and heat while this is occurring, and hears the voice of God tell her she is "chosen." She is then returned to the ship the way she had come, and returned home.

At home, the beings walk around the house with a glowing globe that is apparently magnetized to their hands, and wake everyone from suspended animation. The rest of the family is put to bed, but Betty has a final meeting with Quazgaa, whose one eye goes completely white and whose head turns into that of a bee. He then relates some confusing philosophy to Betty, tells her that she was "chosen" (a common enough theme in these accounts), and he and his cohorts whisk Betty to bed, where she awakes the next day with only a sketchy memory of what occurred.

Betty apparently had other experiences after this, as they were documented in a second book which I have not yet had the pleasure of reading.

The Pascagoula Fisherman

One of the most frightening stories in the annals of Ufology is the abduction tale of two Mississippi fisherman. The story is as follows.

On the night of October 11, 1973, Calvin Parker and Charles Hickson decided to do a little fishing off a deserted pier in their hometown of Pascagoula,

Mississippi. Sometime after dark, the men began to hear a strange buzzing sound, and noticed an odd blue light coming in off of the water. The light then transformed itself into a strange vehicle, which came to hover over the ground about fifteen feet from where the men stood. "Calvin done went hysterical on me," Hickson later recounted.

According to one report I have read, a beam of light shot from the craft and rendered one of the men paralyzed, or, to put it another way, in a state of suspended animation. A door opened in the side of the craft, and three horrific-looking creatures emerged, floating down to where the men stood and grabbing them up. The creatures were described by the terrified men as being about five feet tall and wrapped in "elephant skin," looking like a trio of mummies as they came down. They had long arms ending in claw-like pincers, legs that seemed to be conjoined by their own flesh, and no actual faces. Where a nose and ears should have been there was a "carrot-like growth," a sort of fleshy spike, and they had slits for mouths. In other words, they were floating grotesqueries.

They floated the two men into the craft, where they were laid out on a table and examined by a large electronic eye on the end of a robotic arm. Hickson and Parker claimed the "eye" moved up and down their bodies. Then, approximately twenty minutes later, the examination was apparently over, and the two men, who claimed they were paralyzed during this time, were floated back down to the pier and the craft lifted, flying away into the night. Hickson and Parker, in a state of extreme emotional and mental excitement, jumped into their car and went, first, to the local newspaper, which they found to be closed. Then, thinking better of it, they decided to go to the sheriff instead.

The sheriff, though understandably skeptical, was taken by the extreme emotional duress the two men seemed to be under, and so did something unexpected. He left the two of them together in a room, and went out. Unbeknownst to Hickson and Parker, they were being secretly tape recorded while the sheriff was away.

Suffice it to say, the sheriff was astonished when, later playing back the tape, the men continued to talk about the incident as if it had actually occurred. They were both, clearly shook up by it, and news of the amazing close encounter soon spread nationwide. Dr. Hynek, of CUFOS thought the men had really had a strange and terrifying experience, although he reserved judgment about whether or not the men had actually been kidnapped aboard a UFO.

Parker would later pass a lie detector test.

Travis Walton

The account of Arizona woodcutter Travis Walton has been fictionalized in the science fiction horror film *Fire in the Sky.* Unfortunately, the film got many points wrong, so the story is worth repeating here.

Travis, his older brother Duane, and a group of four other men were cutting trees in the national forest. Riding back in the car, near Heber, they saw what they took to be a UFO hovering in the sky and shining very brilliantly through the trees. Walton, an admitted UFO enthusiast, suddenly jumped out of the vehicle and ran toward the object, which was quite close at this time.

He stood beneath it, when, suddenly, he was "zapped" by a bright beam of light and thrown to the ground. Panicked, the other men sped away, leaving Travis there. When they returned, Travis and the UFO were long gone.

Travis was missing for five days.

The police, at first, suspected foul play, but, a few days later, Travis' sister in Snowflake received a call from a very disoriented Travis, who was outside a phone booth in Heber with only the sketchiest memory of what had happened to him. He was quickly rescued, but continued to be affected by symptoms of disorientation and post-traumatic stress for a long while afterward.

It was only after undergoing the therapy known as regressive hypnosis—a form of therapy controversial because critics contend that it can implant false memories (as in several cases of purported Satanic Ritual Abuse)—that Travis was able to recall in full what happened to him during those five missing days. What he recalled would astound all those who listened.

Travis claimed to have woken up on an examination table, surrounded by small beings with large heads and large human-like eyes. They had small mouths and did not look fully human. Travis, in his panic, claimed that he struck out at one of them, and this allowed him to run from the examination room into another room, where he met a tall, blond human being in a helmet and blue uniform. This being had a calming effect on Travis, and took him for a tour of the ship.

During this tour, Travis was taken to a place that seemed like an airplane hanger, where he saw a number of parked UFOs. Here he met a trio of humans, two men and a woman, all dressed in the same blue uniforms with matching helmets. The human occupants of the UFO of course did much to ease Travis' mind, so he allowed them to put a weird sort of mask over his face. It is here that his memories of the event end.

Travis Walton and the other witnesses would go on to pass polygraph examinations. His case, however, is still considered controversial, and there are many who claim, based on his prior background as a UFO buff, that his story is a hoax.

Whitley Strieber and *Communion*

Undoubtedly, the most influential book on UFOs to be published since the mid-1980s is Whitley Strieber's controversial classic *Communion*, the cover of which bears a haunting illustration of a grey alien visitor. Strieber, a horror fiction novelist who had previously thrilled readers with books like *The Hunger, The Wolfen*, and *Catmagic*, apparently had a very strange series of incidents plague him beginning in 1985, and sought to chronicle the development of his awakening to weird forces in a series of books, of which *Communion* was the first.

The central incident which makes up the story of *Communion* begins on December 26, 1985, at the Strieber's cabin in upstate New York. Strieber awoke in the middle of the night, disturbed by a mysterious whooshing sound that seemed to emanate from downstairs. As he lay in bed, Strieber became certain that a number of people were moving around downstairs, and he checked the burglar alarm system by his bed. Finding that there was no problem with the alarm system, he lay there perplexed, until a strange figure seemed to enter the room.

Strieber described the figure as small, robot-like, wearing a breastplate and a strange sort of skirt, and having a perfect hole for a mouth. The figure rushed toward him, at which point Strieber blacked out, coming to only to realize that he was being carried (or floated) through the woods. It was here, in a sort of hollow depression, that Strieber lay paralyzed, while a being with a face mask and another being in blue overalls did something to his head. Suddenly, Strieber found himself floated above the treetops, and the next thing he knew he was in a very dirty domed "examination room," surrounded by menacing entities.

He was terrified to realize that the entities wanted to insert a long, thin needle into his nasal cavity, and he protested, rather limply, that they would "ruin a beautiful mind." Altogether, Strieber recounts four types of entities: the robot-like being he had seen back in his bedroom, shorter beings with wrinkled blue skin and pug noses, beings approximately five feet tall with almond shaped eyes, and one similar being with button eyes. The beings proceeded to shove a triangular object up Strieber's rectum (at which he says he felt intense anger) and there the memory stops.

The next day, Strieber claims, his mind was a complete blank, save for a convenient memory of a strange owl sitting on his windowsill, staring in at him in the night. Strieber looked for owl tracks in the snow outside the window, but found none; he himself believes this to be a "screen memory," or an implanted memory to cover the horror of the UFO abduction.

Strieber began to experience severe personality changes after this, but he would remain clueless as to the nature of his problem, even though disturbing "flashbacks" and a vague sense of unease pervaded his daily life.

After being given the book *Science and the UFOs* by Jenny Randles and Peter Warrington, Strieber said he was shocked to find the similarities between his own situation and that of alien "abductees" who reported many of the same symptoms. Now convinced that something extraordinary, indeed, had happened to him, he wasted no time in contacting the inimitable Budd Hopkins, the New York artist and researcher who so extensively used regressive hypnosis with abductees, to aid in the recall of their experiences.

There had, Strieber also discovered, been a number of UFO reports in the area of his cabin at the time of his strange experience.

Hopkins explored with Strieber an incident that happened on October 4th, when the Striebers were entertaining guests filmmaker Jacques Sandelescu and his girlfriend, Annie Gottlieb. Whitley remembered that an intense blue light had pervaded the cabin, and that he had assumed from this strange occurrence that "the roof was on fire." He then remembers hearing a loud "bang!" like a rifle report, and later an "immense crystal" hovering above the cabin.

This fantastical stuff was later confirmed by Sandelescu, who, when called about the incident, remembers that he awoke at 4 in the morning, but assumed his watch had stopped, because the entire cabin was lit up as if it was 10 a.m. Strieber furthermore learned of a "dream" his small son experienced, of being carried out of his room by "little doctors." Strieber felt that he was going insane, and the stress of this period, he reports, nearly destroyed his marriage.

The next step on his personal Damascus Road was a visit to Dr. Donald Klein, of the New York State Psychiatric Institute. A battery of psychological and neurological tests were conducted; Whitley Strieber received a clean bill of mental health.

He continued regressive hypnosis, going back to the age of twelve, when, apparently he had been abducted, along with his father and sister, from a moving train. He recounts his early youth, visions of staring down mysterious animals, and reflects upon the restless, "loner" nature of his young adulthood. It was, Strieber claims, as if he was always trying to "escape" from something, or someone. He also recounts further incidents of missing time.

Strieber indulges in a bit of speculation, but the book ends on a hopeful note. It makes for powerful reading, whether you are a believer or skeptic.

Strieber has gone on to chronicle his experiences with the "visitors" (who he is careful never to pigeonhole as conventional "space men") in a series of increasingly strange, surrealistic books.

Afterword

There are those who feel that extraterrestrial visitors came here in the distant past; that they aided mankind in building awesome monuments and creating what we consider civilization, and that they served as the model for the gods, demons, and supernatural beings that populated the ancient world.

There are those who feel that extraterrestrial visitors from another, more technologically advanced civilization have been coming here since 1947; some of these people feel that the aliens are concerned about nuclear weapons and the environment, others that they are preparing us for induction into the "Galactic Federation," and are hoping to move us into more "spiritual" and brotherly realms.

Some people claim that the "extraterrestrials" aren't really that at all, but that they are "inter-dimensional," paranormal, or even demonic entities who have always, and will always be here. With us. To torment us, and be the stuff of our nightmares.

Some people feel that a vast "breeding program" is underway, and that UFO occupants routinely kidnap people to impregnate them with "hybrid children," who are then stolen away to replenish the home world. Still others feel this is all lunacy, that UFOs and aliens are nothing more than Hollywood-driven folklore, and that sightings are simply misperceptions of conventional aircraft, natural phenomena, or the product of over-active imaginations. (Or, experimental aircraft?)

To all of the above, THIS writer says:

Yes.

Watch the skies!
Keep watching the skies!

~The Thing From
Another World
(1951)

Appendix: The Original Introduction

I scrapped the original introduction to this book in favor of another approach. However, I still feel there is a lot of good and valuable information included there, so I include it below.

> "This damn thing becomes an obsession…a fixation. The only way to stop all the nonsense is to stop thinking about UFOs. Get rid of all your files. Take up stamp collecting, or chasing women. The UFO business is emotional quicksand. The more you struggle with it, the deeper you sink."
>
> ~John Keel

This book will make you a believer in…something. I do not promise you that you will be absolutely convinced by all the material contained herein, nor can I promise you that you will ever become one of the thousands and thousands of people who have been so blessed (or, alternately cursed) to experience these strange phenomena firsthand. I make no claims for the authenticity or the veracity of every claim contained herein, nor do I subscribe to any one particular theory of UFO origins over another. Some (most) claim for UFOs an extraterrestrial or interplanetary origin; others, a smaller group, put them in the same place where demons and other denizens of the invisible world dwell. This author doesn't believe in "space men," but what exactly *you* believe is up to you.

I have put this book together as a primer on the subject, and to document some of the more troubling UFO events that are still occurring, primarily in the Midwestern states. I have picked this regional focus to best illustrate the mundane, average nature of most witnesses, as UFOs rarely pick hotshot celebrities, powerful politicians, or eager journalists to manifest themselves to. Instead, they make a big show in front of Joe Sixpack and his bewildered family, right before buzzing back into the great beyond.

On a more troubling note, they sometimes make their mischief by kidnapping cows, dogs, sheep, and, more rarely, people just trying to get a decent night's sleep. The people kidnapped are, invariably, average folks completely mystified by what has happened to them. So what *has* happened to them?

A Few Things to Mull Over

1. UFOs have been appearing since the dawn of recorded history. Cave paintings and etchings may or may not indicate they were here before recorded history. Whatever else may be the case, UFOs have seemingly been here for a very, very long time.

2. UFOs are usually silent, although sometimes a buzzing, whooshing, or beeping noise has been heard to emanate from them.

3. At night, they are brightly lit. During the day, they can appear in any number of shapes or sizes, from the classic flying saucer to spheroid, triangular, delta-winged, etc.

4. In the past, they have been said to drop strange material, such as wispy, web-like strands called "angel's hair," and sometimes even slag. Charles Fort, the great chronicler of unexplained phenomena, reported rains of blood and flesh-like material coming from the sky, and we may assume some of this came from UFOs.

5. UFOs have been known to stall cars, interfere with televisions, radios, and other electronic devices, emit lights that alternately cause conjunctivitis, sunburn, (in at least one case) were said to have strange healing properties, and have even been known to change shape, explode, turn into clouds, airplanes, and flying dragons of the heavens, for all we know.

6. They have been sighted by journalists, teachers, doctors, soldiers, politicians, policemen, airline pilots, astronauts, college professors, and even a U.S. president. They have allegedly invited some folks for cosmic joyrides, and kidnapped others with seemingly no other purpose than inflicting terror and pain.

7. Some claim they genetically engineered mankind to mine gold; others say they are creating hybrid babies to take back to their depleted planet. Some UFO occupants look like Vikings; others like Orientals; still others like "hairy dwarfs," robots, insects, gelatinous blobs, glowing orbs, mechanical stalks of celery, and even miniature comic book characters. Today, they are popularly represented by the image on the cover of Whitley Strieber's bestselling book *Communion*: slender, big-headed beings with long fingers and slits for mouths, two holes where the nose should be, and, most distinctly, huge, black, fathomless almond-shaped eyes. These beings are said to abduct motorists out of cars and sleepers out of their bedrooms.

8. Some claim that the abductions start in childhood; frequently, only "regressive hypnosis" can recover the memory of the abduction.

9. Usually abductions involve painful and baffling "medical experiments," with the victim being taken from their car, or sometimes floated out of their bedroom window (or even through the wall), and laid out on a table in a circular room. These abductions happen primarily at night, but can occur at any time during the life of the abductee.

10. The abductee may have a long, needle-like instrument inserted in their eye, navel, groin, etc. He may have sperm taken, or, in the case of females, will have eggs withdrawn. This may be intensely painful, but the pain and fear can often be controlled by a simple psychic directive from one of the abductors.

11. There may be further experiments; at some point, the abductee may be released from his or her strange paralysis. The abductee will then go through a consultation with the head UFO occupant. This will usually be psychic, as the "Greys" are said to either not speak audibly or be unable to speak. The abductee may

be shown images of apocalyptic destruction via a three-dimensional projector, or have these images put psychically into their minds. They may be warned that, if mankind doesn't change his ways, such destruction is imminent.

12. This is the same message the UFO occupants have been spewing for decades.

13. The abductee may then be taken on a tour of the ship, shown a star map, be told where the "home planet" is, shown hybrid "children" that are claimed to be their own, or have even weirder experiences. All or none of this may happen. The abductee is then returned to their car or their bedroom, their memory erased, often awakening with an implanted or "screen memory" of seeing a strange animal, perhaps an owl or coyote, looking at them.

14. They then experience a downward spiral of fear or depression: have trouble sleeping, experience strange flashbacks and disturbing dreams, experience poltergeist phenomena (such as objects moving, doors slamming, footsteps, foul odors, weird noises), and feel compelled or alternately repulsed by the subject of UFOs. Often they are compelled to take strange walks or drives at night; experience the tell-tale "missing time"; have nosebleeds, strange indentations or scars, or feel their beds shake at night. Some of them experience sleep paralysis, increased psychic activity, or awake seeing a hooded phantom standing over their beds.

15. Alternately, some who experience close encounters find themselves spiritually uplifted, focusing on environmentalism, animal rights, and world peace, and having a better understanding of their place in the cosmos. Many begin "channeling" aliens, write books of "revealed wisdom," or become gurus. Some may simply go mad. We don't know.

The subject of UFOs attracts a lunatic fringe of conspiracy theorists. One such theory holds that the U.S. Government has been working with aliens at the super-secret base called Area 51, back-engineering alien technology that crashed (or was traded) years ago. Some claim, as in the fantastic document called The Omega File by "Branton", that a network of underground bases exist, where military and Grey aliens keep human slaves and perform horrific experiments.

(The theories of New Age guru David Icke are so labyrinthine and hard to explain that one literally needs a diagram to keep up with their ever-shifting focus. Icke posits that there is a grand conspiracy involving Freemasons, "Illuminati," the British Royal Family [who are said to be blood-drinking, shape-shifting reptilians from the lower fifth dimension], the Bilderburgs, the Trilateral Commission, the Council on Foreign Relations, the IMF, the United Nations, nearly every government in the world; Satanists, neo-fascists, Mormons, Zionists, Rothschilds, CIA, FBI, Rockefellers—you get the picture.)

Governments, particularly the United States Government, are said to be hiding their info on UFOs (in many cases this is true), and the US Government is said, of course, to have covered up the truth about the Roswell incident, the "Face on Mars," the ancient structures on the moon, UFOs seen by astronauts, man's extraterrestrial origins, etc.

This author feels that, behind most conspiracy theories there is a raving, paranoid nut fit for the funny farm. Of course, this author is also a fan of Jim Marrs, who may be described as a "conspiracy theorist" by some, but is considered by me, at least, to be of sound mind. Other conspiracy theories you may encounter include those of the late Milton William Cooper, a gun-toting "patriot" who authored a book called *Behold a Pale Horse* which was about UFOs and...well, we're really not sure what it was all about, except that Cooper claimed to have seen UFOs, and that the "New World Order" (a term you may come across in your UFO investigations from time to time) was using belief in UFOs to foment...panic, I guess.

Cooper died in 2001, in a shoot-out with police.

Moving right along, UFOs have inspired a number of religious cults.

Scientology, for instance, while not directly inspired by the "Space Brothers," has a "Genesis" scenario that goes something like this:

A long time ago, in a galaxy far, far away, the intergalactic emperor Lord Xenu took all the bad space aliens, and, in an attempt to cure overpopulation, placed them in space planes that looked like DC-10s without propellers, flew them to a much younger planet Earth, imprisoned them in volcanoes along the Pacific Rim, H-Bombed the volcanoes, then captured the souls of these aliens in giant electrical flypaper in the sky. Then, freezing the "thetans" in a combination of alcohol and glycol, he put them in crates and flew them to an interstellar movie theatre where they watched holographic images of all the religious stories and world saviors...and a helicopter accident, I think.

The souls—the thetans—were then released back on Earth, where they took possession of human bodies, and became responsible for all the terrible ills that we face today. Hence, scientologists are said to have "gone clear," then, progress up various levels of "operating thetan" until they are free of any "body thetans" that might be possessing them.

Bear in mind, the founder of the Church of Scientology was none other than science fiction pulp writer Lafayette Ron Hubbard, who, when not raving about "body thetans" was known to "exteriorize" for a little astral flight to Venus, now and again.

But Scientology is only one of the worldwide UFO religions. There is the rainbow-colored Unarius group, founded by Ruth Norman, a psychic medium who pranced around in flowing "space garb," drove a car decked out like a flying saucer, and generally pretended to be "Queen of Outer Space." She and her husband channeled a long series of intensely boring books and fostered a small cult that dressed in silly costumes and claimed to be reincarnated "emissaries of light" from a variety of alien races. The cult still exists, but Ruth has since departed our dimension.

A somewhat darker bunch are the Raelians, founded by French journalist and contactee Claude Vorilhon, who claims to have met his extraterrestrial contact Rael and been "chosen" (what else?) as the emissary of the "Elohim," or space angels. Or, something.

The Raelians are notorious for their criticism of the Catholic Church and what they feel is "sexual repression," as well as, until recently, using a symbol that looked like a swastika in a Star of David. And, also, for claiming to have actually cloned human beings about ten years or so ago.

Of course, the most notorious UFO cult is the mass-suicided "Heaven's Gate" cult that killed themselves using a combination of Phenobarbital and vodka back in 1997. The group, which dated from the Seventies, was first discussed in the UFO literature by eminent researcher Jacques Vallée in his groundbreaking book *Messengers of Deception*, which documented UFO cults and theorized how they could be manipulated by intelligence agencies and even "shadowy cabals."

The group was founded by music teacher Herf Marshall Applewhite and his friend, nurse Bonnie Lou Nettles, who each found in each other a kindred spirit insomuch as they both loved Biblical prophecy and UFOs. They combined the two, declaring themselves to be the "two witnesses" spoken of in Revelations, and quickly formed a group centered on monastic living and asceticism.

The group traveled the country for awhile, lectured to college students, collected members, lost them, and, finally, sometimes in the eighties, Bonnie Lou Nettles died, leaving Applewhite to lead the group himself. In the ensuing years, he would establish the group as computer programmers (they had, for the time, an elaborate website), and they would make much money from this enterprise. They even inspired a forgotten TV movie.

The group was rigidly anti-sexual (in fact some male members of the group had been voluntarily castrated), probably due to Applewhite's suppressed homosexual tendencies, dressed in identical black clothing, including the infamous black Nike running shoes, and shaved heads. They were apparently big fans of *Star Trek* and its various spin-offs. In an interesting side note, one of the members was actually the brother of actress Nichelle Nichols, who played Uhura on... *Star Trek*.

The group asserted that they were simply extraterrestrial souls trapped in "earthly vessels," and that they needed to shed these vessels in order for the Heaven's Gate "Away Team" to reach the "level above human."

It was the approach of comet Hale-Bopp, and quite possibly the discussion of a "mother ship" hidden in the comet's tail, that finally decided them. The "mother ship in the comet's tail" story was first floated by someone on Art Bell's *Coast to Coast AM* radio program.

The group committed suicide in shifts. Once discovered, the cameras crawled the eerily silent hallways of Rancho Sante Fe, filming row after row of black-clad bodies.

The group recorded a video explaining their sudden need for departure. One member apparently backed out, and left before the stuff went down.

Now, a little more, then we can let you begin your journey.

Classification System

There is a classification system created by Dr. J. Allen Hynek in regards to UFO sightings. Dr. Hynek, a man that once worked for the Air Force's "Project Blue Book" debunking UFO sightings, became a believer, and outlined his system in his book *The UFO Experience.* Here goes:

NL (Nocturnal Lights)

Distant anomalous lights seen in the night sky.

DD (Daylight Discs)

Distant disc-like objects seen during the day.

RV (Radar/Visual)

UFOs seen by radar and visual simultaneously.

Close Encounter of the First Kind (CE1)

A UFO sighted within 500 feet of witnesses, oftentimes interacting with the witnesses in some way.

Close Encounter of the Second Kind (CE2)

A CE1 that leaves physical traces (burn marks, depressions in the soil, broken tee limbs, etc.).

Close Encounter of the Third Kind (CE3)

A CE1 with humanoid occupants seen.

Close Encounter of the Fourth Kind (CE4)

Of course, this list was later modified with the addition of "Close Encounter of the Fourth Kind," which is abduction aboard a UFO.

Special Notes for Survival

If you should ever see a UFO hovering overhead, try and remember as much as you can about the experience. If it should hover directly overhead, for God's sake, DON'T STAND UNDER IT.

If you can, try to get an accurate "guesstimation" of the speed, distance, direction from which the object might have come, and other relevant details, such as the time of day, date, and the weather conditions. You can report it to the National UFO Reporting Center and remain anonymous.

Those with close-up UFO sightings have been known to experience weird, poltergeist-like effects, to experience problems with their telephone and other electronic devices, to receive weird calls, have strange dreams, and experience harassment from kooks, cranks, and even Men in Black.

You may, if you have a close-up UFO sighting, never be the same again. You may have other paranormal experiences, see apparitions, glimpse strange creatures in the woods, or find that you are, unaccountably, interested in conservation and environmentalism all of a sudden.

If you should ever find yourself kidnapped aboard a UFO, just go with the flow and remain calm. There's not much you can do about it, anyway.

Now, I think we've gotten everything else out of the way. Is there anything I've missed? No? Good. We're about to take a trip together, so buckle up, and relax. We're going to fly the unfriendly skies, and take a rocket ride through lands of terror and worlds of wonder. It's a strange universe, and you've just got your passport to Magonia, so keep your eyes open and your mind sharp. Are you ready?

Three…two…one…

Lift-off!

Reporting UFO Sightings or Experiences

If you feel that you've seen a UFO, and wish to report it, here are some places you can report it to:

Mutual UFO network

www.mufon.com

National UFO Reporting Center

www.nuforc.org

IF YOU FEEL YOU HAVE BEEN ABDUCTED ABOARD A UFO, YOU MAY WISH TO CONTACT:

International Center for Abduction Research

(Dr. David M. Jacobs)

www.ufoabduction.com

Endnotes

1 Steiger, 102-104.

2 Stemman, 74.

3 Ibid.

4 Ezekiel 1 (KJV).

5 The famous horror story "The Shadow Over Innsmouth," by H.P. Lovecraft, runs along a similar theme. In the story, a demented sea captain makes a deal with a hideous race of frog-like fish people that live beneath the oceans of the world. He offers them up the women of the tiny Massachusetts seaport town of Innsmouth to breed with, in exchange for good fishing and gifts of gold. The narrator of the story finds himself stranded in Innsmouth, and at the center of a mystery. At the climax of the story, he sees a "procession of the damned" moving through the outskirts of town, as the hideous race assemble and go on a long march to hunt for the interloper. At the end of the story, the narrator finds himself in despair to realize he is a descendant of the mad sea captain, and is probably tainted by the degenerate blood of the hybrid race.

6 Author and UFO guru Jacques Vallée has written much about the "Miracle of Fatima" of 1917, and about the strange similarities between what witnesses described and what UFO experiencers sometimes describe, including: falls of strange material, such as rose pedals; weird music, a flashing disc of fire, and the appearance of an unusual entity. There is no end to the number of recorded miracles, and, apparently, much similarity between certain aspects of the UFO phenomenon and these mystical happenings, imparting an amount of legitimacy to those who claim for UFOs a wholly supernatural origin.

7 Tales of an underground world—Agharti, Schamballa—are rampant in world myth. Stories of underground alien bases are also popular in conspiracy folklore.

8 Stemman, 44-63.

9 "Native Americans, Astronomy, ETs, UFOs." http://www.bibliotecapleyades.net.

10 One interesting fact David notes about the Kachinas is that they may take the form of "any animal, plant, celestial body, or supernatural being."

11 Gary A. David. "The Flying Shields of the Hopi Kachinas," http://www.viewzone.com/flyingshields/ (December 9, 2011)

12 Might Stonehenge and other mysterious ancient monuments not qualify as "traces" of their civilization?

13 Jacques Vallée , *Dimensions: A Casebook of Alien Contact.* (Chicago: Contemporary Books, 1988), 88-89.

14 Stemman, 72.

15 This may not be true, as this author swears he has seen the original photo on a UFO website that collected such antique images. But, that was years ago.

16 Anders Liljegren and Clas Svahn, "Ghost Rockets and Phantom Aircraft" in *Phenomenon: Forty Years of Flying Saucers.* John Spencer and Hilary Evans, eds. (New York: Avon, 1988).

17 BJ Booth. "The Battle of Los Angeles Part 1" http://www.ufocasebook.com/battleoflosangeles.html

18 See the book *The Spear of Destiny* by Trevor Ravenscroft for a really excellent documentation of this.

19 In point of fact, many of the early contactees described UFO occupants that fit the classic, Nordic "Aryan" image as promoted by Nazi ideology: long blond hair, blue eyes, pale skin, and tall, athletic physiques.

20 Coming into the modern era, we have neo-Nazi Ernst Zundel, who, during the Seventies, wrote a pamphlet proclaiming that the Nazis had survived in "super secret bases at the North Pole," and were active in the design and development of UFOs. Or, something like that.

21 Susan Michaels. *Sightings: UFOs* (New York: Simon & Schuster, 1997), 40-45.

22 It is interesting to note that Schauberger's plans captured the attention of Hitler, who offered to finance the device. Schauberger refused; he was a committed pacifist who could not imagine his device being used as a weapon of war.

23 He allegedly took his saucer plans and his family, threw them all into his BMW, and took off. Later, the plans were said to have been stolen from the trunk of his car. Attempts to re-draw them from memory were failures.

24 Again, if it was simply a weather balloon, why the strong-arm tactics on the part of the government?

25 Around 1994, a video surfaced of a supposed "alien autopsy." The video was produced by none other than British huckster Ray Santilli, and showed a quite grisly black and white film of a bloated little body with six fingers, a huge head, large eyes covered by a dark membrane, and a slit for a mouth. Additional footage showed hands rummaging through a lot of debris, supposedly of a crashed UFO, and picking up a sort of dashboard made for a six-fingered pilot. The footage was aired on Fox as part of a special called "Alien Autopsy: Fact or Fiction?" hosted by Jonathan Frakes of *Star Trek* fame. Although it caused a minor stir at the time, the footage is generally thought to be bogus. It did, however, lead to a bumper crop of other faked "alien autopsy" pics.

26 Andy Roberts. "The Legend of the Crashed Saucers" in *Phenomenon: 40 Years of Flying Saucers*. John Spencer and Hilary Evans, eds. (New York: Avon, 1988).

27 Robert Emenegger, *UFO's Past, Present and Future* (New York: Ballantine, 1974), 42-43.

28 Emenegger, 44.

29 Emenegger, 45-46.

30 UFO occupants frequently resort to telepathy to communicate with experiencers today, particularly in the case of abductions, where almond-eyed "greys" are said to communicate with their expressive, frightening eyes.

31 This bears some superficial similarity to the case of Stephen Michalak, a Canadian who was injured by steam shooting from a landed UFO. Michalak, who was knocked unconscious by the blast, awoke with a peculiar grid pattern burnt into his chest, and symptoms of radiation sickness. No explanation has ever been found for Michalak's anomalous burns.

32 The swastika, far from simply being a symbol of Nazism and racial hatred, is actually an ancient religious symbol, and, in fact, may be the oldest religious symbol known to man. It is found on many Hindu and Buddhist temples, and is generally taken to mean good luck whenever it is present. ManWoman, an eccentric artist, has spent his entire life documenting non-Nazi or pre-Nazi uses of the swastika. He is tattooed with swastikas from head to toe.

33 Oddly enough, there are claims that NASA has been hiding evidence of past civilizations on the moon. The author at one time possessed a book making such claims, with a plethora of pictures that supposedly proved that, at least at one time, there was an alien civilization present on or beneath the lunar surface. Researcher John Lear has made astounding claims, on the *Coast to Coast AM* radio show with host Art Bell, that a "mile-long" tower exists at the Mare Crissium crater, wherein a special alien device processes the souls of the dying. Whatever the case, author Jim Marrs documents "telemetric lunar anomalies" such as bizarre vibrations and seemingly tunneled-out layers of sediment on the lunar surface in his excellent book *Alien Agenda*. It should be noted that some people speculate that the moon is hollow and was created by an alien race artificially.

34 Stemman, 89.

35 Ibid.

36 Meier, a one-armed Swiss farmer, took a great number of crystal-clear shots of "Pleidian Beamships," which he said were the result of his being in psychic contact with "Semjase," a beautiful extraterrestrial female. His photos, which are visually remarkable, if not stunning, are often regarded as frauds. Meier has made a number of predictions, some of which are said to have been accurate, and has claimed to be the target of various assassination attempts over the years.

37 Stemman, 80-89.

38 Stemman, 100-101.

39 The smell of sulfur, according to John Keel, often accompanies the appearance of a monster, MIB, UFO occupant, or other paranormal weirdo. In ages past, this smell was called "brimstone," and associated with the Devil.

40 One of the puzzling aspects of this supposed conversation with the Exalted One was, when asked if man would ever walk on the moon, he told Bender that indeed he would. It was only seven short years later that, in fact, man *did* walk on the moon. Prophetic?

41 The editor of this magazine, one Ray Palmer, is the man sometimes credited with creating the UFO phenomenon. In addition to editing *Amazing*, Palmer created a number of flying saucer and paranormal publications, including the granddaddy of them all, *Fate*.

42 Frequently, "reptilian aliens" are reported by abductees as being loathsome presences aboard UFOs. The figure prominently in the conspiracy theories of David Icke. Art imitating life, or vice-versa?

43 John Keel, *The Complete Guide to Mysterious Beings* (New York: Doubleday, 1994).

44 BJ Booth "UFO Crash and Retrieval—Missouri, 1941." http://www.ufocasebook.com/missouricrash.html

45 Edward Ruppelt. "The Chase in Rapid City, South Dakota," in *The Flying Saucer Reader,* Jay David, ed. (New York: New American Library, 1967), 30-34.

46 Emenegger, 52-53.

47 Richard Hall "The Portage County, Ohio, UFO Chase," http://www.ufocasebook.com/portage.html (December 4, 2011).

48 Ibid.

49 www.mnmufon.org

50 There is said to be an extraterrestrial base near Dulce, New Mexico, staffed by Greys and U.S. Military; of course, there are numerous legends of underground races and civilizations. Perhaps Bulwer-Lytton was right.

51 Jacques Vallée, in a computer model, demonstrated that the UFO phenomenon, is essentially a sort of paranormal "misdirection," or an attempt to sow confusion. This was based on a pattern (or rather lack thereof) of a number of sightings over a short, intense period of time.

52 "1971, The Delphos Kansas UFO Landing Ring." http://ufocasebook.com/Kansas.html.

53 Ibid.

54 A common enough occurrence after close UFO sightings, as attested to by Keel and others.

55 "Sheriff Blinded by Light from UFO; Minnesota-1979," http://www.ufocasebook.com/minnesotasheriff1979.html.

56 Matt Losure, email to author, December 3, 2011.

57 http://www.rense.com/general10/filers42501.htm

58 In *Dimensions*, Vallée notes that UFOs, which are usually silent, have been, from time to time, reported to make a humming or buzzing sound, or a sound like a "hive of bees."

59 Anyone who has seen films like *Reanimator* and *From Beyond*, both based on Lovecraft stories, knows with what grotesque and nauseating disgust his creations can be invoked.

60 Simon's book *Dead Names* covers the history of one Necronomicon, from its discovery to its eventual publication. It is a book rich in modern occult history, and is well worth reading. Skeptics argue that the Necronomicon was simply a literary invention of H.P. Lovecraft.

61 Jonathan Titchenal, email to author, November 29, 2011.

62 Randles, Hough, 219-221.

63 Ibid, 168.

64 Keel, Complete Guide, 182.

65 Randles, Hough, 262.

66 Clark and Pear, eds., *Strange and Unexplained*.

67 Keel, *Complete Guide*, 321.

68 Emenegger, 38.

69 Similar cases of falling material from UFOs have been documented by Vallée and other researchers.

70 One book that covers the subject of JFK and what he possibly knew about UFOs is a new book called *JFK and UFO*, published by maverick publisher Adam Parfrey under his Feral House imprint. I know nothing of the contents.

71 Lorenzen, Coral and Jim. 331-332.

72 The author is certain he cannot imagine anyone stepping out of a flying machine so outlandish!

73 Nearly all UFO entities seem to be telepathic, a fact that bodes well for those who claim for them a supernatural or psychic origin. Interestingly enough, there are reports of UFO entities that spoke German (or, at least, a language that sounded like German) and French, and did so audibly. The entities associated with the airship sightings of 1896-97 all seemed to speak plain English. Puzzling.